Liquid Assets

The lidos and open air swimming pools of Britain

Liquid Assets
© English Heritage 2005
Reprinted May 2006, April 2007

English Heritage
is the government's statutory
advisor on all aspects of the
historic environment

Kemble Drive, Swindon SN2 2GZ
www.english-heritage.org.uk

Series Editor Simon Inglis
Design by Doug Cheeseman

Production by Jackie Spreckley at
Malavan Media – creators of the
Played in Britain series
www.playedinbritain.co.uk

Printed by Zrinski, Croatia
ISBN: 978 095474 450 2
Product Code: 51093

Making waves at Finchley Lido,
north London, in September 1931.

Previous page A lazy Sunday
afternoon at Sandford Parks Lido,
Cheltenham, in August 1981.

Liquid Assets

The lidos and open air swimming pools of Britain

Janet Smith

Editor Simon Inglis

Crowds gather for the opening of the Parliament Hill Fields Lido in August 1938, the 12th in a chain of 13 open air pools financed by the London County Council in conjunction with local borough councils between 1922-39. By 1950 there were nearly 70 locations offering outdoor swimming in Greater London. In 2005 only ten remained in use.

Contents

Photographer Martin Parr titled his vivid and, for some, controversial study of New Brighton in the early 1980s 'The Last Resort'. Seven years after he captured this scene at the town's immense Bathing Pool – reputedly the largest in the world, able to hold 12,000 sun-seekers – the whole site was cleared and grassed over. It is now known locally as 'The Dips'.

Foreword

by Tracey Emin

I wish this book had come out fifteen years ago, because then the lido at Margate might have been saved.

I started going there when I was eight, and it was just so exotic. It made Margate seem like the Mediterranean. Not like an English seaside town but somehow incredibly glamorous. It had a diving board that made me think of Elvis Presley.

The pool was shaped like a half circle, with a curved tier of seats overlooking the water, like a theatre. They used to hold all these competitions. And there was a giant inflatable ball in the middle which me and my friends could roll over and around all day.

I remember also that it always felt safe there, because there were lifeguards and because it was a closed-in environment.

Like a haven. Like a sanctuary.

Also great was how the water would alter with the different tides. Because Margate Lido was a tidal pool, a mix of fresh water and seawater, its consistency would change all the time. As kids we used to get quite excited by that.

As an adult I swim almost every day now. When you jump into a pool, whatever negative energy you might be storing up, you just leave it behind at the water's edge. It releases so much stress.

But where I live in east London there's nowhere to swim outdoors, and I really hate that. Swimming outdoors is such an absolutely amazing sensation, especially in winter when the water is heated.

Since I left Margate I've swum quite a bit in the Oasis, in Holborn. That's quite something, swimming in the centre of London, surrounded by buildings, all these people cruising around the pool. I suppose it must be the mix of sun, water and air. It's a very sexy combination.

I've also swum in the lido at Saltdean. I was there once with Julie Burchill, who goes there a lot. Just her and me, and maybe a couple of other swimmers. We couldn't believe how somewhere so fantastic could be so empty.

So I think we have to remind everyone of how important and wonderful lidos are, and in order to do that we have to build more

of them. In fact there ought to be one in every park, along rivers, in every part of the city. I still don't understand why we seem to have stopped building them.

That is why a big ambition of mine is to design a chain of lidos by the Thames, using a mix of river water and fresh water. They would be oval shaped, with an egg-like roof, which opens up when the sun comes out. And when that happened all the radio stations in London would make an announcement. 'The London Ovals are opening!'

A bit like Tower Bridge.

And when you fly into Heathrow the pilot would tell passengers that if they looked to the right they could see Buckingham Palace, and if they looked to the left they could see Tracey Emin's London Ovals.

Most of all, for me, the thought of lidos brings back memories of being happy as a child.

I think everyone should have that in their lives. So we should not be closing lidos. We should be saving them, and building more.

So here's to *Liquid Assets*.

Let the nation swim!

The beacon at Margate Lido, built in 1927, stands sentinel over the north Kent cliffs, long after the lido itself ceased operating in 1977.

Architecture and the elements in harmony at the Jubilee Pool, Penzance. Opened in 1935, renovated in 1993 and now Grade II listed, it is Britain's largest surviving outdoor pool, and possibly the most alluring of all for photographers, drawn – as was Philip Trevennen here – by its concrete curves and cool tones. Beyond the white wall lies the sea, and further shades of blue.

Introduction

by Keith Ashton, S & P Architects

As architects who have specialised in the development of sports and aquatic facilities for over 25 years, S&P have long argued that lidos and open air swimming pools play a vital role in our modern day lives.

Whether we choose to use them for sport, recreation or for social reasons, for the promotion of physical health or just simply for enjoying the great outdoors, the architecture of the pool and its associated buildings has always created a special sense of theatre within our communities.

We are often told as children that nothing clears the head better than a good dose of fresh air.

Coupled with modern research into the benefits of swimming on our physiological state, we might presume therefore that a dip in an open air pool will be even more efficacious.

So it is that just as previous generations were encouraged to 'take the waters', doctors today are again prescribing water-based activities as an antidote to more modern ailments, not least stress. Open air pools may therefore be seen as playing a significant role in improving our well being; our mental as well our physical health.

Whether within an urban park or a seaside town, lidos have also, historically, acted as centres of social interaction. That basic need has not diminished.

Communities still need such meeting places, and it is to be hoped that this admirable book will help to draw people back to the lido experience.

Much of what we know and read of lidos places them in a mainly historical context. But this is only part of the story. Lidos are also part of the future too.

Thanks to tremendous advances in technology, we architects are now able to incorporate more environmentally-friendly methods of heating pools, for example.

We can offer hugely improved filtration systems and ultra violet light processes to improve water quality and hygiene.

By adding temporary domes or retractable roofs, the modern lido can operate all year round, without, we feel, detracting from the look, feel or excitement of the lidos of the past, while at the same time creating sustainable solutions for tomorrow.

Certainly there seems to be no lack of public support. For every derelict lido there is an action group campaigning for its restoration.

That so many facilities have closed their doors over the past few decades amounts to a significant loss to our collective urban space.

We must therefore reverse that process, not only by guarding carefully those lidos that remain, but also by developing new facilities for the 21st century, as part of a strategically planned network of sports facilities that delivers value to the nation.

It is with this in mind that we regard *Liquid Assets* as an invaluable, and long overdue record of Britain's outstanding outdoor swimming heritage.

S &P Architects are proud to sponsor this fascinating book, and in doing so, to play our part in fostering the regeneration and rejuvenation of lidos and open air swimming in Britain.

The Basingstoke Aquadrome – a £13m development opened in 2002 – is one of over a hundred swimming pools, both indoor and outdoor, designed by S&P Architects over the last 25 years, including the National Aquatic Centre in Ireland and the Olympic Aquatic facilities for the London 2012 bid. Keith Ashton is the director responsible for S&P's restoration of the London Fields Lido in Hackney, scheduled for re-opening in 2006.

Chapter One

Georgian and Victorian

Outdoor pools have always been outnumbered by their indoor counterparts. In London small indoor baths, or *bagnios* as they were known, started appearing from 1679 onwards; some being 'hummums' or Turkish baths, others being fed by hot springs. Some also offered accommodation and other more dubious services (*bagnio* being one Italian word for brothel). The first indoor bath to cater specifically for swimming is thought to have been the Bagnio in Lemon Street, Goodman's Fields, opened in 1742. This was followed a year later by the Peerless Pool in Finsbury (*see page 12*), Britain's first recorded purpose-built outdoor swimming baths since the Roman era. Bath Street (*above*) marks its location, just off Old Street.

It has been said that while other countries have a climate, Britain has weather.

But the capriciousness of the elements has rarely deterred the British people from indulging their deep affinity with fresh air and water.

This passion reached its zenith during the 1920s and 1930s, when hundreds of open air pools and lidos were built all over the country. No self-respecting municipality would have been without one. Several boasted two or even three.

Although *Liquid Assets* is primarily concerned with those developments of the 20th century, the story of Britain's outdoor pools truly begins in the 18th century.

Before then, the only known baths large enough for swimming were the *thermae* built during the Roman occupation; for example at Bath (naturally), London's Cheapside, Buxton and Wroxeter.

After centuries of disuse the Roman baths at Bath were revived during the 12th century with the construction of the King's Bath, named after Henry I.

As the church's antipathy towards bathing – with its undertones of indulgence and immorality – gradually faded, plunge baths started to appear in private houses from the 16th century onwards.

Famously, Queen Elizabeth took a bath once a month 'whether she need it or not'.

Meanwhile, of course, our ancestors had long known the pleasures of *al fresco* swimming, in rivers, lakes and ponds. In legend and literature, from *Beowulf* and *Piers Plowman* to Shakespeare, references abound to swimming as heroic, manly, yet also, often, as a metaphor for escape or despair.

The notion that swimming might be healthy in itself, and particularly in sea water, seems first to have emerged during the late 17th century, prompted by the advice of influential physicians.

Thanks to a Dr Wittie's advice published in 1660, Scarborough, his home town, effectively became Britain's first seaside spa town.

Then in Brighton in 1750 Dr Richard Russell published an influential tract on the benefits not only of sea-bathing but of drinking sea water (which, as many people were already used to 'taking the waters' at inland spas, must have made perfect sense).

This drift to the coast appears also to have been prompted by snobbism. As increasing numbers of the middle classes found they could afford to visit the inland spas – a trend so deftly caricatured in the novels of Jane Austen – so the upper classes felt the need to take their custom elsewhere. The Prince Regent's espousal of Brighton from 1783 onwards no doubt fuelled this trend.

Bognor Regis became a desirable destination during the 1780s too, by which time bathing machines – huts on wheels which transported the hirer from beach to water in privacy – had become popular. Margate claims to have had them as early as 1753.

(Before bathing machines sea bathing was conducted openly in the nude, albeit on strictly segregated beaches. One of the earliest recorded examples of 'skinny-dipping' in the sea was off the Lancashire coast in 1709.)

Inevitably the fashion for immersion spread inland.

In the Georgian period this led to the construction of what we would now recognise as purpose-built indoor pools. *Bagnios*, or Turkish-style *hummums* were, however, often deemed little more than *bordellos* for gentlemen. One such was a small 'Roman Bath' measuring just under 5 x 2m, opened on London's Strand Lane in the late 18th Century (and later featured in *David Copperfield*).

Swimming outdoors, by contrast, which had always been popular – in London in the Thames and even in the horribly polluted Fleet River – was about to become safer and, as importantly, more socially acceptable.

The Serpentine Lake in Hyde Park, for example, created by royal command in 1730, was soon popular as a communal bathing pool and playground, for men and boys at least.

Around the same time, in 1743, the Peerless Pool in Finsbury opened to subscribers (*see next page*). One of its selling points was its relative safety compared with swimming in rivers and natural lakes; a theme taken up by many a promoter of purpose-built pools over the next century or so.

Nevertheless, relatively few open air baths were constructed before the 20th century.

Nor did the passing of the 1846 Baths and Wash-houses Act – which effectively signalled the birth of the modern indoor swimming pool – lead to a rush of construction, even though the Act specifically included 'open bathing places' in its provisions.

But by this time, in any case, the route to the sea had started to open up to all classes thanks to the advent of the railways.

Dozens of new resorts became established during this period; at Southport, Clacton, Bexhill and Bournemouth, and most notably of all at Blackpool, which needed three railway stations to cope with visitors at its peak. In these coastal towns, the notion of an outdoor pool would not take root until the early 20th century.

The Georgian and Victorian outdoor baths that we know most about were concentrated in the south and south west.

On the following pages we feature a selection of such examples, including Britain's two oldest surviving public outdoor baths; the Cleveland Baths in Bath, opened in 1815 (*see page 13*) and the Clifton Pool, Bristol, dating from 1850 (*page 14*).

Both have lain disused for several years and have been threatened with demolition, although the latter's future now seems assured.

A number of other, more basic outdoor pools from the 19th century have survived thanks to the efforts of campaign groups.

Among these are the Pells Pool, Lewes, built by subscription in 1860 (*page 157*) and the Cirencester Open Air Pool, opened in 1869 (*page 158*).

But for every historic pool saved, dozens more have succumbed.

Whether outdoor or indoor, the restoration and ongoing viability of Britain's historic swimming pools represents one of the toughest challenges facing modern day conservationists.

It is also one of the more important. Only a handful of Georgian and Victorian outdoor baths survive at all.

Yet without them the story of Britain's 20th century lidos would be quite incomplete.

▲ Britain's oldest extant and still operational, purpose-built open air pool, albeit privately owned, is the **Fellows' Pool**, located in the Fellows' Garden of **Emmanuel College, Cambridge**.

According to college historian Dr Frank Stubbings the pool first appears as a rounded outline in David Loggan's *Cantabrigia Illustrata*, published in 1690, but it may well have been created up to sixty years earlier when a water supply from Hobson's Brook became available.

A plan of 1746 or 1747 shows the pool shaped as now, in rectangular form. A century later a watercolour depicts a small changing hut in classical style.

The pool as seen today dates from repairs carried out in 1855. Certainly one of the bricks lining the tank is dated June 1855.

The thatched changing hut, seen above, dates, it is thought, from between then and 1885.

Seen in the background beyond this hut is the cupola of Christopher Wren's college chapel.

Nowadays the pool's water is crystal clear. But it was not always so. College legend tells how one Fellow, Bennett Melvill Jones (the first professor of Aeronautical Engineering at Cambridge), requested a line to be painted on the floor to guide him through the murky waters as he swam his usual underwater lengths.

Swimming at Cambridge has a longer history than that of the Fellows' Pool. In 1571 the Vice Chancellor, John Whitgift, banned all scholars from swimming in the River Cam, or any river, pond or water within the county, apparently because of the rising number of drownings and accidents.

Undergraduates caught defying the ban were to be flogged in public. For Bachelors of Arts the penalty was a day in the stocks and a fine of ten shillings.

THE PLEASURE BATH,

PEERLESS POOL, CITY ROAD.

Subscriptions.

PLEASURE BATH.		COLD BATH.	
One Year, · · · · · · · ·	£1 1 0	One Year, · · · · · · · · ·	£1 10 0
One Month, · · · · · · ·	0 9 0	One Month, · · · · · · · ·	0 10 0
	Single Bathe, · · · · · ·	1s.	

To all Gentlemen Lovers of Swimming & Bathing. This is to give Notice

That there is discover'd behind the Bowling Green in Old Street, near St Luke's Church, the Bathing Waters of Peerless Pool famous in History, consisting of Crystal Springs, constantly running to waste which are now made into a Grand Pleasure Bath, where Gentlemen may without Danger learn to swim. It is 170 feet long and 50 broad, encompass'd with a Wall, has a fine Gravel Bottom, and is in the middle of a Grove. Waiters will attend to teach Gentlemen to swim, if requir'd. In the said place are two Fish Ponds well stock'd with Carp, Tench and a great Variety of other Fish, where Subscribers to the Bath will have the Liberty of Angling. Subscriptions are taken in at the above Places, and at Chadwell's Coffee House, behind the Royal Exchange, at one Guinea per Annum. The Place has been by the Proprietor many Years us'd as a Garden & by digging a Fish Pond for private Amusement, were discover'd many Springs, from whence issued a surprizing Quantity of fine Water which encourag'd him to try farther, and at a very great Expence he has now brought it to Perfection for publick Use, and he hopes for publick Benefit, as conducive to Health, and as a Means to prevent great Numbers being drown'd, by bathing in dangerous Rivers etc. many melancholy Accidents of which sort have happen'd every Summer near this great city; in the last year's Bill of Mortality there was an Account of one hundred & four. But here the Swimmer may with Pleasure & Safety exercise himself in Waters that are Natural & Pure, & those that cannot swim may securely wade, & with a little Instruction & Practice soon become tolerable Proficients in this delightfull and necessary Art. The whole is made as Commodious as possible for the Use and Entertainment of Gentlemen.

From an advertisement for the Peerless Pool, Finsbury, London, in the early 19th century

▲ Britain's first formalised public outdoor swimming pool since the Roman era is thought to have been the **Peerless Pool** in **Finsbury,** developed by jeweller William Kemp in 1743, immediately north of St Luke's Hospital on Old Street.

Kemp's scheme was based around an existing pond referred to in John Stow's 1603 *Survey of London* as the 'Perrillous pond, because diverse youths swimming therein have been drowned'.

Kemp not only enclosed and lined the pond, but also erected changing rooms and an arcade at the southern end, backing onto St Luke's. Trees were planted on both sides to provide added privacy.

To the east of this pool Kemp created a well-stocked fishing pond where gentlemen were able to sail their model boats, or enjoy ice skating in winter. Kemp also provided a library, in addition to the existing bowling green.

Perhaps the only blight to this idyllic retreat was the close proximity of 'Mr Champion's Vinegar Manufactory'.

But if it was still there in 1826, the pamphleteer William Hone made no mention of it in his description of the Peerless Pool.

'On a summer evening it is amusing to survey the conduct of the bathers; some boldly dive, others timorous stand and then

descend step by step, unwilling and slow; choice swimmers attract attention by divings and somersets, and the whole sheet of water sometimes rings with merriment.

'Every fine Thursday and Saturday afternoon in the summer columns of Bluecoat boys, more than threescore in each, headed by their respective beadles, arrive and some half-strip themselves 'ere they reach their destination. The rapid plunges they make into the Pool and their hilarity in the bath testify their enjoyment of the tepid fluid.'

Peerless Pool closed in 1850 and the site is now occupied by the St Luke's housing estate, bordered by Peerless Street and Bath Street.

▲ In a city renowned for its Roman baths – indeed which owes its very name to these prime liquid assets – we should not be surprised to find Britain's oldest extant public outdoor swimming pool, the Grade II listed **Cleveland Pools**, in **Bath**.

Nor, alas, should we be surprised to find that since closing to the public in 1984, its owners (Bath and North East Somerset Council) have struggled to find for it a viable use. A trout farm occupied the site during the early 1990s. Since then, the site has lain disused; its future now the focus of a campaign led by the Cleveland Pools Trust.

From their researches and those of the Bath Archaeological Trust it can be confirmed that the central feature of the main pool (*above*) – a crescent of ashlar changing cubicles flanking the two storey attendant's cottage – dates back to the opening in 1815, and was at least partly the work of a local architect, John Pinch.

Owing to its location, tucked away in the artisan corner of the Bathwick district, and accessed via a steep path leading down from Hampton Row, the pool was never as fashionable as its original promoters had hoped. A downturn in Bath's fortunes during the 1820s hardly helped either.

Yet they continued to operate as subscription baths for the rest of the century until taken over by Bath Corporation in 1900.

Originally the main pool shown here was D-shaped and fed, via a sluice gate, by the flow of the River Avon, on whose banks the pool is located.

The current pool, shaped like a P, is self-contained, however, having been re-lined by the Corporation between 1900-14.

Among other buildings on the site is a former private bath for ladies, added in the mid 19th century and featuring 'perpetual showers', and a second smaller, rectangular pool. Both this and the showers were fed by iron pipes carrying spring water from under the nearby Kennet and Avon Canal.

Contemporaries of the Cleveland Baths were the Knightstone Outdoor Baths at Weston-super-Mare, 1825-1925, and the Clifton Pool, Bristol, 1850 (see *next page*).

But Cleveland is the oldest survivor, significant not only in British swimming history, but also as a unique Georgian model for the lidos of the 20th century.

The north eastern corner of Bristol's Clifton Pool has been occupied by the Victoria pub since 1867, but the integrity of the original stuccoed classical façade, with its split entablature flanking the central bay, can still be discerned behind the contrasting paintwork. Also of interest is an unusual main door, which features an Egyptian-style architrave. At street level it is hard to imagine that behind this compact frontage lies an outdoor swimming pool.

▲ In the narrow back streets of Clifton, Bristol, easily missed amid town houses and a pub, stands the **Clifton Pool**, a unique example of a building type that was in any case rare; a Victorian subscription bath with an open air pool.

Opened in July 1850, the pool was probably designed by the firm of RS Pope, Bindon and Clark, whose other work in the district includes Brunel House, Vyvyan Terrace and Buckingham Place.

Baths such as Clifton were commercial enterprises, the equivalent of a modern day health club, though they were primarily aimed at gentlemen subscribers.

Entry from 6am to 3pm cost one shilling, including the use of two towels. From 4pm the fee dropped to 4d, with one towel.

Boys under 14 paid half price.

Apart from the pool there were private baths for both gentlemen and ladies, and, according to the *Bristol Mirror*, 'a medicated bath for invalids'.

Yet in certain respects the Clifton Pool and its ilk were about to be eclipsed. The 1846 Baths and Wash-houses Act would soon pave the way for a network of public baths, while a new generation of Turkish Baths – two opened in Bristol in 1859 and 1862 – offered more up-to-date treatments.

To pay its way under various owners one corner of the building was turned into a pub, until in 1897 Bristol Corporation brought the pool into public ownership.

Under its control, in 1930 the pool tank was reconstructed *in situ*. An electrical water heating system was also installed, thought to have been the first of its kind in Britain.

But the real charm of the pool was always its intimate character, secreted in a built-up area and with a first floor gallery overlooking the water. For all its limitations, Clifton Pool was a much loved oasis, and continued to operate until 1990.

Thereafter supporters hoped that the sale of part of the plot (on which the 'Tepid House' had stood until 1960) might yet help finance the pool's restoration. Instead, a firm of developers bought the site and in 1998 won planning consent to turn it into flats and houses.

A prolonged campaign ensued – during which the pool was listed Grade II* – until finally the developers backed down and in January 2005 sold the building on to a restaurant company.

This company now plans to refurbish the pool and add a sauna, relaxation rooms and a restaurant; in essence, returning it to its original function as a place to swim, relax, socialise and escape.

It is an enterprise that will be watched in eager anticipation; in effect, the creation of a modern lido within a Victorian shell.

▶ Five years after the opening of the Clifton Pool in Bristol *The Builder* of November 10 1855 published details of a highly unusual open air swimming baths proposed for the Oxfordshire town of **Banbury**.

The plans, submitted by a Mr Thomas Draper of Banbury, may well have been inspired by a letter published by the journal the previous December. In this letter the anonymous correspondent argued that circular pools were better able to conserve water.

Accordingly, Draper's plans revolved, as it were, around a series a concentric rings.

At the core was a circular, brick-lined boys' pool, 24 feet in diameter, with a 12 feet wide, wedge shaped extension on its south side (on the right as seen in the woodcut shown here). This pool's depth varied from 2'6" to 4'.

Surrounding the boys' pool were two rings of slate roofed buildings, accessed by an uncovered passageway.

These buildings comprised, on the inner ring, the boys' changing rooms and four private baths, and on the outer ring, sixteen changing rooms for men, each with its own doorway facing onto the outer pool.

This was the men's pool, forming an 18 foot wide moat around the central core, some 240 feet in circumference, and with a gravel surface. In depth the water varied from 4'3" to 5'3".

A footbridge spanning this outer ring of water led from the entrance block on the north side to the inner core of changing rooms and baths. The entrance block also provided accommodation for the pool's attendant and 'conveniences'.

Finally the pool was surrounded by a retaining brick wall, on which was a walkway for the attendant,

THE BANBURY SWIMMING BATHS, WITH PRIVATE BATHS ATTACHED.

beyond which a circular turfed embankment 10 foot high enclosed the whole and maintained privacy for its users.

Regrettably no records appear to survive to show the extent to which Draper's plans were followed when the baths were built, or how well they functioned.

All we know is that Banbury's first public baths were indeed built shortly after the plans were published, located on what became known as Bath Road (since renamed Swan Close Road), and that they remained in existence until, in 1867, a company was formed to erect a more conventional oval-shaped pool on the town's Recreation Ground.

The site was subsequently occupied by the Britannia Works.

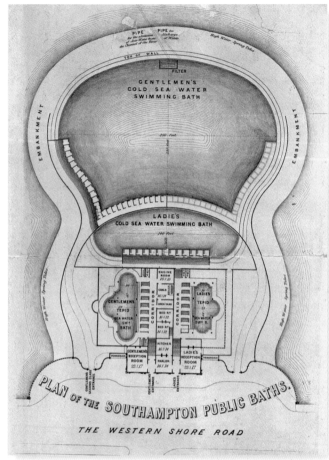

PLAN OF THE SOUTHAMPTON PUBLIC BATHS.

THE WESTERN SHORE ROAD

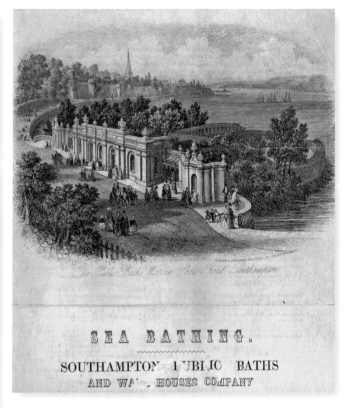

SEA BATHING.

SOUTHAMPTON PUBLIC BATHS
AND WASH HOUSES COMPANY

▲ Another interesting variant from the Victorian era is this surprisingly sophisticated Neo-Classical sea bathing pool designed for the **Southampton Public Baths and Wash Houses Company** by architect John Elliott in 1853.

Sea bathing in Southampton first became fashionable after Prince Frederick tried it during a visit in 1750. But despite the town's best efforts, by the early 19th century its attractions as a resort were losing out to its importance as a port.

This scheme, costed at £4,000, perhaps hoped to compensate for that trend, although the prospectus emphasised that the 'Working Classes' would be admitted at a fee reduced from the daily rate of 6d to just 1d after 5pm.

Two pools for gentlemen and ladies were to be filled with sea water every 24 hours by means of pipes sunk into the Test estuary. Covered tepid baths were also provided, the ladies being staffed by 'a respectable female attendant'.

Sited on the Western Shore Road (now Western Esplanade) at the end of Manchester Street, the baths operated, it is thought, more or less as shown, before being remodelled in 1891-92 (*as shown left in 1910*), and again in 1929.

Thereafter its setting altered radically; a major land reclamation and docks development scheme effectively turning it into an inland pool. Following its closure in the 1970s the site is now occupied by a retail complex.

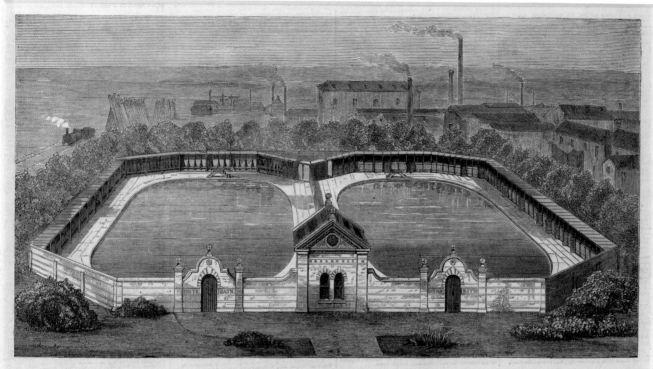

FREE SWIMMING·BATHS AT DERBY, PRESENTED BY MR. BASS, M.P.

▲ As the industrial revolution transformed the urban fabric of Britain, so the need to offer the burgeoning working classes respite from their arduous conditions grew ever more insistent.

By custom ordinary people had only the choice of bathing in rivers, lakes and ponds. Canals and flooded marl pits were also popular. But pollution and water-borne diseases heightened the risks, while drownings were common.

In many towns and cities the 1846 Baths and Wash-houses Act eased the problem. But where local authorities were unable or unwilling to take advantage of the Act's borrowing powers, local philanthropists often had to satisfy the need themselves.

Examples of indoor pools financed in this manner may be found all over Britain; the Hugh Mason House baths in Ashton-under-Lyne, for example (b.1870) and the Memorial Hall Bath in Loughborough (1897).

However, one rare example of an open air pool funded by a benefactor was the **Free Swimming Baths**, **Derby**, endowed by the brewing magnate and local MP, Michael Bass, and opened in 1873.

Designed by George Thompson, the baths consisted of two pools, each 100 x 50 feet, for men and boys respectively, within a walled compound lined on three sides by a range of 129 dressing cubicles. (Bass was throughout his life a true friend of the working man, but

women were still treated as second class citizens, especially when it came to public baths).

Bass paid £2,500 to complete the buildings, on top of the £3,850 he had spent six years earlier on buying the Recreation Ground on which they were located.

That ground is still in use today, on the edge of the town centre. The baths, however, were levelled after the Second World War.

As their name implied, the Free Swimming Baths differed from all known predecessors in two vital respects. They were intended for working people, at no charge.

Both in concept and in spirit, therefore, they may be regarded as true precursors of the 20th century municipal lidos.

Chapter Two

20th Century

Derived from the Latin *litus*, meaning shore, the original Lido was (and remains) an island in the lagoon of Venice, to which the city's elite repaired for fresh air and bathing in the sea. During the 19th century the word came to denote any fashionable beach resort in Europe. Strictly speaking lido should be pronounced, as in the Italian, as 'lee-doh'. In practice, most people in Britain say 'lie-doh'. As to a precise definition of what constitutes a lido, as opposed to an ordinary open air pool, as we shall discover there has never been complete agreement.

The 20th century witnessed the development of numerous specialist and innovative building types, all with their own styles, characters, and, in time, devotees: cinemas, airports, skyscrapers, shopping centres, stadiums, even multi-storey car parks.

To this list we must also add the open air swimming pool, or, as it increasingly became known from the 1930s onwards, the lido.

True, the roots of this building type lie in antiquity, and, as we discovered in the previous chapter, several precedents were created in the 18th and 19th centuries.

But the open air pool of the 20th century was a product of ideology as much as it was of fashion or of paternalistic concern for the welfare of the poor.

As numerous historians and social commentators have pointed out (*see* Links), ideas and social trends emanating from Europe played a key role in this, not least the cult of physical fitness assiduously nurtured in Germany during the late 19th century (albeit for militaristic and nationalistic motives rather than for mere

personal self-development, as is the modern way).

In London today there survives an embodiment of that ideal, the German Gymnasium at King's Cross, opened in 1865 and the venue, four years later, of the first meeting of the Metropolitan Swimming Association, later to evolve into the Amateur Swimming Association.

But while continental influences were undoubtedly important, it would appear that the British needed little prompting when it came to the provision of facilities for outdoor swimming.

By 1900 there were publicly and privately funded, though basic, open air pools in a number of provincial cities, including Southampton, Birmingham, Manchester and Liverpool (*see opposite*). In the capital, thousands of men and boys flocked to municipal swimming lakes.

At Letchworth, the world's first Garden City, a wonderfully

irregular Arts and Crafts building known as the Cloisters was opened in 1907 as a hostel for 20 students, there to study Arts, Sciences and Humanities. Each student was required to take a dip in the open air pool before breakfast.

As we shall show in Chapter Six, two of Britain's leading seaside resorts, Scarborough and Blackpool, started planning their own extravagant open air pools before the First World War.

Scarborough's South Bay pool, the brainchild of the town's Borough Engineer Harry Smith (*see page 58*), opened in 1915, while at Blackpool, the colossal Open Air Baths (*page 62*) was no less grandiose than the Empire Stadium at Wembley which opened in the same year, 1923.

These early lidos – although that name had yet to be applied – with their sunbathing terraces, cafés and spectator areas, may have been created as tourist attractions. Unlike the urban pools

Building for Britain – a 1937 plea for more pools in the interests of the nation.

THE MUNICIPAL JOURNAL & PUBLIC WORKS ENGINEER

Indoor and Open-Air Baths

Municipalities Must Cater for Growing Demand

By ALBERT TEASDALE, General Superintendent, Baths and Wash-houses Department, Manchester

The importance of swimming in the national campaign for physical fitness makes it imperative that up-to-date baths should be provided in increasing numbers by local authorities. In the future, it should be possible for anyone who so desires to be able to bathe in comfort at any time of the year without the need for travelling long distances to the nearest public bath. Once more those who administer local affairs have a responsibility which has immense social and national importance.

and lakes they charged for entry. Nor did their promoters employ the intellectual language of their continental counterparts – for example those of the German *Volkspark* movement of the 1920s.

But their net effect was broadly similar; the popularisation of communal, outdoor living.

Two characteristics of these new outdoor pools are worth noting.

Firstly, they were deliberately classless. Unlike their indoor counterparts, there were no first or second class distinctions. As Sir Josiah Stamp, the Governor of the Bank of England and chairman of the London, Midland and Scottish Railway company declared at the opening of Morecambe's new open air baths in 1936, 'Bathing reduces rich and poor, high and low, to a common standard of enjoyment and health. When we get down to swimming, we get down to democracy.'

Secondly – again unlike most indoor baths built during the Victorian and Edwardian period – Britain's open air pools emerged at a time when mixed bathing was becoming more widely acceptable.

Possibly the last significant ladies-only outdoor pool to have been built was at King's Meadow, Reading, opened in 1903 (*page 166*), and while segregated sessions would continue at certain pools until the 1920s, the very fact that they appealed so strongly to children, and of course to holidaymakers in general, helped to strengthen the notion of swimming as a family activity.

(One consequence of this trend was that men and boys were forced to wear bathing costumes, which was seldom the rule in the single-sex Victorian swimming lakes).

But while the loosening of these class and gender barriers signalled

Burlington Street Free Open Air Bath
(EARLY MORNING THE BATH IS BEING FILLED WITH WARM WATER).

a departure from the past – or at least the Victorian past – other influences were equally at work to ensure that the promotion of open air swimming, *per se*, became enshrined in public policy, at both civic and national level.

By the early 1930s, open air pools had become emblems of municipal modernity and of faith in a brighter, more enlightened future, in much the same way as public libraries had become a generation or two earlier.

Health concerns clearly played a major role in this. »

▲ Although few of Britain's larger industrialised cities built lidos of any note, several were at the forefront of providing basic open air plunge baths in late 19th and early 20th centuries.

The provision at **Liverpool** was typical. The Burlington Street Free Open Air Baths, for example, was constructed following concerns that local boys were swimming in a polluted and dangerous canal.

Costing a mere £700 to build in 1895, it remained in use for some 45 years until being bombed during World War Two.

Entry was free of charge but was limited to boys only under 15.

So popular was Burlington Street that by the time Liverpool acted as hosts to a World Health Conference in 1903, three similar baths had been constructed. (Details of these will feature in a later book in the *Played in Britain* series – *Played in Liverpool* – see Links.)

All were provided as a social service. So, in 1927-28 it is recorded that 84,407 children used the Burlington Street Baths, which cost £368 10s to run. Total receipts for the year were just £1.

▶ Sun worshippers at **Guildford Lido**, shortly after its opening in July 1933. Perhaps one or two of them had seen or even read the cult bestseller of the day, Hans Surén's *Man and Sunlight*, which had first been published in Germany in 1924.

By the time it arrived in Britain three years later – published by Sollux, makers of sun-ray lamps – the book was in its 67th edition.

As Ken Worpole comments in his seminal history of the phenomenon, *Here Comes the Sun* (*see Links*), this may have been due more to the book's images of semi-naked men and women. But its message did tap into the prevailing zeitgeist.

'Greetings to you, you who are sun lovers!' wrote Surén, a former Chief of the German Army of Physical Exercises, in his introduction. 'You bear ardent longings in your hearts! Longings after warm sunshine, blue skies, light and nature; after victorious strength, spiritual loftiness and childlike faith.'

A fag and an ice cream cone too, judging by some of Guildford's sun lovers.

Compared with previous generations these new Britons wore lighter clothes, enjoyed longer holidays and had more disposable income. Sun tans and an outdoor life heralded their entry to an altogether better, brighter world.

» As Alicia Pivaro pointed out in *Farewell My Lido* (see Links) – a 1991 report by The Thirties Society to which we will often refer in this book – during the First World War, when shortages of animal fats led to a higher than usual incidence of rickets and tuberculosis, codliver oil was distributed as a substitute. However, it was soon realised that demand for the oil fell during the summer months.

This in turn led to the discovery that certain nutrients could be supplied by sunlight.

Groundbreaking work in this field had, meanwhile, been conducted by Dr Auguste Rollier at his clinic in the Swiss Alps.

In 1923, he published a detailed account of his methods in a book called *Heliotherapy*. In this, he described the beneficial effects of both natural sunlight and sun-lamp treatment on patients suffering from tuberculosis. Over 80 per cent of patients, he claimed, had been fully healed as a result.

Heliotherapy was just one catalyst for what may be described as the growing cult of 'sun worship'.

Again, this is thought to have originated in Germany, as just one adjunct of diverse social movements that championed, *inter alia*, vegetarianism, hiking, communalism and even nudism. (Tellingly, Britain's first nudist colony, formed in St Albans in 1929, was called the *Spielpatz*, or playground. Naturally it also had its own outdoor pool.)

At a rather more superficial level, fashion also played its part in this new found enthusiasm.

For centuries the possession of a sun tan had commonly been associated with manual labour. One's skin tone denoted one's rank. The paler the better.

In the 1920s that all changed. »

▲ An Italian interpretation of a British lido, by the Neopolitan artist **Fortunino Matania** (1881-1963).

One of the great illustrators of his age, Matania won acclaim for his graphic portrayals of momentous events – the sinking of the Titanic and the Lusitania, the battles of the First World War – reproduced in such magazines as the *Graphic* and *Illustrated London News*.

But in this classically inspired poster commissioned by the Cheshire Lines Railway in the late 1920s he showed his more jaunty side, almost caricaturing the sense of play and romance inherent in lido life at the peak of summer.

Writing in the *Daily Telegraph* in June 2000, Roger Deakin, author of the acclaimed swimmer's odyssey, *Waterlog* (see *Links*), expanded on Matania's theme.

'It must be a sign of our Anglo-Saxon awkwardness about the pleasures of the flesh that we borrowed the word lido from the Italians, just as we took café, restaurant and champagne from the French.

'Like restaurants, lidos are about style and sensuality. Iris Murdoch called swimming pools "machines for swimming in", but lidos are grander, more elaborate.

'Lidos are to swimming pools as lingerie is to underwear.

'Their outrageous fountains and curvaceous terraces celebrate the exuberant beauty of the water they frame, so that a special sense of freedom comes over you when you stand poised to plunge in.

'Lidos have always been designed with a strong sense of theatre... You go to a lido to bathe and to be seen to bathe.'

A little Italy indeed.

▲ Swaying palms and fairy lights at the **Purley Way Lido** in sunny **Croydon** during the late 1930s.

Britain's first open air swimming facility to have been officially titled 'lido' was the Serpentine Lido, named as such by the Labour MP George Lansbury at its opening in July 1930 (see page 26).

However the word may have been commonly understood before then. For example, in a description of the town's new open air pool in May 1928, a reporter from the *Southport Visiter* noted 'one was reminded forcibly of the Lido'.

After the Serpentine's opening, in October 1931 we then find a *Daily Express* report from Hastings, '£60,000 lido for England'.

But the term did not catch on immediately, or universally.

If we take lido to mean an open air pool with a terrace, lawn or beach area for sunbathing, plus a café and some form of spectator viewing area, then the Serpentine was by no means the first of its kind. Numerous earlier open air pools in the north – for example Scarborough, Blackpool and Southport – met all the above criteria, yet their local authorities studiously avoided the term lido, as if it were a southern affectation.

For its part, the London County Council – Britain's most prolific builders of lidos – deliberated for some time over the matter. A circular sent to members of its Parks and Open Spaces Committee in June 1937 stated that the word 'lido' was 'popularly recognised as connoting an expanse of sand with facilities for bathing and for basking in the sun.'

The LCC was therefore urged to use the term in all its documents.

'By doing so, the Council will lend its influence in enriching the English language by a word which may, in time, seem as much at home as earlier Italian introductions, such as concertina, ditto, broccoli, soda, motto, umbrella, salvo and influenza.'

A subsequent handwritten note, dated 25 June 1937, and presumably passed to a fellow committee member, read, 'You can call them lidos now!!'

Despite this, a year later, perhaps mindful that Italy was then in the grip of a Fascist dictatorship, an LCC official still expressed regret that no better English word could be found.

But none could, and to this day 'lido' still remains a useful generic term to denote any open air pool, whatever its range of facilities, swaying palms or not.

》 The credit, or blame, for this is usually ascribed to the French fashion designer and parfumiere, Coco Chanel, who turned the tan into an accessory no woman could possibly be without.

Still within the world of fashion, the introduction of synthetic materials from 1930 onwards allowed swimwear to become lighter, more figure-hugging and, as importantly, less absorbent.

At the same time, swimming for pleasure was an experience that more and more people had the time to enjoy. By the mid 1930s at least nine million British workers were eligible for paid holidays under voluntary agreements with employers. In 1938 these agreements were formalised by the Holidays with Pay Act, entitling all workers to a minimum of one week's paid holiday between May and October (with two weeks for domestic servants).

Of course the 1930s were also a time of high unemployment, reaching a peak of some three million in 1932. To alleviate this crisis the government made grants and low interest loans available to local authorities wishing to carry out works commissioned in the public interest, on condition that they hired unemployed workers.

It was also stipulated that British materials should be used, thus ensuring a flow of orders to suppliers.

And so this combination of economic, social, cultural and political factors resulted in a boom in the construction of open air pools and lidos.

Between 1930 and 1939, at least 180 were built in Britain, added to an estimated 50 completed during the previous decade.

By the end of the decade, hardly a town or city did not have at least one open air facility, however modest. There were 64 within the Greater London area alone (*see Chapter Three*).

Open air pools were even built in relatively small villages, such as Chagford in Devon and Street in Somerset (*see Chapter Seven*).

Here was a phenomenon on a truly national scale.

But then, in September 1939 – for several lidos at the end of only their first or second season – came the war.

Most closed to the public for the duration. A good many in urban areas were put at the disposal of the National Fire Service. Only a handful carried on, such as Uxbridge, which happened to be close to an RAF station.

Some lidos were damaged by enemy action, including Peterborough and Victoria Park. Some failed to reopen for several years after hostilities ended, due to shortages of materials. Saltdean Lido, having been open for only two seasons before the war began, did not reopen until 1964.

But for those that did resume operations in 1945, their popularity reached new heights, as the British people flocked in record numbers to places of sport, recreation and entertainment as a relief from the austerity that now gripped their daily lives.

During these immediate post war years lidos picked up where they left off in 1939, not only as places to swim but as social centres and as places of regular entertainment (*see Chapter Five*).

But this boom was not to last.

One of the first notes of caution was sounded in 1960 with the publication of the *Wolfenden Report on Sport in the Community*.

This concluded ominously that although more swimming

baths were urgently needed, 'as a general rule this provision should be indoor'.

Wolfenden also made the recommendation that 'large barns' be erected to accommodate a multiplicity of sports. Thus was born the idea of the indoor leisure centre, the 'must-have' sporting facility for local authorities from the 1960s onwards.

The advent of cheap package holidays also brought gloom to the nation's lidos.

Foreign travel to warmer climes, once the privilege of the wealthy, raised expectations that an unheated pool on a blustery day could simply no longer fulfil.

As one regular lido user recalled, 'At the time, a water »

▲ Mirroring the mass militaristic spectacles made popular in 1930s Germany and Italy, displays of physical prowess were commonly staged at lidos, such as here at the vast New Brighton Bathing Pool, Wallasey, when 1,200 schoolchildren took part in celebrations to mark the coronation of George VI in 1937.

Members of the Women's League of Health and Beauty, formed in 1930, regularly participated in these events. Familiar in their black and white silk costumes, by 1934 the League had enrolled 47,000 women nationwide.

This cult of fitness gained further ground in 1937 when the Physical Training and Recreation Act set out to provide a network of centres that

would maintain and improve 'the physical well-being of the people by means of exercise and recreation'.

Under the Act a committee offered grants for the provision of 'gymnasiums, playing fields, swimming baths, bathing places, holiday camps and camping sites.'

This was in addition to loans already offered by the Ministry of Health. Between 1934–37 more than £2.5 million was made available for public baths, wash-houses and swimming pools.

But amid all this serious intent, levity was never far from the surface. The highlight of a mass display at New Brighton in 1935 was a slapstick routine in which two men dressed as women were chased by a Keystone cop.

Municipalities were not alone in their passion for lidos, as seen here at the original Butlin's Holiday Camp, opened near Skegness in 1936. Throughout the 1930s open air pools were to be found at roadhouses (or motels) with names such as the Showboat at Maidenhead and the Ace of Spades in Surbiton. Hotels also got in on the act, most notably at the Ocean Hotel, Saltdean, where a substantial open air pool was designed by the same architect, RWH Jones, as the local lido (see *page 146*). Near Littlehampton an entire holiday camp was named the Rustington Lido, to add to its allure.

» temperature of 60 degrees Fahrenheit seemed normal. We didn't know any better. But later, once the family had been to Spain, they certainly didn't want to go into that again.'

Further blows befell the lido during the 1980s.

When Conservative Prime Minister, Margaret Thatcher, assumed office in May 1979, one of her stated aims was to deal with what she saw as the spendthrift habits of local authorities.

This stance led to two pieces of legislation, both destined to have a punishing effect on the operation of public leisure services.

Firstly the Local Government, Planning and Land Act 1980, required local authorities to contract out key council services to competitive tender.

Secondly, the Rates Act 1984 introduced the practice of

'rate-capping', whereby local authorities were penalised if they exceeded their budgets.

When council services were, in due course, contracted out, the new leisure operators soon discovered that lidos made no economic sense. Each required massive subsidies, reckoned in some local authorities to be around £5 per swim. One councillor in the London Borough of Tower Hamlets calculated an even higher figure. He stated that for every person paying the 50p entry fee at the Victoria Park lido, his Council was actually paying a subsidy of £37.

Threatened with rate capping if costs were not radically reduced, councils slashed non-statutory services wherever they could.

Dozens of lidos were axed as a result, particularly in the capital, where the London County

Council's once proud network of thirteen centrally managed open air pools had been handed over to borough council control in 1965.

But even those that did survive continued to suffer from a lack of investment. Maintenance regimes were cut back. Water quality suffered, as did staff morale.

Increasingly lidos would open later in the season and close earlier. Some opened only sporadically, or at short notice, with an inevitable loss of use.

Meanwhile, other areas of legislation added to the burden of lido operators.

The Health and Safety at Work Act 1974, for example, made employers responsible for the safety not only of their staff but of all visitors to their premises.

The Act also established the Health and Safety Commission, whose burgeoning rules have quite transformed the way our lidos operate, and appear.

Diving boards, once a defining feature of open air pools, have all but disappeared as a consequence (*see Chapter Four*). Other restrictions have followed, so that most pools nowadays are plastered with prohibition notices, put up by operators who dare not risk the consequences of any incident.

The European directive, Part-Time Workers Regulations (2000), has had a major impact on staffing. Essentially the legislation gives part-time workers the same employment rights as full-time staff, including sickness benefit, holiday pay and maternity and paternity leave. Since most lifeguards are part-timers, staffing costs have risen accordingly.

Thus within a fifty year period the legislative apparatus affecting open air swimming pools has transmuted from the enabling acts

BUTLIN'S SKEGNESS – *Outdoor Swimming Pool*

Photo: D. Noble, John Hinde Studios.

of the 1930s to the proscriptive regulations of today.

But if the political climate has changed, so too has the real climate. In another reverse from the 1930s, sunbathing is no longer the innocent pleasure it once seemed. Since the detection of a hole in the ozone layer in the 1980s, the number of reported cases of skin cancer in the UK has more than doubled.

So is the lido doomed to extinction in the 21st century?

As of 2005, around 100 open-air pools remain in operation, less than a third of the total recorded half a century ago. (These are listed in full in the Directory on pages 182-83.)

At a time when the health of the British people is the subject of a much wider debate, the consequences of this decline cannot be dismissed lightly.

But in the context of this book, there is of course another issue, and that is the ongoing threat to so many lidos of both historic and architectural significance.

As mentioned earlier, in 1991, The Thirties Society (now The Twentieth Century Society) published *Farewell My Lido*, the first detailed examination of the social history, architecture and survival strategies of lidos in Britain.

Preceding this, in 1982, SAVE Britain's Heritage published *Taking the Plunge*, a wider lament upon the state of the nation's bathing-related architectural heritage, indoor and outdoor.

Neither report made for comfortable reading. As its title suggests, *Farewell My Lido*, in particular, painted a gloomy picture, at a time when only one operating lido, Saltdean, was listed, and dozens more were under threat.

Liquid Assets is, in essence, an update and an expansion of that report, fourteen years later.

To summarise: the final decade of the 20th century brought both hope and frustration.

On the listings front, undoubted progress has been made.

As highlighted in the previous chapter, the Clifton Pool in Bristol was listed Grade II* in 1998, and is now the subject of a restoration programme after narrowly escaping demolition.

To add to Saltdean, largely thanks to pressure from The Twentieth Century Society, SAVE Britain's Heritage and other groups, since 1991 a further twelve open air pools and lidos have been listed Grade II (*see right*).

Of these, eight still function, of which five have been partially or greatly improved since 1993 thanks to the injection of considerable sums of public money, from local authorities, the National Lottery and other funding bodies. A sixth, Brockwell Park, is next for a revamp, in 2005-06.

We may therefore have fewer survivors, but the more historic ones are at least now much better protected and cared for than at any time since the 1970s.

Equally, as we report in Chapter Seven, dozens of smaller, less architecturally significant pools have been rescued from oblivion by the concerted action of local campaigners and volunteers.

So, despite ongoing concerns – for example, at King's Meadow, Reading and Broomhill Pool, Ipswich – there is life in the 20th century lido yet.

For now we conclude by noting the instructive experiences of a select few who have sought Lottery funding for lidos and open air pools during the last decade.

In the 1930s local authorities could call on a variety of public funds for lido construction.

Yet in 2001 an application by the Hampton Open Air Pool in Middlesex for Sports Lottery funding failed on the grounds that outdoor pools were not deemed value for money.

Sport England, which administers the fund, stated that although it does not have a bias against open air pools *per se*, they are unlikely to meet funding criteria unless they specifically widen participation in sporting activity, all year round.

By contrast, the Heritage Lottery Fund has awarded the Jubilee Pool in Penzance £294,300, in 1998, and £492,438 towards improvements planned at Brockwell Park, in 2004.

Both pools are Grade II listed.

How ironic therefore that our surviving liquid assets stand a better chance of being saved for their heritage, rather than for any recreational or sporting value they may be judged to possess.

▲ Despite appearances, hope springs eternal for the restoration of **Uxbridge Lido**, Hillingdon.

Opened in 1935 but boarded up since 1998, the lido forms the focus of a major multi-sports redevelopment proposal for which, as of 2005, funding was being sought by Hillingdon Council.

Uxbridge is one of 13 Grade II listed lidos.

Those that still function are: The Jubilee Pool, Penzance (opened 1935); Tinside Lido, Plymouth (1935); Peterborough Lido (1936); Greenbank Pool, Street (1937); Brockwell Park, London (1937); Saltdean, Brighton (1938); Parliament Hill Fields Lido, London (1938) and Pools on the Park, Richmond, London (1965).

Those that remain closed and awaiting future developments are: the Cleveland Pool, Bath (opened 1815); King's Meadow, Reading (1903), Uxbridge Lido (1935) and Broomhill Pool, Ipswich (1938).

Also listed Grade II is the former lido at Worthing (1925), now a family entertainment centre.

Chapter Three

London

George Lansbury's contribution to open air swimming is commemorated by this plaque at the Lido Pavilion, on the banks of the Serpentine in Hyde Park. As a councillor for Poplar and later a Labour MP and government minister – he was also London's first Commissioner of Works – Lansbury actively promoted the rights of working people to outdoor recreation. Since its creation around 1730 the Serpentine Lake had been a popular swimming lake for men and boys. In 1929, much to the ire of the Park Commissioners and conservative opinion, Lansbury extended the bathing facilities to women too.

The one local authority in Britain that did more than any other to promote the design and construction of open air pools during the 20th century was the London County Council.

A precursor of the modern day Greater London Authority and, before that, the Greater London Council, the LCC governed the capital from 1889 to 1965, from straight-laced Victorian times through to the swinging Sixties.

During that time, directly or indirectly, the LCC had a hand in the design, construction or management of no fewer than six open air pools between 1906-25; seven lido-style pools from 1931-39, and, to cap it all, a children's pool in Southwark, in 1938.

Moreover, these figures do not include a further six open air pools built between 1922-46 by other borough councils whose boundaries fell within the overall extent of the LCC's borders.

Had the Second World War not interrupted its plans in 1939, the LCC might well have gone on to add a further three lidos to its astonishing tally.

Taken as a whole, between the LCC and the individual boroughs, here was an achievement that will surely never be matched in the history of local government in Britain, or perhaps anywhere in the world.

Hardly surprisingly, in the course of all this activity, the design team of the Council's Parks Department – under whose auspices the work fell – developed an expertise that was second to none. As we noted in the previous chapter, the LCC was also directly instrumental in formalising the use of the term lido, in 1937.

In no sense, therefore, has metropolitan bias been a factor in singling out London for a chapter of its own. And should any reader remain sceptical of the contribution made by the capital to our story of Britain's lidos and open air pools, then the map which follows on page 31 will surely prove the point.

When Herbert Morrison, the LCC's chairman from 1934-40, made a vow to turn London into 'a city of lidos', in 1937, it was no idle promise.

By 1951 there were at least 60 open air pools operating in the Greater London area, the equivalent of approximately one per 120,000 people.

This compared with a ratio of one per 161,000 in other parts of England, Scotland and Wales.

Londoners were therefore a third better served than the rest of the country.

But this provision was by no means a new phenomenon. London's first purpose-built pool, as we read in Chapter One, is thought to have been the Peerless Pool in Finsbury, which operated from 1743-1850. We also know that swimming was popular in the Serpentine Lake from 1730 onwards, as indeed it was in the Thames and London's other rivers and ponds from time immemorial.

As highlighted on the opposite page, London also had a network of swimming lakes created in the latter half of the 19th century; at Victoria Park, Brockwell Park, Plumstead Common, Clapham Common and Hampstead Heath.

But for the LCC its first link with a purpose-built facility came in »

▶ In no other city during the Victorian era was outdoor bathing as well catered for as London.

As mentioned earlier, the capital's first formalised swimming lake was the Serpentine, created in Hyde Park in 1730.

William Tayler, a footman, describes in his diary a walk on 25 June 1837: 'Went to the Serpentine River to see the bathers. There were many hundreds just got out and dressing themselves before I got there, as I was rather late and they are obliged to get out of the water at eight o'clock.'

(As bathers generally swam naked, this early morning limit was aimed at protecting the sensibilities of more refined park users. It also deterred men from lingering during working hours.)

'I walked round the water and counted all that was in then, and I counted 347, therefore I should suppose there is about 1,500 - 1,600 men and boys bathe in the Serpentine on a Sunday morning, beside what bathe in other waters around London.'

According to the Royal Humane Society's Annual Report for 1844, that number had risen to 'at least 8,000 bathers every day' during the hot summer of that year.

But as Tayler reported, the Serpentine was not the only swimming lake in the capital. At least four other locations were immensely popular, namely at Brockwell Park, Plumstead Common, **Victoria Park, Hackney** (*shown above c.1899*), and in north west London, at Parliament Hill and Hampstead Heath.

The practice of swimming at Victoria Park began a year after the park opened in 1845, when, to the dismay of the park's sponsors, hundreds of men and boys dived into the new boating lake.

Realising that this demand had to be met, a separate bathing lake was excavated, 300 feet long, with a concrete lining and hedged surrounds. Two boatmen were placed on duty to keep order and rescue those in difficulty.

As at the Serpentine, the lake was made available only between 4-8am on summer mornings.

Unsurprisingly the water quality rapidly declined, and in 1876 a larger lake, 650 x 127 feet, was created elsewhere within the park.

Every morning, it was said, 30,000 gallons of fresh water were pumped into its vast expanse.

The older, smaller pool was, meanwhile, put at the disposal of women, perhaps the first time this had been done anywhere in Britain.

Victoria Park's lake and those in south London were closed in the early 1930s, when stricter standards for water quality – set out in the 1936 Public Health Act – came into effect. At Victoria Park the direct result was the construction of a new lido in 1936 (*page 114*), followed by Brockwell Park (*page 138*) a year later.

At their peak these Victorian swimming lakes must have presented an awesome spectacle.

According to the LCC, on one summer morning an estimated 25,000 male bathers were counted before 8am at Victoria Park.

In August 1909 the *East London Advertiser* added this reflection.

'Five thousand boys lined the edge of the lake, the left foot forward ready to dive or swim. Some looked puny and emaciated, their thin, sapless limbs telling the awful tale of life in the mean streets of London.'

Today, three swimming ponds on Hampstead Heath remain in public use (*see page 171*), as does the Serpentine.

▶ Capital losses – three London pools from amongst the 58 that are known to have closed at various times during the 20th century.

The **Millwall Open Air Pool** (*right*), opened in 1925 and was one of six built or co-financed by the LCC before the advent of the Council's more elaborate lidos of the 1930s. All were no frills designs with plain retaining walls and stepladder diving stages, but no cafés or sunbathing terraces.

Millwall was badly damaged during the Blitz and was eventually demolished in the 1960s.

Southall Open Air Baths on Florence Road (*centre*) was a relatively early creation, by Southall Norwood Urban District Council; opened in 1913, rebuilt 1930, and shown here after closing in 1982.

One of London's longest running lido-related disputes centred upon the **Twickenham Open Air Pool** (*below right*), scenically located on the Thames Embankment, facing Eel Pie Island.

Opened in 1935, alas its virtues were insufficient to save it from closure in 1981, and for 24 long years thereafter it formed a magnet for vandals and seekers of picturesque dereliction.

After three planning enquiries, its failure to gain a listing, and numerous unsuccessful attempts to redevelop the site, the pool was finally levelled in 2004.

Open-air Swimming Baths, Twickenham.

» 1906, when, after two years of bargaining, Wandsworth Borough Council finally persuaded the Council to release land at Tooting for an outdoor pool, and to pay £200 a year for its running costs.

The pool itself was built as part of a scheme to provide work for unemployed men in the area.

A similar motive led the LCC to return to outdoor pool construction, in 1922, as levels of unemployment soared after the First World War.

As detailed by Elain Harwood in *Farewell My Lido* (*see Links*), by this time the Council was controlled by a group of Conservative councillors who called themselves the Municipal Reformers.

It was their decision to commit the LCC to build and manage its own pools in three London boroughs, at Highbury Fields, Peckham Rye and Southwark Park.

All three were built by unemployed workers, funded by the Ministry of Labour, and were opened in September 1923.

But where it could, the Council still preferred to enter agreements similar to the one at Tooting, whereby the local borough footed the bill for construction materials and shared the running costs.

Three further pools built on this basis were at Silvertown (1922), Eltham Park (1924), and Millwall (1925).

Meanwhile, independently of the LCC, three London boroughs proceeded to build their own pools; at Bellingham (1922), White City (1923) and Poplar (1924).

All London's pools of the 1920s were basic, rectangular designs with rudimentary changing facilities. Compared with their seaside counterparts, in Blackpool or Southport, for example, they were certainly utilitarian.

Also, they were segregated, at least until 1927, when mixed bathing was finally permitted at certain times, albeit with an entry fee. (They were otherwise free.)

Another common factor in the 1920s was that London's pools all operated on the 'fill and empty' principle. That is, they would be filled and then emptied only when the water had become unacceptably murky.

As can be imagined, this system led to quite distasteful conditions – see the section on Tooting Bec, for example (*page 52*) – forcing the LCC to experiment with filtration systems, first at Highbury Fields and Peckham, in the late 1920s.

'It is scarcely possible to exaggerate the improvement from the point of view of the bather,' commented the Parks Committee on seeing the results.

In 1931 the LCC embarked upon a new phase of construction, starting with two similar designs at Kennington Park in 1931 and London Fields the year after.

Both differed from their predecessors in that they were architect-designed, fully enclosed brick compounds with purpose-built changing rooms (rather than lean-to cubicles), first-aid facilities, integrated filtration systems – including a new type of tiered aerator, or fountain (*see page 37*) – and pools set at a standard size of 165 x 66 feet.

No doubt inspired by the opening of the Serpentine Lido in 1930, they also included areas for sunbathing. London Fields even had its own café.

Although it cannot be stated for certain, it is likely that both Kennington Park and London Fields were the work of two architects employed by the LCC's Parks Department.

Certainly their designs shared numerous characteristics with later designs that definitely were ascribed to the pair.

The two men were Harry Arnold Rowbotham and TL Smithson.

According to Elain Harwood in *Farewell My Lido*, Rowbotham had joined the LCC in 1902 and was responsible for an extensive range of shelters, cafés and other small buildings in London parks.

His and Smithson's London lidos form a distinct sub-genre within the overall context of British lidos; hard to place stylistically – being only faintly Art Deco, yet patently Modernist in character – and certainly never copied anywhere outside London.

Indeed compared with the stadium-like concrete arenas being built in such places as Hastings and New Brighton, London's new lidos were decidedly restrained. And inexpensive.

Hastings cost £60,000 in 1933, New Brighton £103,000 the year after. By contrast, the LCC's next and most ambitious lido, at Victoria Park in 1936, cost just £26,000.

Both Victoria Park Lido and its near twin, Brockwell Park Lido, replaced swimming lakes that were finally rendered obsolete during the particularly hot summers of 1933 and 1934.

By the time Brockwell Park opened, however, in July 1937, a major change in policies had taken place at the LCC. A new and ambitious Labour controlled administration had decided that, following the success of Victoria Park, instead of trying to negotiate with reluctant local boroughs to co-finance and build new pools, the LCC would take over the entire process itself; design, construction and management. »

▲ Officials from Hackney Borough Council line up to see young swimmers open the season at **Victoria Park Lido** in 1952.

The London Metropolitan Archives contain many such images of civic pride; of mayors cutting ribbons, of dignitaries handing out medals at galas, of minor celebrities turning out to judge diving competitions.

Victoria Park Lido (*see page 114*) was a typical Rowbotham and Smithson design for the LCC; that is, a rectangular brick compound with rounded corners, a main entrance on one side, a café opposite, and a fountain at one end – indeed similar in plan to **Parliament Hill Fields Lido**, shown below. (The original drawings on which this plan was based are reproduced on page 154.)

No trace of Victoria Park Lido survives. Since its demolition in 1990 a car park occupies the site.

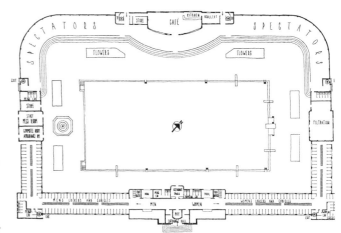

>> Not only that but it also pledged that in future no Londoner would have to walk further than a mile and a half to their nearest lido.

On 12 July 1937 *The Times* published a map showing how the plan would be implemented, with seven new lidos to add to the 14 already in operation.

To implement this plan would, it was estimated, cost £150,000.

'In March,' declared Herbert Morrison, 'I promised the people of London that the new LCC would make London a City of Lidos. Here we are.'

The immediate plan was to build five lidos, at Parliament Hill, Charlton, Battersea Park, Ladywell Recreation Ground and Clissold Park. These would be complemented by a sixth, to be be built by the local authority in Paddington.

This would make a total of 22 lidos within the LCC's boundaries, including the Serpentine; hardly enough to be within a mile and a half of most Londoners, but a fair spread all the same.

But the chain would never be completed.

Parliament Hill Fields and Charlton were duly opened in 1938 and 1939 respectively. But once war broke out the remaining three never left the drawing-board.

After the war other priorities – homes, schools, hospitals and so

on – assumed greater importance, and by the time building materials and funds were available once more for non-essential buildings, in the 1960s, the impetus for lidos had, as elsewhere in Britain, dissipated.

Thus, only two outdoor pools have been built in London since the Second World War: the Oasis in Holborn, which had been started in 1937 but opened in 1946 (*see page 173*) and the Pools on the Park, in Richmond, in 1965.

That same year Herbert Morrison died, coincidentally within days of the LCC's abolition and its replacement by the Greater London Council.

Within a few years Morrison's City of Lidos had split asunder.

Responsibility for most of the pools passed to individual borough councils, few of whom could afford, or knew how to manage these deteriorating assets.

In 1975 there were 50 outdoor pools in the Greater London area.

Today, just eight remain, plus the Serpentine and the swimming ponds on Hampstead Heath.

Of these, three are surviving Rowbotham and Smithson designs; Brockwell Park and Parliament Hill Fields, both now Grade II listed, and Charlton.

A fourth, London Fields, is scheduled for re-opening in 2007 (*see page 169*).

▶ Opened in May 1939, **Charlton Lido** was the last of the LCC pools to be built, and the last designed by Rowbotham and Smithson.

In plan it consists of the standard LCC rectangular brick compound, but with notable differences in its elevations; for example, a semi-circular bay (*right*), with a splendid, though non-functioning clock, forming the poolside entry.

Another variant is the location of its two fountains, set into one of the boundary walls (*see page 37*).

Failures in its disinfection plant have caused it to be closed in recent years, although it opened in 2005 after £67,000 worth of repairs. But without a listing, and with some £500,000 still needed for other work, its long term future must remain a cause for concern.

London, the 'city of lidos' – shown here are the 68 full-size lidos and open air pools so far identified as being open for public use during at least part of the 20th century. For a fuller listing of their locations see the Directory on page 176.

The numbered locations (in black) denote facilities no longer in operation. The lettered locations (in green) denote facilities in use as of the summer of 2005.

(Based on Ordnance Survey map
© Crown Copyright. All rights reserved.
English Heritage, 100019088, 2005.)

1. Alexandra Park Open Air Baths
2. Barking Open Air Pool
3. Bellingham Open Air Pool
4. Bexley Open Air Pool
5. Blue Pool, Hillingdon
6. Bromley Open Air Pool
7. Charles Crescent Lido, Harrow
8. Compton Leisure Centre, Northolt
9. Craven Park Lido, Willesden
10. Durnsford Road Lido
11. Ealing Northern Sports Centre
12. East Ham Open Air Baths
13. Edensor Baths, Chiswick
14. Eltham Park Lido
15. Enfield Lido
16. Erith Outdoor Pool
17. Finchley Lido
18. Geraldine Mary Harmsworth
    Lido, Lambeth
19. Gladstone Park Pool, Willesden
20. Highbury Fields Lido
21. Houndsfield Lido, Edmonton
22. Kennington Park Lido
23. King Edward's Pool, Willesden
24. Kingfisher Pool, Woodford Gn
25. Kingsbury Lido
26. Lagoon Pool, St Mary Cray
27. Larkswood Pool, Chingford
28. Leys Open Air Pool, Dagenham
29. London Fields Lido, Hackney
30. Martens Grove Pool, Bexleyheath
31. Mill Hill Swimming Pool
32. Millwall Open Air Pool
33. Peckham Rye Bathing Pool
34. Poplar Open Air Baths
35. Purley Way Lido, Croydon
36. Roehampton Open Air Baths

37. Ruislip Lido
38. Silvertown Open Air Bath
39. Southall Open Air Bath
40. Southwark Park Lido
41. Surbiton Lagoon
42. Teddington Lido
43. Tottenham Lido
44. Twickenham Lido
45. Uxbridge Lido
46. Valence Park Lido, Dagenham
47. Valentine's Park Lido, Ilford
48. Victoria Park Lido, Hackney
49. Wandle Park, Croydon
50. Wandsworth Open Air Pool
51. Wealdstone Open Air Baths
52. Wembley Open Air Baths
53. West Ham Lido
54. West Hendon Lido
55. Whipps Cross Lido
56. White City Lido, Hammersmith
57. Wimbledon Open Air Baths
58. Yiewsley Pool

A. Brockwell Park Lido
B. Charlton Lido, Hornfair Park
C. Hampstead Heath Ponds
D. Hampton Heated Open Air Pool
E. Oasis Sports Centre, Holborn
F. Park Road Pools, Hornsey
G. Parliament Hill Lido, Gospel Oak
H. Pools on the Park, Richmond
I. Serpentine Lido, Hyde Park
J. Tooting Bec Lido

Chapter Four

Design

Stunt diving into just 15 feet of water at Morecambe's aptly named Super Swimming Stadium in the early 1950s. For the view from the top, see page 51.

In 1938 the Royal Institute of British Architects staged an exhibition at its London headquarters called 'Health, Sport and Fitness'.

In the exhibition catalogue, the RIBA President, HS Goodhart-Rendel, summarised its aims.

'Everywhere in Europe [sport] has become recognised as a necessary ingredient in the life of a healthy nation.'

Architects, he urged, should play their part in providing the 'appropriate buildings' to serve that need. By doing so, they would be acting as 'the preventive officer of ill-health and disease.'

Yet despite these aspirations, the truth is that most 20th century open air pools were designed not by architects but by borough engineers or surveyors.

There were exceptions.

In London, as we read in the previous chapter, Harry Rowbotham and TL Smithson of the London County Council's Parks Department design team, produced a series of lidos that expressed Modernist ideals in a functional style.

Kenneth MB Cross, who together with his father Alfred, specialised in indoor pools, and who was President of RIBA from 1956-57, was another.

Combining with Cecil Sutton, Cross designed one of the finest lidos of the period, the aptly titled Super Swimming Stadium at Morecambe in 1936 (see page 126).

In the 1938 edition of his seminal book, Modern Public Baths, published by the Amateur Swimming Association, Cross criticised the way local authorities commissioned open air baths.

'In many cases sufficient importance has not been attached to the employment of properly trained, practising architects, and the delegation of this work to officials whose business is not architecture but surveying or engineering, frequently results in schemes which are both costly and unattractive in appearance.'

But if this were a little harsh, it is true that the use of in-house engineers meant that apart from London, no single individual or group of designers ever worked on more than one or two pools.

Moreover, none might be considered amongst the leading practitioners of their day.

Had it been otherwise, perhaps more would have survived until the present day. On the other hand, the use of in-house designers did result in an extraordinary diversity of styles and approaches.

At Scarborough, St Annes and Peterborough, Italianate influences were at work. At Blackpool and Southport the Beaux Arts style held sway.

There were echoes of Frank Lloyd Wright and Willem Dudok in the distinctive brick compounds found only amongst the LCC lidos of the 1930s, whereas at Finchley and Purley neo-classical details formed a bridge between municipal conservatism and burgeoning modernity.

But overall, it has to be said, the majority of pools were of little or no architectural merit. Dozens were simply rectangular in plan, surrounded by shed-like changing rooms and cheap fencing.

The style most associated with lidos at their best, during the 1930s, was that of Art Deco. »

Penzance Bathing Pool

▲ Although the most common plan remained the simple rectangle, Britain's open air pools and lidos of the inter war period took diverse forms; partly to facilitate a variety of uses, but also to enhance their aesthetic appeal.

For example at **New Brighton** (*top left and page 86*), built in 1934, the D shaped pool – with its shallower, beach side forming the curved portion – was extended with a deeper rectangle to accommodate competitions, water polo and, in its centre, the diving pit. As can be detected in the photograph, these varying depths are reflected by the darkness of the water.

At **Macduff** in Scotland (*top right*), built c.1935, the tidal pool was divided into two sections, for adults and children. Southampton's pool adopted a similar layout (*see page 16*), but to segregate male from female swimmers.

In **Enfield**, north London (*above right*), built in 1932, the elliptical, stadium-like plan of the outer walls enclosed a rectangular pool, with cutaway steps leading into the water and a fountain, or aerator, placed opposite the diving stages.

A departure from these more formalised, symmetrical layouts was the triangular shaped **Jubilee Pool** in **Penzance**, built in 1935

(*above left and page 92*) and still in use today after a major refurbishment in 1993.

Its designer, the Borough Engineer Captain Frank Latham, claimed that he adopted the three-sided plan after witnessing the pattern of ripples formed as a seagull alighted on the sea.

Tidal pools such as Penzance and Macduff provided an ideal haven for swimmers, without the costs of having to install water circulation equipment.

Other interesting pool layouts can be seen at Uxbridge (*page 106*), Plymouth (*page 108*) and Saltdean (*page 146*).

BATHING POOL, PRESTATYN

▲ Before the onset of Modernism, stylistically Britain's open air pool designers played safe with holidaymakers' expectations.

Prestatyn Bathing Pool opened in 1923 and designed by the distinguished partnership of Howard Morley Robertson and John Murray Easton, featured a classical pavilion, facing onto an unusual irregular shaped pool. Although a lido in all but name, having a café, sunbathing terraces and viewing areas, it was only renamed as a lido after being substantially remodelled in 1960.

Kenneth Cross and Cecil Sutton's **Super Swimming Stadium** at **Morecambe** (*below*), opened in 1936, showed in both name and plan how the larger lidos of the 1930s adopted many of the design principles of modern stadiums, with grandstands, VIP viewing balconies, restaurants and defined circulation routes to maintain separation from wet and dry zones.

In a similar vein, Portobello, in Edinburgh, also dating from 1936 (*see page 120*) might easily have been designed as a small arena for football or rugby.

» As is often cited, the model for this trend was the Piscine Molitor, a classic Art Deco pool complex opened in Paris in 1929 and designed by Lucien Pollet.

As it transpired, none of its British successors actually followed the Piscine Molitor's form, characterised as it was by galleries enclosing the outdoor pool, like a town square, with an indoor pool adjoining.

But in its use of rendering, faience work and tiling, the Paris pool undoubtedly ushered in the notion, and the spirit, of the modern 'urban beach'.

Until then Britain's more elaborate open air pools were found in coastal resorts.

Thereafter, inspired by the Piscine Molitor, and by other examples from Germany and Italy – where Mussolini initiated a major construction programme of sports complexes and pools – Britain's lidos took on a quite different appearance.

As in other Modernist buildings of the period, features that came to characterise the lidos of the 1930s were flat roofs, rounded corners, metal-framed windows and white,

or off-white rendered walls, often with blue or green detailing.

Prime examples of lidos in this guise were at New Brighton, Hilsea, Plymouth, Portobello, Morecambe and Ipswich, all of which are featured as case studies in Chapter Six.

Arguably the Modernist style reached its high point in 1935 with the unveiling of the De La Warr Pavilion in Bexhill-on-Sea, by Erich Mendelsohn and Serge Chermayeff.

Intriguingly a model of one of the architects' earlier proposals for the pavilion – currently on display at the V&A Museum's RIBA Architecture Gallery – shows a small circular outdoor pool in front of the pavilion.

Alas that part of the scheme was never built, and neither Mendelsohn nor Chermayeff nor any of their noted contemporaries in the International Modern movement were ever commissioned to design a lido.

But if they had, they could hardly have improved upon Saltdean Lido, which echoed the De La Warr Pavilion's streamlined forms and curvilinear frontage.

Designed by the architect RWH Jones and opened in 1938, Saltdean may be considered the crowning glory of the 1930s lido phenomenon. In 1987 it became Britain's third lido-related structure to be listed, following on from Weston-super-Mare's classic concrete diving board, which was controversially demolished in 1982 (*see page 134*), and the Worthing Lido (*page 172*).

Saltdean, the Weston diving board and many other 1930s lidos were examples of how the use of reinforced concrete was ideally suited to pool design. Here was a material that offered flexibility, yet

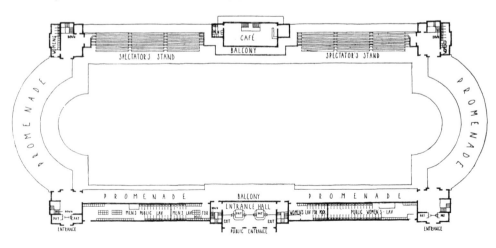

was robust, allowed for smooth, unadorned surfaces, and not least was, at its best, ideally suited to outdoor structures.

When considering the design of lidos, the most common elements are as follows.

The pool itself, or tank, which may take almost any form. (Maintenance of the tank and the prevention of leakage is perhaps the single most troublesome apect of a lido's operation. As shown on page 157, however, the use of stainless steel linings may yet offer a solution to this problem.)

Other than at tidal pools, water filtration systems have been standard at lidos since the 1920s.

Although their inner workings are unseen by users, they do include one design feature that was common to lidos of the inter war period; that is the aerator, or fountain. Tiered like a wedding cake, they are most commonly circular set in an octagonal base (*see page 37*).

Other elements of a lido that vary in form and extent are the sunbathing terraces or lawns, cafés, spectator areas (few of which survive), entrance blocks and dressing rooms. These buildings, either singly or combined, offer the designer the most scope for expression.

The final element once common to all open air pools and lidos are the diving boards.

In many locations – at LCC pools in particular – these were standard issue accessories, bought off the shelf and purely functional.

However at certain lidos the diving boards, invariably formed from reinforced concrete, were finely tuned pieces of sculptural engineering.

Several are featured within this book (*see, for example, pages 38-39*),

not least the aforementioned one at Weston-super-Mare (*page 136*).

Its loss, still keenly felt, and that of several other lost 1930s treasures – most notably at New Brighton, Portobello, Morecambe and Chingford – remains a matter of deep regret. Only in the last decade or so does it seem that the lido's true worth, in both architectural and social terms, has been finally recognised.

Thus the preservation, and ongoing maintenance of those that survive must remain firmly on the nation's heritage agenda.

But at the same time it would be wonderful to imagine that Kenneth Cross's challenge, issued in 1938, might yet be taken up by one of our leading architects of today.

Aqua electrics at the Broomhill Pool, Ipswich (*top*) in 1938. Floodlights and underwater lamps were commonly installed at 1930s lidos, helping to attract large numbers of swimmers and revellers on hot summer nights. Purley Way Lido in Croydon (*see page 98*) was especially well lit. At Blackpool (*above*) the illuminations were for the benefit of tourists rather than swimmers.

We specialise in **REINFORCED CONCRETE**

OPEN-AIR SWIMMING BATH at Commonweal School, Purley, Surrey. *Architects: Elms & Jupp, F.F.R.I.B.A.*

AERATOR FOUNTAIN at Enfield Open-Air Baths. Similar Fountains have been erected at Hornsey, Barking, Guildford, Hunstanton, etc.

SPIRAL STAIRCASE at Barking Open-Air Baths.

SWIMMING BATHS

Aerator Fountains
Non-Slip Curbing
and
Cast Stone Work

and we are proud of a fine reputation for good work.

BRADFORDS
F · BRADFORD & CO · LTD
REINFORCED CONCRETE ENGINEERS

ANGEL ROAD   EDMONTON · N · 18
TELEPHONE:— TOTTENHAM 4267 (3 LINES)

HOLLOW BLOCK FLOORS : WATERPROOFING · REINFORCED CONCRETE STAIRCASES :: CAST STONE · GRANOLITHIC PAVING

▶ First introduced during the mid 1920s, the fountain, or aerator – or even cascade as it was sometimes called – forms the last stage of the water-cleansing and purification process, adding air and therefore a touch of sparkle to the water before it is re-circulated back into the pool.

In common with diving boards, fountains had an aesthetic appeal to match their practical value.

Constructed from concrete and often circular in plan on an octagonal base, fountains provided pool and lido designers with a useful point of focus for poolside landscaping and terrace layouts.

They also looked wonderful when lit at night, as was the case at Finchley Lido in London (*see page 76*), Purley Way in Croydon (*page 98*), and Tinside Pool at Plymouth (*page 108*), where the floodlit cascades with their ever changing coloured lights formed part of a nightly display for passing tourists. (Tinside still stages light shows today.)

One of the leading suppliers of fountains was the Leeds Fireclay Company. Formed in 1889 and with a showroom in London, the company originally specialised in the manufacture of glazed bricks and decorative tiles.

Its first fountains – costing £115 10s. each – are thought to have been those supplied around

Reinforced concrete allowed engineers to give full rein to their creativity when it came to lido design, as exemplified by Bradfords & Co's spiral staircase and chute installation at Barking in east London (*left*).

1927-28 to the London County Council at its recently opened pools at Southwark Park, Highbury Fields and Peckham Rye, where until then – as was the practice at all but a few pools, indoor and outdoor – the tank was simply filled, and then emptied, only when the water became too murky for comfort (usually after a week or so).

By contrast, the new filtration systems, each of which cost around £3,000 to install, were able to circulate the water in a typical pool once every five or six hours.

Soon every lido, such as **Larkswood** (*below*) was boasting about the quality of its water.

For many years fountains drew swimmers, young and old, to sit on their inviting stepped tiers and to cavort in their spray. The archives are full of such playful images. Fountains were part of the fun of open air swimming.

And even for those unwilling to get close, they provided attractive water features in their own right.

Nowadays, however, although numerous original fountains still remain in use, few are left unscreened in one way or another.

Accidents, and in one instance, at Tooting Bec, the drowning of a child, resulted in stricter health and safety guidelines that advise pool operators either to modify or withdraw from use any water feature that is 'misused'.

Fountains were supplied in various shapes and sizes, and were generally sited on the paved areas closest to the shallow end. But they could also be located within the pool itself, as seen at Tinside, Plymouth (*see page 108*) and here at Ilkley Lido, Yorkshire (*above*) – a rare example of a still unscreened fountain. Also unusual is this wall-mounted aerator, one of two still functioning at the former LCC lido at Charlton, in London (*left*).

Design

▶ In 1903, the Amateur Diving Association described diving as 'the art of entering the water in a graceful manner'. By the 1930s, advances in the use of reinforced concrete allowed diving stages to attain a grace of their own, such as here at **Black Rock** in **Brighton**, by engineer D Edwards in 1935.

Edwards' design may have been modelled on a similar 10m board at Scarborough's South Bay pool (*see page 60*), which itself was remembered not only for its daring angle but also, according to divers, because it swayed in high winds.

Less artfully, standard diving stages were supplied by **Wicksteed & Co.** of Kettering (still a leading maker of playground equipment).

This galvanised tubular steel diving stage (*below*), from their 1936 brochure, could be supplied with three, four or five boards, at prices from £97 10s to £125.

◀ Diving stages at lidos and open air pools are all but extinct today, the victim of stringent safety requirements introduced in the 1970s. At many pools not even a modest 1m board is permitted.

Britain's first pupose-built diving stage was erected at the Highgate Pond on Hampstead Heath in 1893, where, five years later, a demonstration of 'fancy diving' by two Swedes, Otto Hageborge and Charles Mauritizi, helped to popularise the new sport.

For designers of both indoor and outdoor pools, there soon evolved a set of recommendations for board heights and appropriate water depths. Oddly, in Britain at least, while the heights were always expressed in metres – as they were set at international level – the depths were given in Imperial measures. (Britain's pools went fully metric only in the 1960s).

By the 1930s the minimum ratios were set at 8'6" (2.6m) of water depth for a 1m springboard, rising to 14' (4.3m) for a 10m fixed board. In practice most larger lidos had diving pits 15' deep (4.6m).

Nowadays greater depths are mandatory; for example, 3.5m minimum for a 1m board, and 5m for a 10m board.

Following a number of deaths at pools, however, diving pits must be separate from swimming areas.

The dramatic diving scenes found throughout this book will therefore never be repeated in any open air pool today.

As to materials, advice in the 1930s stated that springboards were to be made of Douglas Fir, Oregon or British Columbian Pine, while firm boards were to be pitch pine or teak, treated with linseed oil. All boards had to be covered in coconut matting.

— FRONT ELEVATION —

◀ Diving stages helped to define a swimming pool's character, and clearly offered designers terrific scope. But few remain.

This slender, arched diving stage at **Stroud**, in Gloucestershire (*left*) is a poignant reminder of its larger counterpart, once standing at Weston-super-Mare (*page 136*).

Less celebrated (*above left*) was the concrete behemoth at **West Ham Lido**, East London, built in 1937 and demolished 50 years later. It must have taken some clout to flatten.

Portishead, Somerset (*above*) features a stunning concrete board dating from 1962. But because safety guidelines require guardrails to be fitted to platforms over 2m high, its steps have been removed.

It more than bears scrutiny as an artwork in its own right, however.

Elsewhere, springboards survive at Aldershot, Petersfield and Gourock in Scotland (which also has a 3m board), but in this risk-conscious age their use is strictly controlled.

A rare 5m board can also be found at Faversham, where the pool has actually been deepened to allow its retention.

Finally, Broomhill Pool, Ipswich (*see page 142*), still has its original 1938 5m diving stage, but as the pool is currently closed, it breaks no rules.

Chapter Five

Lido Life

ROY FRANSEN
EUROPEAN HIGH and FIRE DIVING CHAMPION

Lidos and open air pools today attract a wide range of people for an assortment of reasons.

Far more than just offering a place to swim – whether one is clocking up the lengths or simply idling in the shallow end – they offer space to sunbathe, to socialise, and for many, mental as well as physical space in which to escape from the world outside.

As Tracey Emin puts it in her foreword to this book, lidos are 'like a haven, like a sanctuary.'

Which is why we today can scarcely imagine turning up to our local lido – should we be lucky enough to have one – to see a man set light to himself on a platform 60 feet high, before diving, head first, in flames, into a pool whose depth is only just enough for a diving board half that height.

Or, into a tank of burning oil.

Fearless Roy Fransen did both, and on a regular basis, as he toured Britain's lidos with his 'Sensational Dive of Death', witnessed by thousands of awestruck spectators and holidaymakers during the late 1940s and 1950s.

Bob Bradborn, the Liverpool lumberjack, rehearses his famous log-rolling act at Enfield Lido in the late 1930s. After performing various head stands, somersaults and other log-related feats, Bob would challenge members of the audience to see how long they could stay upright. There were always plenty of takers. But none managed more than nine seconds.

In those days, life at the lido was rarely quiet. Indeed if this book had a soundtrack it would actually be quite raucous at times.

For while a midweek dip at a suburban lido in modern day London, Penzance, Guildford or Cheltenham might promise for some, inner peace, harmony and tranquility, at the majority of the nation's lidos, 'fun, fun, fun' has always been the order of the day.

And sometimes, the night.

That was when many a lido switched on its fairy lights, turned up the music and transformed itself into a magical oasis.

Lidos were modern. Lidos were sexy. Lidos were unlike any form of pleasure park the British public had ever known. In Portsmouth, bus conductors used to call out 'Hollywood!' as the stop for Hilsea Lido approached.

As we learnt in earlier chapters, every major lido tried to draw crowds to water polo matches,

diving competitions, swimming galas and the like. But in the north west – in Blackpool, Morecambe and New Brighton – open air pools functioned like a cross between a lido, stadium and amusement park. Anything to bring in punters when the weather failed, which of course it so often did.

So they hosted fitness classes, water spectaculars, beauty contests and Roy Fransen stunts. Until eventually, in the 1960s, they discovered that, in the words of Oscar Wilde, the problem with being fashionable is that sooner or later one becomes unfashionable.

Forty years later, there are signs of that wheel of fortune turning once again. As we will later read of Stonehaven (*page 84*) and Brockwell Park (*page 138*), to name but two locations where the nightlights still occasionally burn, there is life in the lido yet.

The Dive of Death perhaps we can live without.

As the British public cast off the cares of wartime and flocked in record numbers to sports events, amusement parks and cinemas during the late 1940s, lido operators decided to capitalise while the going was good.

Their inspiration was the Aquacade Review, launched by impresario Billy Rose at the New York World Fair in 1939, and starring Johnny Weissmuller, the 'Aquadonis', opposite Esther Williams, his 'Aquabelle'.

In a format that would later be turned into a 1944 Busby Berkeley Hollywood classic, *The Bathing Beauty*, hundreds of synchronised swimmers performed in lavish, water-based entertainments.

Here was a spectacle perfectly suited to Britain's stadium-like lidos, and for a decade or more until the late 1950s troupes of performers would travel from pool to pool, thrilling crowds with their rousing routines.

One such Aqua Revue, produced initially by Roy Fransen, featured acts with names like the Gorgeous Aquabelles, The Aquabats, the Aqua Loonies and The Awkward Bats ('the world's craziest diving team'), before Fransen himself closed the show with his trademark death-defying dive in flames.

At Scarborough a Water Follies show, staged on Tuesday and Wednesday mornings, starred Betty Slade, a former world professional diving champion.

A producer of one of the revues staged at the **Super Swimming Stadium, Morecambe** during the 1950s emphasised the financial necessity for such extravaganzas.

'Since the first season's experience (in 1936) it was found that some subsidiary activities would be necessary, apart from swimming and bathing, to fully utilize the baths, owing to dull days and the water temperature.'

In a good year, he noted, Aqua Revues could yield £6,000.

One of the participants in these revues was Liz O'Neill, also from Morecambe, who in the 1950s joined a troupe of 16 girls calling themselves the Aqua Lovelies.

In addition to synchronised swimming they also performed song and dance routines.

'It was not as glamorous as it looked,' she recalled at the age of 73. 'There were two weeks of rehearsals and sometimes, even in May, there would be ice on the water. You really had to steel yourself to go in.

'But now I feel a lot healthier than a lot of women of my age, and I'm sure the cold water has a lot to do with that.'

The Aqua Lovelies underwent a punishing schedule of up to four shows daily from May to September.

'But the crowds were fantastic,' remembered Liz, 'and by the end of the season you felt really great.'

Being an Aqua Lovely was also well paid. Liz received £16 a week, virtually the same as most top professional footballers of the day, Stanley Matthews included.

But as the television age took hold and attendances at lidos started their inexorable decline during the early 1960s, like most novelty shows, the charms of the water shows eventually faded.

Poignant confirmation of this decline is provided in the diary of RP Yeoman, the Pondmaster, or pool manager, at the Portobello Open Air Baths in Edinburgh, where there were seats for around 6,000 spectators.

On 4 July 1962, Yeoman noted: 'Roy Fransen Gala at Pool. 722 paid. *Not so good*.'

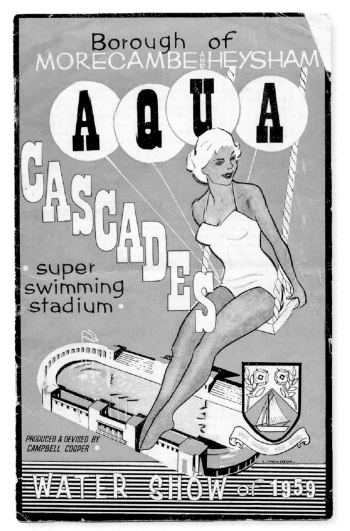

▲ A packed crowd fills the **Open Air Baths** at **Blackpool** in the early 1960s, for yet another lido staple of the post war period.

It cannot have been easy for the audience to gain much of an impression of the beauty queens parading on the distant stage, and yet such contests were popular fare at lidos and open air pools all over Britain for some 40 years.

Probably the first such contest was held at the Super Swimming Stadium in Morecambe, within weeks of VE day, in the summer of 1945. Over 4,000 people attended the first grand final, organised by Morecambe and Heysham Council and sponsored by the *Sunday Dispatch* newspaper.

As the annual contest drew more entries – eventually being renamed Miss Great Britain – heats were held every Wednesday, with the winners being presented their prize by whoever happened to be starring at the Winter Gardens that week.

It was a ritual captured on celluloid in a 1960 film version of a John Osborne stageplay, *The Entertainer*. A still from the film (*right*), shows fading music hall comedian, Archie Rice, played

Mannequin Parades

<table>
<tr><td>

LANCE & LANCE,
High Street.

Miss CRISP (in charge)
Miss MARY FLETCHER
Miss J. VERNON BROWNING
Miss PAT PRATTON
Miss MARJORIE BENWELL
Three LONDON MANNEQUINS

Displaying Satin and Cotton Telescopic Swim Suits, Viennese Novelty Swim Suits, Jacquard Fancy Swim Suits.

</td><td>

WALKER & LING,
High Street

Miss JAMES (in charge)
Miss MARJORIE GREEN
Miss BETTY FRANCIS
Miss NAOMI SPARROW
Miss DOREEN McLEAN
Miss BETTY HARDCASTLE
Miss ANN HUNTER

Displaying the 1937 range of Wolsey, Minster and Jaeger Swim Costumes.

</td></tr>
<tr><td>

SHOW OF SHOWS GIRLS
Knightstone Pavilion

Miss IZNA ROSELLI
Miss STEPHANIE FIELD
Miss PEARL BRYAN
Miss GLADYS MANNING
Miss DAPHNE POLGLASE
Miss OLIVE PAYNE
Miss LEONI CODY

Displaying a selection of the Latest Styles in Swim Suits, by " Ribbolastic," " Morley," " Windsor Water Woollies " and " Wolsey."

</td><td>

B. T. BUTTER,
High Street

Miss COUSINS (in charge)
Miss MARGARET HODGSON
Miss GWEN TEMPLE
Miss BERYL TEMPLE

Three other Ladies and a Troupe of Juniors will also exhibit

</td></tr>
<tr><td>

MARKS & SPENCER,
High Street

Miss JANET MUSGROVE
Miss KITTY WHATLEY
Miss C. JOHNSON
Miss J. THOMAS
Miss L. FORFAR
Miss E. EDWARDS
Miss R. EVANS

Displaying 1937 Fancy Knit and Striped Costumes, Beach Shorts, Trousers and Sun-tops.

</td><td>

WESTON SPORTS HOUSE,
High Street (John Moore)

Miss E. UPSHALL
Miss CREED
Miss CRANDON
Miss SPENCE
Miss K. FRANCIS

Displaying the latest range of " Bukta " Swim Suits.

</td></tr>
</table>

by Laurence Olivier, compering a beauty contest at the Super Swimming Stadium, when suddenly he falls for the charms of a butcher's daughter from Burnley (Shirley Ann Field, on the catwalk).

Unlike the stageplay the film flopped. But fleeting glimpses of this wonderful pool, demolished in 1976, make it well worth the price of a video rental.

◀ Ribbolastic! A page from the official souvenir programme for the opening of the **Weston-super-Mare Bathing Pool**, on 1 July 1937, lists the participants in 'A Parade of Bathing Fashions for 1937', laid on by local retailers as part of the afternoon's celebrations.

The very names, of both the mannequins and their swimwear, are redolent of 1930s Britain; a time when all young ladies were a Miss, and manufacturers were beginning to incorporate newly developed synthetic materials into their latest lido fashions.

So that ladies could show off their suntans in evening wear, the new all-in-one ranges – the bikini had yet to be invented – featured scooped backs and narrower straps. Colours of the day were navy and white, cream, grey or black, with red trimmings adding a touch of gaiety.

Mannequin parades apart, the programme included diving displays – from Weston's magnificent new diving stage (*see page 136*) – races, a display by the Bristol Water Babies (Neta, Mary, Audrey, Molly and Eileen), and 'a display of physical culture' by the Women's League of Health and Beauty (motto: Movement is Life!).

Some 4,000 people attended, a figure repeated when the show was staged a second time that same evening.

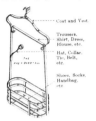

The system is now being marketed in this country by the patentee, Mr James Sieber. It is known as the " Hyg-Gard-All," and the holder is illustrated here. It is of solid construction, being of ⅜ in. to ¼ in. gauge steel strip. The

Coat and Vest.

Trousers, Shirt, Dress, Blouse, etc.

Hat, Collar, Tie, Belt, etc.

Shoes, Socks, Handbag, etc

height over all is 2 ft. 10 in., length of basket 1 ft. 3½ in., width of basket 6¾ in. and depth 5 in. Each holder weighs 4½ lb. to 5 lb.

The disposition of the garments is indicated on the illustration, from which it will be seen that the clothes hang neatly and compactly straight on the holder. This assists in speedy changing.

For an installation of 400 holders a minimum of 20 cabins should be provided.

The holders are stored on a framework of light 1 in. steel tubing, 7 ft. high by 1 ft. 8 in. wide, the length depending on the space available. This will accommodate 16 holders to the yd. The space required for 100 holders, including gangway, is about 10 sq. yd.

The framework has the advantage of being economically installed and of being readily dismantled during the close season. On the other hand, it may be used for cloakroom purposes during the latter period.

One attendant only is required to service 400 to 500 holders.

There is no doubt that the system will prove a sound investment for those establishments that find their cabin accommodation taxed.

▲ Few lido users over the age of 40 will have forgotten the wire baskets commonly used for clothes storage. Before the introduction of James Sieber's patented *Hyg-Gard-All* system (presumably meaning Hygienic Guard All), in the mid 1930s, each bather retained his or her own cubicle, thereby limiting the numbers that could be accommodated. The baskets changed all that, allowing turnover to increase dramatically.

▲ Young holidaymakers at the **Open Air Baths** in **Blackpool** are put through their paces by a somewhat portly announcer (seen on the left, issuing instructions over the microphone) in the late 1940s.

In most cases lidos offered an ideal environment for families, at a time when few Britons enjoyed more than a week's summer break, and fewer still holidayed abroad.

But note the gathering of spectators in the stands, and absence of a lifeguard on the platform between the children's section and the rest of the pool.

Such a scene is hard to imagine today, in so many ways.

Even less likely is that such a photograph could be taken at all.

Modern measures for the protection of children have resulted in most pool operators prohibiting the use of cameras, while in extreme cases, this has even led to grandparents being forbidden to photograph their grandchildren.

The domed building in the background is the Grand Pavilion of the South Pier, designed by TP Worthington and opened in 1893, but destroyed by two fires, in 1958 and 1964.

SWIMMING POOL, PORTOBELLO.

▲ One remarkable characteristic of lidos built during the inter war period – at least those located in coastal towns and resorts – concerns the sheer number of people who attended not to swim but simply to spectate.

We may perhaps understand why the people of Portsmouth chose to hire deckchairs for the day at **Hilsea Lido** (*above*). This was, after all, an urban beach, a place of fresh air, fun and sociability.

But to pay to perch on a hard wooden bench for hours on end at the **Portobello Baths** in Edinburgh (*right*) or at the Open Air Baths at Blackpool (*opposite*), or indeed at any of the other major pools where grandstands dominated the scene – that seems harder to understand, and inevitably gives rise to some uncharitable thoughts.

Yet it cannot be denied that in their early years, the number of paying spectators at many of Britain's lidos far outstripped those actually using the pool.

Of the 500,000 or so people who passed through the turnstiles in Blackpool's first season, in 1923, only 94,403 were actual bathers. During Portobello's opening year in 1936, spectators outnumbered swimmers by two to one, earning the pool an estimated extra £10,000 in ticket receipts.

At Weston-super-Mare, opened the following year, it was reckoned that 9d in every shilling earned derived from spectators; that is, 75 per cent of the total revenue.

Of course many individuals were drawn purely by curiosity. These were, after all, remarkable buildings.

Some pools were also entertainment centres in their own right, even when no actual events were being staged. Margate, for example, had puppet shows, six cafés, and wonderful sea views.

Nevertheless, at a time when images of the undressed or even half-dressed human form, were far less in evidence in everyday life than they are today, the lure of the lido must have seemed irresistible to many, whatever their tastes or personal leanings.

▶ As in many northern climes Britain maintains a longstanding, though undoubtedly eccentric tradition of outdoor swimming in the depths of winter.

Probably the most celebrated participants of such icy escapades are those members of the **Serpentine Swimming Club** whose annual Christmas Day race in the Serpentine Lake in London's Hyde Park is illustrated here in the 1916 edition of *Swimming* (one of the illustrious *Badminton Library of Sports and Pastimes*, published by Longmans, Green).

The 'Serps' staged the first race in their year of formation, 1864, having set out their aim to promote 'the healthful habit of bathing in open water throughout the year'.

Early winners were rewarded with a gold medal. This was replaced in 1904 by the **Peter Pan Cup**, donated to the club by the author JM Barrie.

Then, as now, the Peter Pan race takes place over an agonisingly long 100 yard course, in water temperatures usually below 4°C (39°F). Nowadays, hardly surprisingly, entrants must prove that they are habituated to such extreme conditions by competing in at least three other winter events.

This would therefore preclude joining in the Christmas Day swims held at either Hampton Open Air Pool, or at Sandford Parks, both of which are heated all year round.

But they might try the unheated Parliament Hill Fields Lido, which stays open on winter mornings, the swimming ponds at Hampstead Heath, or **Tooting Bec Lido** in south London, where two gentlemen from the South London Swimming Club are seen breaking the ice before embarking on their Christmas Day swim (*right*), some time during the 1920s.

SERPENTINE CLUB—CHRISTMAS MORNING.

(At another south London lido, Brockwell Park, where the tradition is no longer kept up, the Christmas Day swimmers used to call themselves splendidly the 'Brockwell Icicles'.)

While outsiders may view the practice as pure madness, regulars swear by the physical, mental and spiritual benefits of ice cold dips.

'What's the point of looking at the thermometer?' asks Janine Rhodes in *The Hungry Winter Swimmer* (*see Links*).

'Just going in warms you up, makes you feel all tingly and expands the mind.'

It also, presumably, whets the appetite for the Christmas turkey.

◀ Bathers at the newly opened **Twickenham Baths** in May 1935 try to work out the air and water temperature from this unusual, and possibly unique 'Rototherm'.

Soaring summer temperatures played an important role in encouraging local authorities to build open air pools during the 1930s, the peak temperatures being recorded during the summers of 1932-35 inclusive, when July and August averages often tipped 30°C (86°F), particularly in 1933.

Indeed it was these heat waves that finished off the swimming lakes at Victoria Park and Brockwell Park, where the water quality dipped below standards newly set by the Ministry of Health.

In the 1930s it was rare for pools to be heated, whereas today, 80 per cent of all outdoor pools heat their water. Most maintain an average temperature in the range of 65-75°F, although two miles from Twickenham (which closed in 1981), Hampton prides itself on a tropical temperature of 82°F all year round (*see page 162*).

Unheated pools, meanwhile, can also reach the 65-75°F range at the height of summer, which in recent years has been higher than ever.

August 2003, for example, was the hottest since records began.

Bad news for the planet, no doubt, but good news for Britain's lidos.

▲ Workmen apply finishing touches to the **Morecambe Super Swimming Stadium** prior to its opening in July 1936. (Whether these men were the two lucky ones chosen by ballot to attend the laying of the foundation stone the previous October is not known.)

Annual maintenance forms a significant part in the life, and running costs, of an outdoor pool.

Cracks in the tank must be repaired; the floor and lines may require repainting, and the filters cleaned out and overhauled.

If major work is not required pools are generally left full over the winter. But even then, frost and ice can cause the concrete to crack. A high water-table, such as at Peterborough, can even 'break the back' of a pool.

Emptying and filling the tank is a lengthy process. For example it takes a week to drain Tooting Bec Lido of its one million gallons (approximately 4,550 cubic metres), and a week to refill it.

In 1908 this process cost £25.

By 2005, with water charges costed at roughly £1 per cubic metre, that cost had risen to £5,000.

▼ Since the days when be-suited boatmen patrolled the Victorian swimming lakes for strugglers and mischief-makers, the lifeguard has, quite literally, been the lifeline of Britain's open air pools and lidos.

But standards today go far beyond those that applied in times gone by, when virtually any fit youth could turn up for a summer season and spend it sunbathing or chatting up the girls. (One such youth was the actor Sean Connery, who had a brief spell as a guard at the Portobello Baths in Edinburgh.)

Under guidelines issued by the Health and Safety Executive (*see Links*), much stricter criteria apply today. At the very least, no pool may open to the public without the presence of at least one qualified lifeguard, while for pools measuring 50 x 20m or more, a minimum of four is recommended, rising to six whenever the pool is crowded.

For a typical local authority lido on a busy summer's weekend, that can require a great deal of planning. No pool manager likes to delay opening, or turn away swimmers if guards have not turned up. At smaller community pools (such as featured in Chapter Seven), the onus on voluntary lifeguards is even greater.

Becoming a lifeguard is not just a matter of knowing how to berate teenagers or blow a whistle.

In order to achieve the required standards – a National Pool Lifeguard Qualification, for example – guards must swim 100m on their front and back without stopping. They must cover 50m within 60 seconds and be able to surface dive to a depth of at least 1.5m.

They have to be trained in rescue, recovery and resuscitation techniques. They must understand basic legal issues and know how to conduct risk assessments and, finally, demonstrate observation and supervision skills, which is where the whistle comes in.

Having achieved the requisite qualification, they must then be reassessed every two years.

But at least they no longer have to wear white coats and hats, as was de rigueur before 1939.

Instead, as recommended by international guidelines, bright red shorts or skirts and a yellow top are now standard.

Thus the lifeguards of today stand out, in more ways than one.

Barking Lido advertises in the *Municipal Journal* for a Head Attendant in 1937 (*top*) while at Parliament Hill Fields (*left and above*), lifeguard Mari Timony perches on what remains of the lido's original Wicksteed 3m diving stage. The stage is named Alwyn's Tower in memory of a former lifeguard who died in a road accident in May 2003.

Chapter Six

Case Studies

On this part of the page readers can find key facts relating to each case study. Where the buildings are listed, the date of listing is added in brackets. All sizes are in feet and inches unless otherwise stated. The volume of water is given in gallons (g), so that 1m g means one million gallons.

This chapter consists of twenty seven case studies of lidos or open air pools constructed between 1906 and 1938.

All were either publicly funded or intended to be available for use by the general public. Private facilities have not been included.

The case studies are presented in the chronological order of their opening dates.

Each has been selected according to a variety of different criteria, as follows:

Historic significance – judged in terms of the building's importance in relation to national, regional and local factors.

Architectural quality – based on an assessment of the building's design merits, its place within the overall development of 20th century swimming pool architecture, or its use of innovative or unusual features.

Form – as far as is possible we have tried to select a representative sample of the main building styles adopted during the period in question.

Context and location – the selection includes examples from cities and towns of varying sizes and character, located in as wide a geographical spread as possible, so as to provide a mix between urban and suburban, inland and coastal locations around England, Scotland and Wales.

Development – how the planning history and subsequent fate of certain examples informs our wider understanding of the history of open air swimming in Britain, or is relevant to the current debate on conservation and future management.

Concerning the identity of the architects and engineers named within the case studies, it should be noted that with only a few exceptions it was common practice for only the Borough Engineer to be credited.

In practice, of course, whole teams of architects, engineers and building specialists working for the municipality would have been actively involved. As such these backroom boys must remain the unsung heroes of our tale.

No doubt some readers will be sorry to see their particular favourite omitted, and it can be taken as read that given more space we would have featured many more examples.

In this respect it should be noted that Chapter Seven (*see page 158*) provides summaries relating to a further eleven pools that are either smaller in scale – several being in village or rural locations – or of less architectural interest, but where the involvement of community groups, past or present, serves to provide useful lessons for campaigners and conservationists currently active.

Finally, on the thorny issue of nomenclature – the use of the terms 'lido', 'baths' or 'pool' – we have endeavoured to adopt the titles most commonly given by local people. But in truth they have long been interchangeable.

▶ An original 1930s turnstile made by the Salford engineering company Baileys – one of many supplied to lidos between the wars – still greets swimmers at **Stonehaven**, Aberdeenshire (*right*).

From there, a helping hand (*above left*) leads to the water.

For a history of British turnstiles see *Played in Manchester*, the first in the *Played in Britain* series.

Living the high life at the Super Swimming Stadium, Morecambe, in the 1950s. Many of the pools featured in this chapter formed part of a regular circuit for divers, swimmers and entertainers during the golden years of British lidos.

Case Study

Tooting Bec Lido, London 1906

Architect HJ Marten
Cost £8,000
Size 300' x 100' x 3'-7'
Water freshwater, 1m g
Opened 28 July 1906

Tooting Bec Lido was the first open-air pool to be purpose-built in a London County Council park. Opened on the eastern edge of Tooting Bec Common in 1906, it was, in the capital at least, decades ahead of its time.

Here, I should declare an interest. Tooting Bec Lido is where I swim and this is where my passion for lidos began, even though I had swum in many other outdoor pools before. It is still the only place in London that I know where everyone smiles.

And no wonder: the huge expanse of water, its inviting 'blueness', the bright seaside colours of its cubicle doors, the surrounding green of the trees, the chirruping of the birds and, above all, the open space in an otherwise crowded city. Admittedly, the rush of the trains on the London to Brighton line can intrude on this idyll, but that soon becomes a background rumble.

Tooting Bathing Lake, as the lido was originally called, was the brainchild of a local rector, the Reverend John Hendry Anderson, who became mayor of Wandsworth Borough Council in 1904. Inspired by the popularity of other swimming lakes at Brockwell Park, Clapham Common, Hackney and Hampstead, he and other Wandsworth councillors argued that with 250,000 residents, the borough sorely needed its own facility. This need had grown since the construction of a large LCC housing estate at Totterdown, begun in 1903.

Other boroughs had built their own lakes without grant aid from the LCC. But Wandsworth needed extra finance, and for the LCC to make available the chosen site within Tooting Common.

Anderson became Mayor of Wandsworth in 1904, and after two years of failed negotiations with the LCC, a breakthrough was finally made in early 1906, shortly after Anderson had assumed the chairmanship of the Works Committee of the Central Unemployed Body for London (CUBL). This voluntary organisation arranged short-term work projects, especially during the winter months, to ease the distress of the poor.

Under the deal agreed, the CUBL would provide the labour and cover wages, which eventually cost £4,300. (The commissioning of open air pools in order to provide work for the unemployed became common in the 1930s. But in 1906, this was a first.)

For its part the LCC would release the site for the lake, which it now stipulated should measure a massive 30,000 square feet, fifty per cent larger than Wandsworth had originally proposed. It would also meet maintenance costs, estimated at £200 a year.

Wandsworth would in turn provide the building materials, plans and site supervision, which in the end totalled £3,400.

Work on the project started in March 1906 and took five months to complete. »

The original entrance to the Tooting Bec Bathing Lake, at its southern end, facing Tooting Bec Road. Note the embankments flanking the entrance, made up from spoil excavated during the construction process, and used to shield the lake from the adjoining Common.

The building of **Tooting Bathing Lake** in 1906 was an early example of a work creation scheme for the unemployed.

Nearly 400 men – most of them local – were paid 7d per hour for a 43 hour week. This was one penny more than the London County Council's standard rate because the work was considered more physically demanding than the usual 'levelling and turfing'.

All the digging, for example, was done using picks and shovels, with the excavated soil being shifted by wheelbarrows to form the surrounding embankment.

As a result of their efforts the workmen were, according to the Central Unemployed Body for London, 'improved in physique, capacity and zeal'.

But plenty dropped out. Of the first 145 men recruited 70 gave up soon after. Some were not fit enough, but one ask to be excused as he was 'nervous of water.'

To seal the lake's floor Portland cement was laid on bituminous sheeting, while the sides were concreted using timber formwork. Stone flagging was then laid for the lake's surrounds.

The lower image, taken from the same vantage point, looking north, soon after the opening, shows the rudimentary nature of the bathing lake, with just an open-fronted corrugated iron 'dressing shed' on the east side, backing onto the London to Brighton railway line.

Note the presence of the rowing boat. This was not for public use, but for the attendant, Alfred French, to rescue any swimmers in distress.

This he did in 1907, winning a Royal Humane Society award for saving two men from drowning.

Even so, like all attendants of the period, French always wore a suit, collar, tie and cap while on duty.

Handwritten note on photograph:
Bashing Pond
Tooting Bec
Common
Streatham

alfred French
bath attendant
diving after
the Pond was
declared open

28 July 06

▲ Baths attendant Alfred French takes the first dive into the **Tooting Bathing Lake** on 28 July 1906, watched by the assembled dignitaries, including Evan Spicer, the LCC Chairman, Alexander Glegg, the Wandsworth Mayor, and the Reverend John Anderson.

According to the *Wandsworth Borough News* French was followed into the water by hundreds of small boys, who 'heedless of the presence of members of the fair sex, unblushingly undressed and were sampling the quality of the water long before the "big guns" had departed.'

This unblushing behaviour was only a foretaste of things to come.

Within days of the opening, complaints from local residents started to pour in concerning the 'dirty condition of some of the bathers', many of whom walked barefoot across the Common to reach the pool.

One man wrote to Wandsworth Borough Council stating that the lake was being 'stormed by the riff-raff from slum-land'. Another said he was 'unable to enjoy a bathe in company with boys and men who are filthy both in clothes and person.'

Spitting seems to have been a particular bugbear. 'It should be absolutely prohibited in the water,' wrote one correspondent, 'but it is found floating on the water and over the whole cement surrounding the bath.' Another begged the LCC to ban spitting, 'especially on Sundays'.

Another cause for complaint was rats. One bather described his disgust when he picked up his wet costume and 'found that it was covered in vermin.'

But if conditions were not to everyone's satisfaction, the lake was nevertheless hugely popular. It was also free of charge. Records for the 12 weeks of summer in 1908 show more than 112,000 entrants (an average of 1,500 per day).

However, of these 112,000, only 3,000 were female, and for a simple reason. While men and boys were allowed to swim from 6am onwards (only until 9am on Sundays), women were restricted to Tuesdays, from 7.30am. A petition signed by 54 local women in 1907 to increase these hours was flatly refused.

As to attire, 'Male persons over the age of ten years will be required, when bathing, to wear bathing costumes or drawers, and females will be required to wear the costume approved by the Amateur Swimming Association.'

》 Looking at it now, Tooting Bec's new swimming lake appears to have been quite primitive; a vast, rectangular basin of cold water and very little else. No changing cubicles, no fountain, no café and certainly no filtration system.

Indeed Wandsworth Borough Council had specifically refused an offer from a Mr Bell to fit a pair of filters to keep the water clean.

This parsimony proved to be a false economy, however, and to add to the complaints already flowing in from the public about other standards at the bathing lake (*see left*), swimmers were soon up in arms about the stagnant and unhygienic nature of the water.

Arthur Tate, now in his 80s, remembers swimming at the lake in the summer of 1929. 'The water was so green,' he recalls, 'that when you stood up you couldn't see your feet. Swimming under the water was through a green haze.'

With no filters the only solution was therefore to empty the tank and re-fill it; a major operation for a pool holding one million gallons. The first record of this being done was in March 1908 when it cost £25. (By 2005 the cost had risen to £5,000.)

But for all its drawbacks, Tooting Bec's new swimming lake soon became an integral part of local life.

Within a few weeks of the Lake opening, for example, the South London Swimming Club (SLSC) was formed there. Its regular Sunday morning races became so popular during the early years that midweek heats had to be held at 7am on Wednesday mornings.

This is no longer necessary, but thanks to the club the Sunday morning race remains sacrosanct and is still keenly contested, all year round.

Since those early years the swimming lake has undergone various improvements.

The first, and most radical occurred in 1931, with the installation of a filtration plant and aerator (or fountain) as part of an LCC programme of upgrading all their pools to meet new Ministry of Health hygiene requirements.

A café, a simple concrete block, opened in 1936. Thus the bathing lake evolved into a lido.

Less welcome was the introduction of entry charges; 6d for adults, 3d for children.

The advent of mixed bathing also changed the tone. No longer could men and boys simply strip off in public. Instead, they had to use one of the newly installed changing cubicles with doors.

One member of the SLSC, Charles Roskilly, expressed his frustration in this verse of 1934.

So now we have our comforts and
The water's always clear,
We've Rules and Regulations, too,
With penalties severe,
Within a nasty wooden hutch
Swimmers remove their clothes
Without a permit signed and sealed
A man can't blow his nose.

We can't do this; we can't do that,
The LCC say 'No'.
We can't dress here, we can't dress there,
In cages we must go.
The lake was built for honest men,
But we're becoming slaves.
The LCC rules swimmers though
Britannia rules the waves.

But if SLSC members were unhappy then, in later years they would prove to be the lido's saviours.

In the 1990s, when Wandsworth wanted to close the pool during the winter, the SLSC negotiated

a deal allowing the club to run the pool off-season, employing lifeguards and carrying out maintenance for six months of the year. The fear was that if the pool closed, it might never re-open.

Indeed this long-term link with a committed user group has been the single most important factor in keeping the pool open when so many other lidos have closed.

More recently, Wandsworth Council has honoured its predecessor's pioneering efforts in 1906 by investing heavily in Tooting Bec Lido, spending some £500,000 on upgrading the facility between 1999 and 2002.

A small children's paddling pool has been added behind the café and, more dramatically – and controversially – a striking new entrance and changing-room block built adjacent to the shallow end of the pool, the opposite end to the original entrance.

Yet one feature has not changed. While elsewhere pool sizes have shrunk, to save money, Tooting Bec's considerable dimensions remain as they were in 1906.

This alone, added to the coolness of the water, makes the lido particularly popular amongst serious swimmers, for example triathletes and would-be Channel swimmers, who can often be seen training in the early morning.

Other activities regularly staged are canoeing, tai chi, yoga and keep-fit classes.

Nor are these activities confined to just the summer months.

Routine maintenance apart, remarkably, Tooting Bec Lido has managed to remain open 365 days of the year, including Christmas Day, Boxing Day and New Year's Day, even in wartime.

Over the course of ninety nine years in existence, that adds up to quite a liquid asset.

Although the sundial adorning Tooting Bec's café frontage appears to date from the same era as the fountain – installed by the LCC in 1931 – it was in fact made in 1994 from aluminium and plyboard by Michael Halliday, a member of the South London Swimming Club. In common with the lido itself, the club celebrates its centenary in 2006, when no doubt more bubbles will fill the air of this most enchanted of British lidos.

▲ Completed in 2002 at a cost of £500,000 to Wandsworth Borough Council, the new entrance to **Tooting Bec Lido** – on the west side of the pool, facing Tooting Bec Common – was designed by William Martin & Partners.

The design is intended to evoke the curvaceous Art Deco style of the 1930s and thereby call to mind the heyday of lidos, even though this particular pool pre-dates that era by some thirty years.

Cement render, galvanised steel, glazed blocks and steel doors have all been used to make the building as vandal-proof as possible.

The re-siting of the entrance from the southern, or deep end of the pool, to be nearer the shallow end, was partly done to conform with Health and Safety guidelines.

However this change in emphasis aroused strong feelings and resulted in the holding of a public enquiry.

Many swimmers lamented the loss of that breathtaking, first view down the full length of the pool as one entered, while conservation groups objected to the new entrance's jarring effect on views across the Common.

▲ Apart from its new entrance, **Tooting Bec Lido** is almost instantly recognisable to swimmers thanks to two distinguishing features.

First is the sheer scale of the tank. Measuring 100 feet (30.7 metres) from west to east, the width is greater than the length of most indoor pools. Those without the stamina or heart to tackle Tooting Bec's prodigious 300 foot length are therefore still swimming a respectable distance.

Second are the distinctive multi-coloured doors of the changing cubicles, so evocative of the seaside and virtually a trademark for Tooting Bec.

The first cubicles at the pool consisted of a simple corrugated-iron roofed shelter, fronted by canvas curtains.

Doors were added only in the 1930s when mixed bathing became the norm. Initially painted green, they acquired their current cheerful colour scheme in 1981.

The trees behind the boxes were planted on the surrounding embankment so that, as required by the LCC, the lake would not 'detract from the natural beauty of the Common' which lay beyond.

Case Study

South Bay Bathing Pool, Scarborough 1915–89

Architect Harry W Smith (*above*)
Cost £5,000
Size 350' x 190' x 2'-7'
Water Seawater, 2m g
Opened 21 July 1915
Closed 1989
Demolished 2003
On site now Public park

Having evolved as a popular spa town during the Georgian period – being one of the few European spas where visitors, including the Prince of Wales, could both take the waters and then take to the water – by the early 20th century the North Yorkshire coastal town of Scarborough was struggling to compete with more fashionable health resorts elsewhere in the country.

Harry W Smith, borough engineer from 1897-1933, saw the provision of outdoor swimming pools as a way to reverse this trend. In 1900 he told a meeting of Scarborough engineers:

'The advantages of a bathing pool are manifold, and briefly may be summed up as follows.

'A reduction of the risk of sea bathing to a minimum: bathing is possible at times when, owing to the rough seas, it would be risky to do so; more commodious accommodation and comfort can be provided for the bather than is possible in a bathing van; facilities for the holding of swimming galas and carnivals, with the attendant revenue to be obtained therefrom.'

Thirty years later those same arguments would be used during Britain's lido-building boom.

Harry Smith was thus well ahead of his time.

He must also have been persuasive, for under the 1900 Scarborough Improvement Act, the Corporation arranged to borrow up to £8,000 from the government, repayable over 45 years, specifically for the construction of bathing pools.

That same year Smith led a deputation to St Helier, Jersey, to inspect their facilities.

The result was a decision to build not one, but two outdoor swimming-pools: one in Scarborough's South Bay and one in the North Bay.

It took a full twelve years of debate and prevarication to start on the first of these two – designed by Smith himself – in April 1914.

Located at the foot of the South Cliff, below the newly opened Italian Gardens (also designed by

Smith), the pool was in effect an elaborate extension of a sea wall completed in 1912 to protect the base of the cliff from erosion.

Perhaps for that reason alone, despite the outbreak of hostilities a few months later, construction work continued, before the pool was finally opened on 21 July 1915.

Although a midweek afternoon in wartime, it was also Wednesday half-day closing in Scarborough, enabling several thousand people to attend the official ceremony. Hundreds more watched from the clifftop above.

On that first day, £46 7s 6d was taken in admission money.

One corporation official called the pool, 'the greatest and most attractive improvement made in the history of the town.'

As well as the rudimentary facilities of dressing-boxes (137 in all), there were hot and cold showers, lined by glazed tiles, first aid rooms and a separate block for the pumping plant and laundry.

With its Italian gardens and winding paths, its colonnades, terraces and tiled roofs, Scarborough's South Bay Bathing Pool bore a distinctly classical air, forming an elegant counterpart to Joseph Paxton's Spa, further up the Esplanade.

The Mayor, Councillor Graham, pronounced the new bathing pool as a modern facility without equal. 'I do not know where anyone could look to see anything approaching it,' he declared.

In fact it might well have been the largest open air pool in Europe.

But Scarborough's pride and joy was not without its drawbacks.

Firstly, its position at the foot of the cliff was by no means ideal. It lay half a mile south of the end of the promenade, and several hundred yards from the South Cliff Tramway – Britain's first funicular railway (opened in 1873) – which linked the Esplanade with the Spa and sands below.

Secondly, the Bathing Pool would prove to be rather primitive by later standards. There was, for example, only a low retaining wall around the outer edge, dividing the swimming area from the sea (which at high tide would flood the pool and thereby keep it filled wih fresh seawater). Spectators would sit on this outer wall, despite the risk – which would not be countenanced today – of falling into the sea.

But the pool was not yet complete. Recognising that it needed other revenue-earning facilities to remain viable, after the First World War the Corporation added a café, restaurant and more seating for spectators on a terrace gouged out of the cliff face.

Further up, on a second terrace, would be sited three blocks of holiday bungalows for rental.

In 1933-34, the whole pool was modernised at a cost of £20,000. This included excavating a deeper tank and adding three distinctive fountains within the pool, as part of an improved filtration system.

But the most prominent addition was a steeply angled 33 feet high reinforced concrete diving stage; a work of art in itself and ideal for breathtaking displays to entertain holidaymakers. Professional showmen would perform hair-raising stunts such as being set alight on the top board before diving dramatically into the water below (see page 40).

In 1938 meanwhile, a mile or so away, the North Bay Pool was finally opened adjacent to the popular Peasholm Park. Apart from occupying a more sheltered location, this more modern pool offered heated water, a considerable advantage over its southern counterpart.

From the 1960s onwards the number of bathers at the South Bay Pool dwindled. On a hot day, 2,000 or more might visit. But in the poorer summer of 1978, for instance, this dropped to a paltry 200 or so.

By then, the pool's physical condition was deteriorating, and Scarborough Borough Council began to weigh up its options. As well as the two local pools, it was also responsible for the open-air pool at Whitby.

A Save the Pool campaign was launched and a stay of execution achieved until 1981, when the pool remained closed for the summer season. A year later, the council granted a reprieve and reopened the pool, at a cost to ratepayers of more than £42,000. But its days were numbered, and the South Bay pool finally closed in 1989.

Attempts to have it listed subsequently failed, and in 2003 the pool was infilled.

Scarborough's North Bay Pool does survive however, as the Atlantis water theme park.

▲ Scarborough's South Bay, shortly before the revamp of the **Bathing Pool** in 1933. Along the shore can be seen the Grand Hall and Spa, partially designed by Joseph Paxton.

Although not ideally placed for holidaymakers, Harry Smith planned the pool to have a dual purpose. Tidal erosion of the South Cliffs had required the construction of a sea wall in 1912. By adding the pool, its two million gallons of contained seawater effectively acted as a buttress to the sea wall, as well as helping to divert the tide.

Tinside Pool in Plymouth (see page 108) performs a similar role.

SCARBOROUGH
IT'S QUICKER BY RAIL
Full Information from any L·N·E·R Office or Agency

▲ For the people of Yorkshire and the north east, Scarborough offered refinement and clifftop scenery unlike any of the west coast resorts.

This railway poster from 1932 was one of several by artist Edmund Oakdale, commissioned by the London and North Eastern Railway to promote east coast holiday destinations.

Along with all seaside lidos, Scarborough's Bathing Pool offered a regular fare of entertainments, using the distinctive diving board, added in 1934, to full effect.

During the 1930s the Water Follies Show, featuring the celebrated Aqua Belles, took place on Tuesday and Wednesday mornings. As well as dancing girls, the show featured the world professional diving champion, Betty Slade, who had competed at the 1936 Olympics in Berlin.

Costing 2s for adults and 1s for children, the shows proved immensely popular. Crowds of up to 4,000 people attended, with many more able to watch from a clifftop vantage point for free.

▲ After its closure in 1989 Scarborough's **South Bay Bathing Pool** lay becalmed and untended for 15 years, its terraces weathering like the harbour of an ancient port.

Ironically, a lifeguard had to be employed to prevent people from swimming in it.

Finally, in 2003, shortly after this photograph was taken, the pool was infilled with 60,000 tons of rubble and its derelict buildings demolished, courtesy of a £900,000 grant from Yorkshire Forward (the regional development agency), plus £300,000 from Scarborough Borough Council.

The site is now grassed over (*left*) for use as a public park.

Case Study

Open Air Baths, Blackpool 1923–81

Architects JC Robinson and F Wood
Cost £80,000
Size 376' x 172'
Water Seawater, 2m g
Opened 9 June 1923
Closed 1981
Demolished 1983
On site now Sandcastle Waterworld indoor leisure centre

Six weeks after the opening of the Empire Stadium at Wembley in April 1923, Britain gained its first glimpse of what might well be called a swimming stadium.

Whilst elsewhere in Europe, work was proceeding on a new generation of municipal sports complexes incorporating both stadiums and open air pools – at Lyon, Frankfurt, Dresden and Hamburg, for example – on Blackpool's South Shore arose an aqua arena of quite astonishing proportions and grandiosity.

Said to have been the largest swimming pool in the world, and also to have been based on the Colosseum (though in fact it appeared closer in form and scale to the smaller arenas of Verona, Nîmes and the 1807 Arena in Milan), the design was a far cry from what Blackpool Corporation had originally intended.

In 1917, as the town prepared for life after the Great War, it considered building two identical, rectangular open-air pools, at both ends of the promenade, costing an estimated £32,000 each. As we learned earlier, Scarborough had drawn up similar dual-pool plans of its own a few years earlier. But wartime stringencies and a requirement that local authorities curb expenditure on capital projects forced Blackpool's plans to be shelved.

After the Armistice a complete re-think, no doubt influenced by a post war boom in the leisure business, resulted in the decision to build just one large facility, with the capacity to stage international swimming events and form a major attraction for residents and visitors alike.

Apart from its sheer scale, the revised plan was characterised by its sweeping colonnade of Doric columns flanking a central, Beaux Arts domed entrance and café. This had a pergola-style roof terrace, open to the elements.

Ranged around the pool and accessed from a concourse measuring one third of a mile, were no fewer than 574 dressing-rooms for bathers, plus seated tiers able to accommodate around 3,000 spectators on three sides of the water.

Nothing of its like had ever been seen before.

The pool itself, filled with filtered sea water, was semi-elliptical in plan, but with a straight edge on the seaward side. This was designed for competition swimming. The curved side was shallow for use by children.

So ambitious was the eventual building that it was not completely finished in time for its grand opening on 9 June 1923. It also rained so hard that morning that the man chosen to take the first dive into the pool thought better of it and turned up in top hat and tails instead.

Hardly an auspicious start to what the Corporation was trumpeting – albeit with good reason – as 'the finest pool in the whole world'.

In *Athletic News*, a Manchester-based weekly, Francis Wood, Blackpool's Borough Engineer and Surveyor, won glowing praise.

'There was no such structure to give him any guidance, to suggest a plan or to contribute even a hint. Mr Wood has been practical, and yet he has been picturesque.'

But a letter that has recently come to light points to another man being responsible for the design. J C Robinson, chief architectural assistant in Wood's office from 1920 onwards, stated unequivocally in a job application letter of 26 August 1924: 'During the time I have been in Blackpool I have designed the architectural part of the New Open-Air Bath.'

This suggests that Robinson was responsible for the poolside buildings while Wood dealt with the engineering details. (That the Borough Engineer was solely credited at the time was, however, quite commonplace.)

But whoever took the credit, there could be no doubt about the pool's popularity.

By the end of its first full season in 1924, more than half a million people had paid to go through the turnstiles. Yet of those, only 94,403 were actual bathers. The rest were spectators and visitors simply drawn to the building as an attraction in itself. By May 1929, Blackpool Corporation was able to announce that an astonishing four million people had visited the pool in the six years since it opened.

In 1935, autumn illuminations were introduced (see page 34), floodlighting the cascades in changing colours, and, of course, helping to extend the season.

This annual spectacular continued until about 1950.

But as early as the mid-1960s, certain local councillors were starting to brand the pool as a white elephant. One went so far as to declare that the days of open-air pools were over altogether.

There thus followed proposals to build a roof over the pool or to convert the site into a sports stadium. Other suggestions made in subsequent years were to turn it into an exhibition centre, a skateboard rink, an amusement centre and even a concert venue.

As the pool's deficit grew ever larger, the final axe fell in 1983.

Three years later in its place arose the £11 million Sandcastle Waterworld, an indoor pool complete with slides, shutes, wave makers, themed party areas and water maintained at a constant sub-tropical 84 degrees F.

▲ 'What Wembley Park is to football so Blackpool's new bath will be to swimming,' wrote one observer in 1923, the year both the stadium and the **Open Air Baths** opened.

Certainly the pool area was as long as a football pitch, and almost as wide. The seated areas were also purpose-built for spectator events; galas and diving competitions, and from the 1930s onwards, beauty contests.

The pool's other attraction was its convenience. All along the north western coast low tides require swimmers to take long treks out across the sands to reach the water's edge. Open air pools, at Blackpool, Lytham, Southport and the like brought the sea to the people, whatever the time of day.

▶ A Lancastrian temple to Neptune – Cyril Farey's 1923 watercolour of the **Open Air Baths** (on display at Blackpool's Grundy Art Gallery) offers a reverential, almost ethereal image of sun-kissed, classical formality, set against the chimneys of the South Shore's guesthouses beyond.

It is as if the baths were more ornamental than recreational. Not a single swimmer sullies the surface.

Farey (1888–1954) was both an architect and a leading perspectivist of the 1920s. Here he is clearly also an idealist.

In the distance can be seen the approach to TP Worthington's South Pier (opened 1893 as the Victoria Pier), the Blackpool Tower (b. 1891-93) and its short-lived rival, the 'Gigantic Wheel', erected by the Winter Gardens in 1896 but dismantled in 1928.

AIR BATH, BLACKPOOL

▲ Blackpool's **Open Air Baths** may have lacked a sophisticated title – it was built before the term lido became common – but its Beaux Arts styling was much in vogue in the early 1920s.

This early image suggests that the main pavilion originally had a pergola shading the first floor café (unless the roof was simply unfinished at that point). Also seen is an attendant in a rowing boat.

Note the range of vantage points provided, to accommodate as many paying spectators as possible, and, also rather like a stadium, the provision of terraces and a sunken walkway around the pool (*shown opposite in the early 1950s*).

The baths were demolished in 1983 (*left*), at a cost of £500,000.

Case Study

The Knap Bathing Pool, Barry 1926–97

Architect J Pardoe & Major ER Hinchsliff
Cost c.£25,000
Size 360' x 90' x 1'-7' 9"
Water Filtered seawater, c.1m g
Opened 1 May 1926
Closed 1997
Demolished 2004
On site now Grass

The headland on which the Knap Bathing Pool was sited goes by the name of Cold Knap.

It would have been a fair description of the pool itself.

Even Great Western Railways hedged its bets in a 1930s' poster, advertising Barry as 'The Bracing South Wales Resort' that offered 'Varied Enjoyment'.

That measured endorsement notwithstanding, the Knap was one of the largest open-air pools in Britain.

It was built, as were so many, by unemployed men. In Barry, however, they were employed on the 'docket system', under which they were paid not in cash but with vouchers which could only be exchanged at selected local shops.

Although built by Barry Urban District Council, the finished pool was at first leased to a Mr MW Shanly. Little is known about him other than that he also had a concession in London – for hiring out deckchairs in Hyde Park.

In April 1926, shortly before the pool opened, the Barry Amateur Swimming Club was formed. It made the Knap Pool its base and,

perhaps hoping for favourable terms, invited Shanly to become its first president.

The club organised several swimming galas, competing against other local clubs such as the aptly named 'Newport Shiverers'. Later, the pool was also the venue for international water polo matches, diving displays and beauty queen contests. In 1939, with the help of a boom to shorten the pool to 50 yards, it also staged the British Games (in which, alas, the Welsh team finished last).

From a design standpoint the Knap's most interesting feature was its chalets and changing-rooms, added in 1937.

Designed by the Borough Architect and Surveyor, Major E R Hinchsliff, who was said to have been an admirer of Le Corbusier, they were built in concrete in two arcs on either side of the pool, with stepped flat roofs and brightly coloured doors.

Behind the 38 chalets lay a further arc of changing cubicles.

Each chalet was leased out annually at a cost of one guinea (£1.05) to Barry residents and two guineas for non-residents. Unsurprisingly this led locals to fear that the Council would give preference to outsiders.

According to Tom Clemett, a Barry resident for more than 50 years, 'The chalets became more like holiday cottages, with Calor gas stoves, tables, chairs and sun loungers being stored in them.

'A family atmosphere pervaded the area with children sitting and playing together.'

Other improvements made during the 1930s included the installation of pumps, enabling the one million gallons of water to be circulated in just over 12 hours, a vast improvement on the original sluice gate system that relied on the ebb and flow of the tide.

After the Second World War control of the Knap reverted to the Council, and over the next two decades it remained a popular attraction. During the early 1950s

Laid out in two crescents flanking the long rectangular pool, the Knap's chalets provided a welcome windbreak for their occupants and were much sought after. Indeed by 1960, even though the annual rent had risen to £40, there were still so many applicants that the Council had to allocate them by ballot.

up to 3,000 people a day were recorded as attending over Bank Holiday weekends.

But by the 1980s, numbers were falling and the pool took on a neglected air. Realising that it was increasingly at risk, more than 15,000 local people signed a petition to save it.

But water was found to be leaking from the basin, while the pump and filtering equipment fell into an advanced state of disrepair.

Vale of Glamorgan Council concluded that a smaller pool should be built instead, this time with heated water.

After a series of public meetings, the old pool finally closed in 1997. Shortly afterwards, the Council set up the Knap Pool Restoration Group, involving both councillors and local residents, to find a way forward. An application for lottery money – most probably from the Heritage Fund – was seen as the best bet.

Local businessman Armando Armelin became chairman of the group. Having grown up in Barry he was concerned that a building of architectural and historical importance was about to disappear for good.

'Successive local authorities might have done more over the years to prevent its decay,' he later recalled. 'But the issue was not simply one of economic viability.

'The Knap was a public amenity for the people of Barry and for tourists, too. It was also one of the last great lidos in Europe and for that reason should have been kept.

'A restored pool would have brought more people to Barry. It could have become the Blackpool of South Wales.'

Armelin was convinced that the only way to secure the pool's future was to get it listed by Welsh

Historic Monuments (CADW). Victoria Perry of The Twentieth Century Society lent her support, describing the Knap Pool as a 'wonderful asset to the town'.

She was particularly concerned that the chalets might disappear and argued that they were architecturally important because 'the sweeping shapes, white surfaces and bright colours anticipated the avant garde forms of continental Modernism.'

Despite their sustained efforts, however, they failed to convince CADW, who announced in August 1997 that it did not believe that the Knap possessed 'the quality we would look for in a building of this type and period'.

A second pool was never built, and the Knap Pool was finally demolished, together with the much loved chalets, in 2004.

The Knap's chalets formed the focus of a tightly knit community of locals and holidaymakers. Two beaches and a boating lake were also close at hand. Now only open parkland occupies the site.

Case Studies

Margate Lido, Cliftonville 1927–77

Architect Mr Palmer
Cost £60,000
Size 250' x 150' x 2'-9'
Water Seawater
Opened 24 June 1927
Closed 1977
On site now Sand

While the majority of open air pools and lidos featured in this book were publicly funded, the pool at Cliftonville – the smart end of the north Kent resort of Margate – was the result of what we would now call a Private Finance Initiative.

John Henry Iles, a noted brass band enthusiast and former journalist who had built Britain's first roller coaster at Blackpool in 1906 (and who went on to become a leading figure in the amusement park industry between the wars, including at Wembley and Manchester's Belle Vue), had already set up Margate's Dreamland complex in 1919.

A year later he leased from Margate Corporation the nearby Clifton Baths Estate, famous for its hot salt water baths. Here he set about building new baths, cafés, restaurants, a cinema, concert hall and even an oyster lounge.

He then resolved to add an outdoor pool, such as already existed at Scarborough and Blackpool.

However Margate Corporation baulked at this. They felt it would detract from Cliftonville's genteel image, and for two years Iles' plan was delayed by legal wrangling.

Yet by the time the pool finally opened in the summer of 1927, Corporation aldermen were only too happy to point out that the 'improvements have not cost ratepayers a farthing, but will bring them in untold gold.'

They added, apparently without a hint of irony, that for Margate to progress municipal and private enterprise would have to go 'hand in hand'.

Three maroons, or flares, were fired at the opening ceremony: one for the King, one for the Mayor and one for Margate.

The pool itself was semi-circular in shape and covered an area of approximately 37,000 square feet. It protruded on to the beach and had a diving-stage at the furthest point from the promenade.

Sea water entered the pool through four sluice gates. The ebb and flow of the tide meant that the pool could be emptied and filled every day.

Standing guard over the pool from the heights of the promenade above was a tall beacon, emblazoned on all four sides with the word 'lido' (*see left*).

As well as terraced seating for 'thousands of onlookers', Iles also installed electric lighting.

The *Isle of Thanet Gazette* enthused, 'Bathers will be able to indulge in their aquatic frolics even at night.'

And they did. On hot summer evenings the pool sometimes stayed open until midnight.

From the 1930s onwards, the pool played host to the usual seaside entertainments: swimming and diving displays and 'ornamental floating formations' (better known today as synchronised swimming).

There were also variations on the beauty contest theme,

'British Throughout' reads the caption on the back of this postcard, thought to date from the 1930s, the heyday of the nation's lidos. Margate Lido was known particularly for its range of quirky cafés, laid out on terraces cut in to the cliff above.

BATHING POOL AND CAFE. CLIFTONVILLE

including Miss Calf and Ankle, Miss Sports Girl, Miss Mermaid and, even more obscurely, Miss Grace and Bearing, and Miss South Seas Siren.

In 1935, meanwhile, at around the same time the pool became known as Margate Lido, the facilities were modernised to meet Ministry of Health hygiene requirements. For example, a 500 feet long culvert was dug out to sea, allowing water to be channelled into the pool even at low tide. Also added was a laundry, so that hired towels and costumes could be washed daily.

The changing accommodation was redesigned and 2,000 rather smart galvanised steel and white enamelled lockers were installed, each fitted with coat hooks, trinket bowls, mirrors and even ashtrays.

But swimming was only one element of the activities available.

On a series of terraces rising above the pool were no fewer than six licensed cafés with seating for about 3,000 people.

In addition, there were pitches for six orchestras, whose music not only serenaded the onlookers but was relayed down to the pool by loudspeakers.

Artist Tracey Emin, who grew up in the area during the 1960s, remembers it well.

'It's where I learned to swim, flirt and fight every summer,' she recalled in the *Guardian* in July 2003. 'But the lido wasn't just a pool, it was an amazing tiered structure that accommodated tiny bars, tea rooms, a puppet theatre, ice cream parlours, gift shops ...'

Nor was the lido the only local place to gather.

Two more outdoor pools were created on the foreshore: at Walpole Bay and Marine Terrace Sands. Both opened on 18 June

1937, and although less elaborate than the Margate Lido, being hardly more than concrete basins to collect sea water, they were considerably larger.

Walpole Bay Pool was a vast 450 x 400 feet and Marine Terrace Sands 320 x 250 feet.

The aim, said the mayor, was 'to provide facilities for the expert swimmer to enjoy himself whether the tide is in or out, and at the same time to enable children to paddle or bathe in perfect safety.'

Of the three pools, Walpole Bay was to have the shortest life, closing in 1957. Margate Lido itself closed in 1977. Marine Terrace Sands followed in about 1990, although the remains of all three are still visible today.

When asked why the Lido had closed, the reply from one local resident was blunt and to the point: 'Because no-one went there anymore!'

Margate Lido shown on a postcard dating from the late 1920s (*top*) and the same view today (*above*). A mosaic on the seaward side reads Lido Sands. Note that as well as the pool, Margate's pier, designed by the great Eugenius Birch in 1853, has also since gone, the victim of a storm, in 1978. The lido beacon on top of the cliff (*opposite*) still survives.

Case Study

Sea Bathing Lake, Southport 1928–89

Architect AE Jackson
Cost £65,000
Size 330' x 212' x 0-9'
Water Seawater, 1.4m g
Opened 17 May 1928
Closed 1989
Demolished 1993
On site now Shopping mall

A railway poster from 1932 was unstinting in its praise.

The travelling public were exhorted to go to Southport – the so-called 'Paris of the North' – in preference to any other European destination, for one very simple reason.

Not the majestic boulevard and tea-rooms of Lord Street or the delights of the Victorian ironwork pier. Not the glorious Sands or the exclusive Royal Birkdale golf course.

Instead, the finest attraction in Southport was its open air swimming pool.

'Swimming pool is far too prosaic a name to describe the magnificent temple that Southport has built to the goddess of air and water and sunshine. Here the youth and beauty of the town disport themselves in the most elegant surroundings and men and maidens meet in the pleasant cafés surrounding the pool to talk about the concert that is over, or the dance that is to come.'

If the description sounds somewhat overblown, so was the Sea Bathing Lake itself.

A clear echo of Blackpool's Open Air Baths, completed five years earlier, the structure resembled a Roman amphitheatre with, at its heart, a giant pool.

In fact, the new bathing lake was marginally smaller than its predecessor, Southport's original Sea Bathing Lake (*shown left*). This opened in 1914 and measured a massive 400 x 200 feet.

But in the ever competitive tourist and holiday market on the north west coast, size was not everything, and so, no doubt spurred on by Blackpool's example, in 1926, Southport Corporation decided to replace the earlier lake with a more sophisticated pool, using the latest filtration systems and located in a more sheltered site in Prince's Park, next to the Marine Lake and close to the pier.

Another motive for approving the scheme was that it promised work for some 300 unemployed local men.

The opening ceremony was performed on 17 May 1928 by the Earl of Derby, Lord Lieutenant of Lancashire, whose racing colours of black and white set the tone for the ribbon cutting ceremony. The girls chosen to present him with red roses also wore black and white costumes.

One of the first swimmers was 13 year old Enid Wright. 'I was one of a group of children who swam the first length of the pool after it was opened by Lord Derby,' she told the *Southport Visiter* in January 2003, at the age of 90. 'It was a lovely thing to be asked to do.'

Her efforts were then followed by a mannequin parade of ladies wearing costumes made of silk and taffeta from a local store.

'One was reminded forcibly of the Lido,' commented the local newspaper at the time (thus providing us with one of the earliest known references to the world lido in connection with a British open air pool).

A prominent feature of Southport's Sea Bathing Lake was the colonnade fronting the café. This served a double purpose, providing shelter for spectators on a wet day and a covered stage for the band, which had the choice of playing either inwards towards the café or outwards toward the Lake.

VIEW FROM THE TERRACE, NEW SEA BATHING LAKE, SOUTHPORT.

SOUTHPORT
Cheap fares to Southport daily by the
LIVERPOOL OVERHEAD RAILWAY
"THE MOST INTERESTING ROUTE"

The most elaborate structure at the new Lake was the café which, as at Blackpool, had a glazed dome roof, topped by a globe.

According to the opening day programme, an 'orchestra' would play at the café every afternoon during the bathing season from 2.30-5.00 pm. On the opening day itself, St Hilda's Band took the stage, playing a selection of light classical and popular songs.

On either side of the café were small shops selling sweets, tobacco and newspapers. From here to the men's and women's changing rooms, strictly segregated at each end of the pool, ran a covered arcade or verandah, 230 feet long, 12 feet wide and with a green tiled roof. Protruding from underneath the tiles were white wooden spars, intended to add to the garden-like atmosphere of the surroundings.

This walkway enclosed the western half of the pool – backing onto the sea – in front of which were rows of terraced seats for around 2,500 spectators. 》

The Liverpool Overhead Railway, or 'Ovie' – for whom Alfred Lambart created this poster in the 1930s – was Britain's first electrically powered elevated railway, in 1893, and the first to use escalators and automatic signalling. It also remained independent of British Rail before closing in 1956.

The terraces were lined by cream-coloured flagstones, with red-brick risers. Beyond the Lake, spectators looked out over the gardens and lawns on the far side of the pool, and beyond that, to Prince's Park and the promenade.

The two-storey changing-room blocks at the north and south ends of the pool were deemed highly advanced for their time.

Rendered in rough cast cement to harmonise with the café exterior, they contained 120 pitch-pine cubicles, lined with terazzo tiles to a height of nearly six feet, and above that, buff coloured bricks to the ceiling. Best of all they were centrally heated by circulating hot water.

Mike Benton, a teacher now living in Liverpool, recalls going to the Sea Bathing Lake in the late 1940s and early Fifties. 'We didn't have holidays like people do today. When summer came, lidos were the place to go. Southport was Spain on Merseyside. It was the highlight of the year.'

For young people, it was also a good place to socialise. 'Lidos were the open-air equivalent of dance halls,' says Benton.

Bryan Naylor, who virtually brought his family up at the pool and campaigned hard in the 1970s and '80s to keep it open, believes lidos provided an often overlooked social service.

'They helped to keep crime down,' he says. 'Young people had somewhere to go and enjoy themselves in a legitimate manner. Drug-taking was unknown.'

In common with most seaside lidos, Southport staged beauty contests in the summer: the Miss English Rose competition for adults, and Miss Rose Bud for girls. There were also comedy acts by teams of highly skilled divers.

As open air swimming became less popular – one Head of Tourism in Southport blamed the 'diabolical weather' – so inevitably the number of users at the pool diminished.

Bryan Naylor suggested retaining it but covering it with a dome, creating what he called an Aquadome. This idea was rejected, so Naylor built his own mini-version in his back garden.

By the early 1980s, Sefton Council was losing around £40,000 a year on the pool and decided to lease it out to a private company. The company managed only four years and thereafter a succession of other enterprises on the site also failed.

In 1989, the Sea Bathing Lake was finally closed and after four years of increasing dereliction, it was finally demolished in 1993.

The site of what was once called Southport's 'wonder lake' is now occupied by a shopping mall.

▶ Southport's **Sea Bathing Lake** was located on the western, or seaward, side of Prince's Park, with its covered walkway – linking the café and both end changing room blocks – providing much needed shelter from the chill sea breezes.

In this image Marine Drive, which runs parallel with the coastline, can be seen heading northwards up through the Southport Sands into the distance, towards the Ribble Estuary.

Running across the centre of the photograph, from the Promenade on the right, out towards the sea, is the approach road to Southport Pier (out of view to the left).

Beyond this approach road lies the Marine Boating Lake, and beyond that, just a few of the many golf links that dominate the sands on this stretch of the coast.

As can be seen from the air, the oval shaped pool of the Sea Bathing Lake had shallow sides, increasing in depth only towards the central section, which measured 330 x 56 feet.

At the Ladies' End (nearest the camera), the highest diving-board was 8' 6" high, with a water depth below of 6 feet, whereas the men's diving-board opposite was nearly twice as high, at 16' 6", with 8' 6" of water below. These measurements had been set by the Amateur Diving Association in 1915 (see Chapter Four).

Case Study

Finchley Lido, London 1931–93

Architect Percival T Harrison
Cost Main pool £23,000;
children's pool, £7,000
Size Main 165' x 80' x 3' 6"-10';
children's 165' x 80' x 1'-3'
Water Freshwater, heated, main
456,250g; children's 138,000g
Opened Main 7 September 1931;
children's 12 July 1934
Closed 1993
Demolished August 1994
On site now Finchley Lido Leisure
Centre (includes small open-air pool)

Laid out on what remained of Finchley Common – once a notorious hiding place for highwaymen, thieves and fugitives – Finchley Swimming Pool was possibly the most advanced of its type when first opened to the public in September 1931.

At its official inauguration by the Mayor of Finchley on 26 March 1932 it was declared to be 'the latest type of bath,' with a state-of-the-art purification and filtration system and not one, but two cascades for aerating the water. Up to 90,000 gallons could be circulated per hour.

As a result, Percy Harrison, the Borough Engineer responsible for the design, was able to boast, 'Clean water day is *every* day.'

Not only that but there was a heating system too, making Finchley the first warm water pool in the capital (even if, in reality, it struggled to reach a tepid 60-65° Fahrenheit).

There was also generous provision for at least a thousand sunbathers, prompting the *Finchley Press* to refer glowingly to the pool's 'Lido-like facilities.'

Alas, moments after the ribbon was cut, it started to rain.

Not to be deterred, two years later the facility was extended, with the addition of a children's pool. This was separated from the main pool by a curved arcade and a cascade of water, designed to take advantage of the sloping site.

During the Second World War the pool's pioneering heating system was taken out of use.

Finchley's moment of glory was yet to come, however. In 1948 London stepped in at the eleventh hour to host the first Olympics of the post war period.

Unlike today's Games, precious little funding was available for sophisticated venues, but Finchley's pool was deemed to be just right for sharing the men's water polo tournament with the Empire Pool at Wembley.

(Women's water polo had to wait until Sydney in 2000.)

Temporary stands were erected on three sides of the main pool, and perhaps because these were the first Games to be televised, a yellow ball was trialled for greater visibility.

In total Finchley staged ten games over four days. (More had been scheduled but four of the 22 teams failed to arrive.) Among the participants were the eventual gold medallists, Italy, plus France, Spain, Sweden, Greece, India, Australia, Argentina and Chile. Finchley also staged Egypt's defeat of the Great Britain team.

Welcoming contestants to the event, a souvenir brochure painted an idyllic picture.

'The Open Air Swimming Pools at Finchley are situated in a very pleasant environment adjoining the Great North Road.

'They have been constructed on rising ground, on the north side of a shallow valley, and in lay-out and design, full advantage was taken of the open prospect to the south and south-east.

'From a terrace, which is one of the pleasant features of the premises, there is an unbroken view across to the low ridge of Fortis Green and Muswell Hill, with the Alexandra Palace and the BBC's television tower forming an interesting feature on the sky line about two miles away.

'Adjoining the premises on the north and east sides is an extensive open space, a large part of which the Council has maintained in its natural state, where hawthorns bloom and lend to the pools an effect of being situated away from urban surroundings.

'The Open Space was acquired for public recreation in 1925, and seven years later a tablet commemorating this acquisition and laying out was unveiled by HRH the Duke of York, now King George VI, when he also visited the swimming Pool.

'A bowling green and pavilion, eight hard tennis courts and a putting green add to the facilities for recreation.

'This part of Finchley in the little valley below the swimming »

▲ **Finchley Lido** as pictured in the 1948 Olympic brochure, showing the unique dual-pool layout. The elliptical children's pool was actually fifteen feet lower than the main pool.

Despite the construction of a new pool, leisure centre and car parks on the site in the 1990s, together with a David Lloyd Indoor Tennis Centre to the immediate

north (*that is, top left*), the open land to the south and east remains undeveloped as a nature reserve and the Glebelands Open Space.

Note the unusual two-sided concrete grandstand at the top of the photograph. Built in 1930 and accessed from Summers Lane, it is still in use, by Wingate FC on one side and Finchley Rugby Club on the other.

>> pools and on the rising ground beyond, is rich in trees, and as seen from the environs of the pools the landscape appears to be singularly free from buildings.

'Here and there a church spire rises above the trees and adds interest to the scene. Being fully open to the south and so well situated, the grounds are particularly attractive, and bathers and others can enjoy a freedom from the restriction of urban surroundings which cannot be rivalled by any other pool so near to the centre of London.'

Certainly the Finchley Lido, as it subsequently became known, was extremely popular.

In 1947, nearly 195,000 people paid to swim there, more than 11,000 of them in a single day.

In 1964, the total was not far short of 220,000.

Yet by the summer of 1990, by which time adult admission trebled from £1.30 to £4.00, the figures had dropped to 80,000, despite later opening hours.

When regular users first heard of closure plans, in 1983, a petition quickly attracted 5,000 signatures. That helped win a temporary stay of execution. But by 1990 the threat had grown.

Nor were the campaigners' efforts helped when, within the space of one July weekend that year, an 18 year old boy drowned and a 16 year old broke his neck.

At the inquest into the boy's death, a verdict of accidental death was returned. But there was much criticism of the pool's management. The water had apparently been so murky that no-one realised that he had failed to re-surface. His sister labelled the lido 'a death trap'.

Both incidents may well have been the last straw for Barnet

▲ London's northern suburbs were well served by open air pools, at Mill Hill, Bounds Green. Edmonton and Hornsey. But none was as extensive or elegant as **Finchley**.

As described earlier, the main pool, entered via the lodge (*top*), sat on a rise with a grass terrace offering clear views southwards.

To this was added the elliptical children's pool (*above*), on the lower part of the site, some fifteen feet below.

Opened by the Lord Mayor of London, Sir Charles Henry Collett, on 12 July 1934, this shallower pool, built to a maximum depth of 3' 6", was divided from its neighbour by two elegant curved arcades, each housing changing rooms for girls and boys respectively.

But the real delight was the provision, between these arcades, of a cascade of water, tumbling from the upper level to the lower.

On summer nights, when the pool did not close until 10pm, or later during heatwaves (having opened at 6.30am), floodlights illuminated the water, with coloured bulbs adding a particularly magical touch to the cascade.

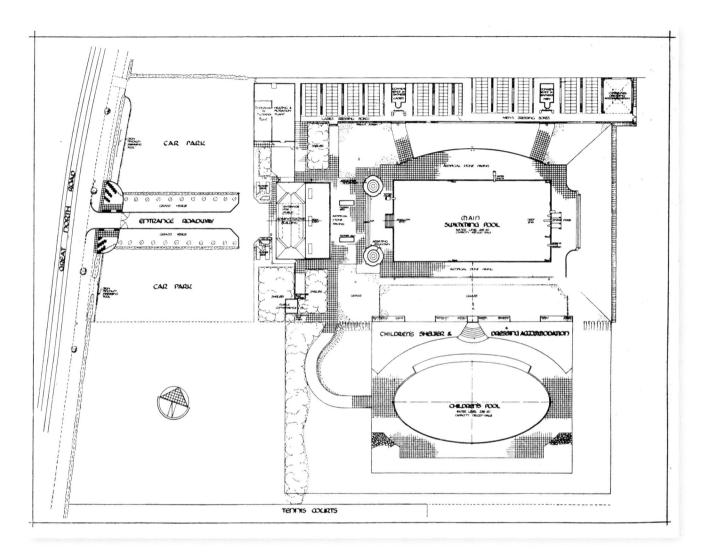

The plan contains the following labels:

GREAT NORTH ROAD

CAR PARK

ENTRANCE ROADWAY

GRASS VERGE

GRASS VERGE

CAR PARK

HEATING & FILTRATION PLANT

LADIES DRESSING BOXES

MEN'S DRESSING BOXES

ADMINISTRATIVE BUILDING

ARTIFICIAL STONE PAVING

MAIN SWIMMING POOL

ARTIFICIAL STONE PAVING

GRASS

CHILDREN'S SHELTER & DRESSING ACCOMMODATION

CHILDREN'S POOL

TENNIS COURTS

Borough Council, which had in any case been discussing plans to replace the lido with a leisure complex. The two pools were by then reckoned to be soaking up an annual subsidy of £150,000.

In July 1992 Mike Gee, one of the founders of the Finchley Pool Preservation Society, made an impassioned plea in the *Independent*.

'When you go to the lido, you're part of the planet. You are part of the sun, the wind, the rain. Nature! Blackberries! Daffodils opening! Birds flying down for food! The trees turning brown! You don't get these in a leisure centre...'

But to no avail. In 1996 the Finchley Lido Leisure Centre opened in its place, comprising a hotel, restaurants, a bowling alley and multiplex cinema. In one corner of the site there are also two indoor pools and a fitness centre, operated by Greenwich Leisure Ltd (who run six other centres in the borough of Barnet).

In the centre's backyard is a small open-air pool; 'a mere puddle' as described by one former lido user, compared with its once proud Olympian predecessor.

Percy Harrison's plan of Finchley Lido, after the addition of the children's pool in 1934. Access to the site was from the Great North Road (now the A1000, or High Road).

Case Study

St Leonard's Bathing Pool, Hastings 1933–86

DIVING PLATFORMS, HASTINGS & ST LEONARDS BATHING POOL, 9TH.

Architect Sidney Little
Cost £60,000
Size 330' x 90'
Water Seawater, 1m g
Opened 27 May 1933
Closed 1959
Reopened 1960 as holiday camp
Closed 1986
Demolished 1993
On site now Wasteland

They called Sidney Little the 'Concrete King', and for fifteen years or so he cast his spell across the East Sussex town of Hastings – a town that could never decide whether it wanted to be a working fishing port or a modern resort.

It was Little, who, as Borough Surveyor from 1926-50, oversaw a £3 million redevelopment of the sea front, including a twin deck promenade in which crushed glass formed part of the concrete walls. (Hence its nickname, Bottle Alley.)

The Concrete King built sea walls, reservoirs, roads and no fewer than three underground car parks.

And in 1933 he built an open air swimming pool on the seafront of St Leonards – the upmarket part of town – that dared to rival the northern giants of Blackpool and Southport in ambition, and scale, and far outstripped any of its contemporaries as an expression of rugged concrete modernism.

It was, in short, a lot of lido for a little kingdom.

It even made the nationals.

'£60,000 lido for England,' ran the headline in the *Daily Express*

when the plans were first revealed in October 1931 (and that was some years before the word lido had caught on).

As the photographs show, in design it was effectively a stadium on the waterfront, with water rather than turf in the centre.

On the street side tiered seating accommodated 2,500 spectators, curving inwards at the corners around the D-shaped pool. Underneath this was a gymnasium and inevitably, given Little's involvement, some underground parking.

Opposite, running parallel with the shoreline, was a covered promenade with segmental archs and sliding screens fitted with Vita glass to shelter bathers, should the wind blow in from the sea.

At one end a poolside café was decorated in shades of apple green and orange and furnished with highly fashionable Lloyd Loom tables and chairs.

All this was at ground level.

At rooftop level a concourse linked all four sides, providing a sun terrace that was to be bedecked with brightly coloured canvas chairs and large sun umbrellas. This, commented the local newspaper, achieved a 'lido effect' for what was otherwise 'the acme of engineering perfection.'

Yet despite Hasting Council's proud claim to have built the biggest and best pool in Europe, the St Leonard's Bathing Pool – for it was never officially called a lido – was to enjoy an unusually brief life.

An unusual 10m diving stage dominated the Hastings pool and was popular for championships and training. In this 1950s image the diving pit has been cordoned off while a water polo match takes place. Most of the larger pools were designed to stage the sport, which required a maximum playing area of 90 x 60 feet.

BATHING POOL

WILTON HOTEL

Indeed it only made a profit in its first year of operation, and as early as 1946 the Council offered it out to commercial interests.

None came forward until the pool was closed in 1959, and re-opened the following year as a privately-run holiday camp.

Subsequently renamed the Hastings Holiday Centre, this offered chalet hire for up to 300 guests, many of them holidaymakers from London looking for a cheap break. Even in the 1970s, a week's stay cost only £68 for full board.

By the early 1980s its appeal had waned, however, and when the pool sprang a leak, Sidney Little's lido was put out to grass.

The Council revoked the lease in 1986 amid speculation that a marina was to take it place. Instead, it lay empty for seven years before being bulldozed.

Dennis Carrington, the last owner, shed few tears.

'We never broke even,' he told the *Hastings and St Leonards Observer*. 'What's the good of an outdoor pool in this country? Nobody would be foolish enough to build one today.'

August 1933 and an exercise class takes place on the roof terrace. Note how the pool was designed for diving and water polo in the centre, with fixed booms to separate the deep and shallow sections (as seen also at Hilsea). On the beach side small concrete chalets were built for hire, many of which are all that remains on the otherwise vacant site today.

Case Study

Guildford Lido 1933

Architect JW Hipwood
Cost £13,000
Size 50m x 28m
Water Freshwater 500,000g
Opened June 21 1933

Guildford Lido, like so many open-air swimming pools of the 20th Century, was built using unemployed labour. Unusually, however, its funding did not come from central government but was raised locally.

The man credited with this initiative was Alderman William Alfred Harvey, Mayor of Guildford, who in November 1932 launched a fund to help the six hundred local men who were then on the dole.

Harvey sent letters to every household in the town urging those lucky enough to be in work to make 'a gesture of brotherhood to our townsmen' and donate one per cent of their annual earnings to the Mayor's Work Fund.

'Every shilling means an hour's work,' went the campaign slogan.

Clearly the people of Guildford were moved by his appeal. In just over twelve months the fund raised £7,720, thereby providing 590 unemployed men with 150,500 hours of labouring.

Only building projects deemed of value to the community were eligible for consideration, and all had to be approved by the Council.

Which made a proposal for the construction of an open-air pool a popular one. Indeed the idea had been mooted in 1930 but then shelved owing to the recession.

Now it was revived, only one note of dissent was heard, from the vicar of the nearby St John's church, concerned lest swimmers disturb his parishioners at prayer.

In total, 120 men were employed on the project, which from start to finish took just six months.

Set in a generous four and a half acres parkland site, the new lido provided what the Council still describes as an 'oasis in the heart of Guildford'.

At the opening ceremony, Mayor Harvey spoke of the trend towards 'out-of-doors and sunworshipping'.

'These grounds,' he announced proudly, 'are a token of what this town thinks about health and fitness and its liabilities to provide for those under its care.'

And with that he disrobed and took the first dive into the pool.

Seventy years on, Guildford Council has remained true to Harvey's commitment.

In the mid-1990s, with expensive repair bills looming, the future of the pool looked very much in doubt. Seeking possible salvation from the National Lottery, applications were made to both the Sports Lottery Fund and to the Heritage Lottery Fund.

To no avail. The former was turned down because the pool is open only during the summer months; the latter because the lido was considered to have no buildings of architectural merit.

But just as local residents rallied to Mayor Harvey in 1932, so in 1997 the Friends of Guildford Lido succeeded in persuading the Council of the lido's value to the community.

So successfully that since 1997 Guildford Borough Council has

Guildford Mayor William Alfred Harvey OBE leads the way on opening day in June 1933, casting off his ceremonial robes and chain to take the first dive.

spent £1.6 million on a series of refurbishments. This has included relining and retiling the pool itself, and slightly shortening it to the standard 50m Olympic length for competition events.

The water filtration plant, the café and main entrance have all been modernised, and a gym installed, thereby bringing in revenue all year round.

The next refurbishment phase, scheduled for 2006-07, should see the provision of new changing-rooms.

Although the lido is still owned and maintained by the Borough Council, in 2005 its operation was taken over by a private leisure company, Spectrum, who run the town's award winning indoor leisure centre nearby.

▲ Eschewing Modernism for a vernacular style more in keeping with the Home Counties, **Guildford Lido** had its own superintendent's lodge on nearby Lido Road (owned privately since the 1970s).

Inside the lido, all is trim and tidy and, it would seem after the vicar's concerns in 1933, in harmony with the neighbouring St John's Church.

Case Study

Open Air Pool, Stonehaven 1934

Architect RR Gill
Size 165' x 60' (main pool)
Water Heated seawater, 290,000g
Opened 2 June 1934

Stonehaven Open Air Pool, near Aberdeen, is one of dozens of small pools whose value as a liquid asset far outstrips its modest architectural merits.

It is also the most northerly lido in the country (if one excludes the Trinkie Outdoor Pool at Wick, a natural seawater pool.)

Opened in 1934, after a Poll of Householders had been held in the town, Stonehaven's pool has undergone a series of upgrades over the years.

During its first season, when the water was neither filtered nor heated, only 20,000 bathers turned up, although a further 60,000 paid to watch them shiver. With surprising speed, Stonehaven Town Council installed a filtration and sterilisation system, as well as heating. As a result, the number of bathers more than doubled and the total number of tickets sold over the season exceeded 100,000.

In more recent years the opening of an indoor leisure centre nearby appeared to have sounded the death knell for the pool, especially when attendances dipped to only 13,500 in 1992.

Perched on top of an incline a few hundred yards inland from the North Sea, the pool at Stonehaven is accessed via a boarded walk from the town's harbour. Once through the turnstile a high wall protects swimmers from the chill winds that can and do blow in from the sea. Not on this sunny day in the late 1930s however, by the looks of it.

Its jolly appearance today therefore represents a remarkable turnaround in its fortunes.

When Aberdeenshire Council took over responsibility for the pool in 1994 they deemed its running costs of £90,000 a year too high a burden for ratepayers and mothballed the pool for a year.

Two dozen supporters soon banded together to form the Friends of Stonehaven Pool, and the fightback began.

First came a survey which showed that the number of visitors who cited the lido as their sole reason for coming to Stonehaven was in the region of 45,000. Closure of the pool, argued the Friends, would be an economic body blow to the town.

The campaigners also stressed the health benefits of taking exercise in warm, salty water.

Victory for the Friends came in instalments. In 1997, they undertook to carry out the day-to-

day maintenance of the pool and were able to offer the voluntary services of plumbers, welders, joiners and electricians. This alone saved the Council around £20,000.

Eventually an official partnership agreement between the Friends and Aberdeenshire Council was signed in May 2000.

Under this agreement, Aberdeenshire Council provides a capital budget for the pool and pays for lifeguards, while the Friends take responsibility for marketing and routine repairs.

William Munro, Area Manager for Aberdeenshire Council and himself a keen swimmer, recalled, 'I had great confidence that a partnership with the Friends could work, but it has exceeded even my expectations.'

'We now have partnerships with a number of other community groups. We provide them with small grants, and find it has engendered a much greater level of

THE BATHING POOL, STONEHAVEN.   B.2215.

civic pride. But Stonehaven Pool is the flagship.'

According to Mary Mitchell, Chairman of the Friends, the financial situation has improved too. The pool costs around £30,000 to run each season and needs about the same number of people going through its doors.

After the hot summer of 2003, however, the pool made an exceptional profit of £27,000.

One of the Friends' best initiatives has been the revival of the pool's traditional midnight swim, held every Wednesday throughout the summer from 10pm until midnight or later.

When I succumbed to the offer of a 'swim under the stars' in 2001, I was astonished to find a long queue. Some swimmers had travelled from Aberdeen, others from Dundee, over 50 miles away, just for the pleasure of a nocturnal dip. For many this was a regular weekly fixture. There was a mix of ages – and in one case, three generations of one family – though teenagers were in the majority.

Music played over the pool's loudspeakers as we swam in a party-like spirit. Multi-coloured bunting wafted in the late night breeze.

A people's pool in every sense, and, as we shall learn in Chapter Eight, one of many such success stories in Britain today.

Come rain or shine, the water at Stonehaven stays heated to a luxurious 85° F – just one reason why the Scottish Tourist Board classifies the pool as a four star attraction. The lively colour scheme helps too.

Case Study

The Bathing Pool, New Brighton 1934–1990

Architect L St G Wilkinson
Cost £103,240
Size 330' x 225' x 0'-15'
Water Seawater, 1.75m g
Opened 13 June 1934
Closed 1990
Demolished May 1990
On site now wasteland

'The greatest bathing arena in the world' or, 'one of the biggest white elephants in Wallasey'.

What a difference 30 years can make.

Opened by Lord Leverhulme in 1934, the Bathing Pool on King's Parade, New Brighton – on the north eastern tip of the Wirral peninsula, facing Liverpool Bay – was one of the largest lidos ever built in Britain, occupying a prime seafront site of 4.5 acres.

It was also one of the best appointed, as might have been expected from a town that prided itself as one of the leading holiday destinations in the north west. (Until 1921 it had a tower that was taller than Blackpool's).

Yet despite this, when the idea had first been mooted in 1927 – at the same time as Southport was planning its own grandiose pool – there was fierce opposition.

The proposal put forward was actually for two open air pools on the New Brighton seafront; one on King's Parade, in the town centre, and a smaller one a mile westwards, by Harrison Drive.

For the next few years the debate swung for and against the proposal within Wallasey Town Council, before the pressing need to provide work for unemployed men in the area finally tipped the balance.

A government loan enabled the Harrison Drive pool to go ahead in late 1931, and this was opened the following June, by the Earl of Derby. Indeed it was named after him thereafter.

Designed by the Borough Engineer, L St G Wilkinson, the Derby Pool was a substantial structure, with a rectangular pool 330 feet long and a two tiered pavilion and terrace shielding bathers from sea breezes.

For many small towns this alone would have seemed quite adequate. But New Brighton's ambitions as a resort spurred councillors on to proceed with the larger pool in 1933.

This time Wilkinson appeared to spare no expense.

Quite simply, his new Bathing Pool was a colossal structure, even larger than that of Blackpool's, completed a decade earlier,

with a stated capacity for 12,000 spectators (although some accounts claimed 20,000).

The main entrance block on King's Parade – its Art Deco façade 238 feet long – contained administration offices, common rooms for both male and female lifeguards, a pool manager's apartment and a committee room. The latter led out on to a balcony offering a fine view over the diving end of the pool.

Flanking the entrance were six shops. One sold bathing costumes. Another offered a photographic service. A third sold high-class chocolates, advertised in those less politically correct days as 'Black Boy Chocolates'.

Changing rooms were light and airy with 'glasscrete' ceilings, and horizontal, metal-framed windows.

Also included was a first aid centre equipped with two 'wards', each containing two beds for those taken ill at the pool (or along the Promenade).

Yet another room was for 'drying people's clothing after accidental immersion.' »

VIEW OF THE NEW BRIGHTON BATHING POOL

◀ Seven years in the planning, but well worth the wait. The **Bathing Pool** at **New Brighton** set new standards for lido design in Britain.

At its opening ceremony in June 1934 (*below*), an estimated 12,000 spectators attended a two hour spectacular, watched over by Lord Leverhulme – whose family fortune had been made at nearby Port Sunlight – plus the Mayor of Wallasey and sixteen of his counterparts from other town councils around the north west.

'A dazzling kaleidoscope of colour,' filled the vast arena, reported The *Wallasey News.*

New Brighton, it declared, was now 'Britain's premier garden city by the sea'. There was even excited talk of holding the next Olympic Games there.

But the pool's designer, L St G Wilkinson, had concerns of his own, knowing that the site was too close to the beach for comfort.

In an article in the *Municipal Journal & Public Works Engineer* in June 1938 he described the pool as having 'a rather bad foundation, partly of running sand.'

A correspondent in the *Wallasey News* voiced the same fears.

We have an old, old parable,
On building on the sand –
But perhaps my fears are
"groundless",
And I may not understand.

THE MAIN ENTRANCE

▲ The classic 1930s entrance block to the New Brighton **Bathing Pool** (*top*) was rendered in 'snowcrete' and decorated, as were all exterior walls in the building, with a band of green faience work (glazed tiles).

Extensive use of 'glasscrete' glazing bricks also flooded the interiors with light, such as in the two-storey café (*above*).

Clearly, this was no ordinary municipal pool.

» In its first year of operation, the New Brighton pool set records that would never be matched.

On 7 July 1934, a sun-drenched Saturday three weeks after its opening, an astonishing total of 34,560 people paid to enter.

Within a month of the opening, the aggregate total of admissions stood at 350,000. By the end of the season that figure had risen to nearly one million, earning Wallasey Town Council £14,358 in ticket receipts.

But of course it could not last. The following year, as the novelty wore off and spectator numbers dropped by 300,000, total receipts fell to £10,650. Poor weather was another factor.

Even at this early stage, one Wallasey Town councillor was sufficiently concerned to propose that the pool be converted into an ice rink during the winter months. His proposal was heavily defeated, but the idea of roofing over the pool would be discussed many times in the years ahead.

In common with many lidos of the 1930s, New Brighton had a towering diving stage; 10 metres high, facing a pit 15 feet deep (the minimum recommended by the Amateur Swimming Association).

Inevitably, young men liked to show off to the crowds by spicing up their dives with acrobatics.

In 1937 this led to the pool's only fatality. Wilfred Bennett, a 28 year old from Birkenhead, attempted a handstand dive off the top board and collided with another swimmer in the water. He died the following day.

Other than this, however, New Brighton's pool enjoyed six comparatively successful summer seasons before the Second World War broke out. After the immediate post war boom,

however, the tide gradually turned.

Barbara Bell, whose grandparents, parents and children were all enthusiastic swimmers at New Brighton, has vivid memories of their regular visits during the 1960s and 1970s.

'New Brighton was simply magnificent. On hot days you would have to queue to get in, despite the pool's huge capacity.

'Once inside any non-swimmers in the party would claim a wooden bench, whilst the swimmers would rush to the changing rooms.

'I can still remember the smell of those changing rooms. Salt water and cheap talcum powder!

'Another marvellous thing about New Brighton was the way the concrete sloped down into the water like an artificial beach. It was even painted a sandy colour to add to the effect.'

But by the 1980s, as attendances continued to fall to around 30,000 a year, down from an average of 85,000 during the early 1970s, and as New Brighton itself fell victim to the growing availability of cheap continental holidays, plans were hatched to build an indoor leisure complex on the site, just as had been done at Blackpool in 1983.

One architect wrote to the *Wallasey News*, urging that there be no alteration to the existing structure. 'It may be shabby for want of a coat of paint,' she wrote, 'but it is not ugly.'

A Save New Brighton Baths campaign was duly formed, but suffered an acute setback in February 1990 when severe storms damaged the pool's already uncertain foundations.

Repairs, previously estimated at £1 million by the Merseyside Development Corporation, would now be even costlier.

A further blow fell weeks later

when an attempt to have the pool listed was refused by the minister responsible, Lord Hesketh.

And so, opened by one lord, buried by another, Britain's largest open air pool was demolished, and the site grassed over.

Now known locally as 'The Dips', it has lain vacant ever since.

But perhaps not for much longer. Wirral Borough Council,

in conjunction with a development company called Neptune, have drawn up plans for the entire redevelopment of the New Brighton promenade, involving, *inter alia*, the creation of a new lido in part of the existing Marine Lake, the rest of which would be infilled and sold off for private homes on the sea front, with a superstore and car park alongside.

For many, that is a price too high to pay for a new lido. For others, any measure to revive the beleaguered town would be welcome.

One ideal place to mull over these differences lies a short distance along the promenade.

It is the former pavilion of the Derby Pool, now converted into a pub.

A magnificent view of the New Brighton Bathing Pool's main pavilion in 1934. This and all other black and white images of the pool in this section are from the Stewart Bale Ltd Photographic Archive, held by the Merseyside Maritime Museum. More of this wonderful collection will be featured in our forthcoming title, *Played in Liverpool*.

Case Study

Sandford Parks Lido, Cheltenham 1935

Architect Gould Marsland
Cost £16,000
Size 50m x 27m x 0.9 - 2.75m
Water Freshwater, heated, 500,000g
Opened 25 May 1935

If any town conjures up a picture of prosperous middle England, it is the Regency spa town of Cheltenham in Gloucestershire.

Cheltenham's famous waters were discovered in 1716, but it was a visit by George III in 1788 that confirmed the town's status as one of Britain's leading spa resorts, characterised by its elegant Royal Crescent and Georgian terraced houses which today form part of an extensive conservation area.

It is still possible to take the waters in the Pump Room in Pittville Park to the north. But a park on the eastern side of town offers a much more pleasurable aquatic experience.

Sandford Parks Lido consists of three pools; a main pool and two smaller ones for children, set in 4.5 acres of landscaped grounds with lawns, flowerbeds and paved terracing (illustrated on page 1).

The lido opened in 1935, on land that had been bought by Cheltenham Council and then used as allotments. According to Annette Denison's history of the pool (see Links), it is unclear whether the original intention was to build an open air pool on the site. But the idea, if not the location, had certainly been mooted some years earlier.

During excavation of the site, the builders unearthed peat deposits which had to be replaced with concrete before construction of the pool could begin.

The lido's design itself was by the Borough Engineer, Gould Marsland, who, as is evident, had a particular interest in water engineering. (Marsland, who was also responsible for the Whaddon Estate and the suburb of Hesters Way, is otherwise credited with sparing the town from the encroachment of tower blocks.)

For the lido's first season, there was no café, but a marquee that was accessible from both the pool and the park. The £1,000 that raised helped to fund a permanent café in 1936 (also designed by Marsland). A paddling pool was added at the same time.

Sandford Parks remained open throughout the Second World War, attracting up to 90,000 visitors a year. One of them, a sergeant evacuated from Dunkirk, described the pool as 'heaven after hell.' It was, however, hit by a bomb later during the war, which damaged the children's pool.

In more recent times, the lido was first threatened with closure in the early 1980s, only to be spared following protests and petitions from users and local residents.

By 1996, however, Cheltenham Borough Council had identified around £250,000 worth of repairs, including a new filtration system.

Calculating a life expectancy of only ten years for the pool, it concluded that the outlay could not be justifed, and instead handed its operation to a group of dedicated supporters, who formed a limited company with charitable status, Sandford Lido Ltd.

To help the company get started the council allocated annual grants worth £40,000, as well as some financial help with repairs. Crucially the council also agreed to let the new operators retain the income from the large car park adjoining the pool.

Julie Sargent, Chief Executive of Sandford Lido Ltd, reckons this amounts to at least £85,000 a year.

'A secondary stream of income is really important,' she says.

'As well as the car park, we have the rental income from a private gym on the site and we contract out the café in the summer.'

Over the past ten years, with the help of grants from the council and a variety of foundations, the trustees have spent a total of £350,000 on repairs and maintenance. A further £500,000 overhaul of the main pool is planned for the near future.

Despite the financial headaches, Sargent believes outdoor pools can be run successfully as charities.

'In many ways, it is much easier for us than the council,' she says.

'Councils have other facilities to worry about and tend to look at their lidos only at the time of opening, whereas we can concentrate on it for twelve months of the year.'

Ron Coltman, now in his seventies, has enjoyed a lifelong association with the pool. His father took him to the opening ceremony and he still recalls the excitement of being allowed to hurtle down the slide into the sparkling water below. In his teens, he took a job looking after the wire baskets and later still, became pool supervisor.

'I still get a buzz in the spring,' he says, 'when we are preparing to open for a new season.'

Taking the waters, 20th century lido style – Sandford Parks from the air in 1947 (*top*), showing the site's quatrefoil plan and curving service block and café, and more recently (*right*), a steamy sunrise view from the main entrance, with the lido's two playful dolphin litter bins framing the fountain.

Case Study

Jubilee Pool, Penzance 1935

Grade II Listed (1993)
Architect Capt. Frank Latham
Cost £15,000
Size 330' x 240' x 3-15'
Water Seawater, 1m g
Opened 31 May 1935
Closed 1993
Re-opened 1994

Advertised as 'the first and last lido in the UK' the Jubilee Pool's claim to prominence goes beyond a mere geographical quirk.

Opened in 1935 to mark the Silver Jubilee of George V, the pool is a beautifully understated Art Deco treasure, its curvaceous outer walls rippling gently out into Mount's Bay on the south west tip of Cornwall, ten miles from Land's End.

Passing through the entrance at street level and dropping down the stepped terrace towards the pool, one's first impression is of the cool, man-made white and blue tones of the water and its surrounds, set against the lapping waters of the bay.

It is as if a giant deckchair has collapsed in the wind.

The Jubilee Pool's architect, Captain Frank Latham, is said to have been inspired to create a triangular pool by the sight of a seagull alighting on the water. It is an image hard to equate with the finished design, but a poetic one all the same and one fully in keeping with the spirit – the *genius loci* – of the place.

Latham had held the post of Borough Engineer and Surveyor in Penzance for 35 years when he was asked to design the pool.

Before Penzance, he had worked in Margate, so had considerable expertise of coastal locations.

At an initial cost of £15,000, the Jubilee Pool was extraordinarily cheap. This was partly because no concrete was laid on the floor of the pool. In effect Latham enclosed what was an existing sandy cove, already popular with swimmers.

The fact that the pool was filled with sea water also helped to reduce costs, seven sluice gates being constructed to control the inflow at high tide.

Penzance Town Council was clearly pleased with Latham's efforts. In the official town guide for 1935, it asked in rather purple prose, 'Who's for a dip in the southernmost bathing pool in the British Isles, amidst the opal-tinted girt of the English Bay of

Naples crowned by the island features of St Michael's Mount?'

But the pool's dramatic setting was also its achilles heel.

Surprisingly, relatively little steel reinforcement was incorporated within the pool's concrete walls, and although they were clearly streamlined to offset the pounding of the sea, over the last 70 years the structure has needed continual monitoring and repair.

The most serious incidence of this occurred in March 1962 when violent storms struck the Cornish coast. Part of the sea wall was breached, allowing sea water to flow uncontrolled into the pool.

Fortunately Penzance Town Council reacted with commendable urgency, and the pool was able to open as usual that summer following major works.

By the late 1980s, however, the pool's structural problems had worsened, so that, owing to leakage, the water level was now dropping at a rate of around

Crowds gather at the Jubilee Pool for its opening on 31 May 1935. In the foreground is the roof of the Sailors' Institute, built by a local landowner in 1908 to provide a welfare service to seamen. To the left of the pool the Penzance war memorial is visible.

fifteen inches per day. To stem this clearly required another extensive programme of repairs, a measure that Penwith District Council (who had taken over responsibility for the pool in 1974) were now reluctant to finance.

Instead, as part of a scheme to redevelop the nearby harbour area, the Council had granted planning permission for an indoor leisure complex, to be known as the Water Fun Centre.

It was then suggested to the developers that a better place to locate this new complex would be the Jubilee Pool site itself.

The resultant design, which included a large, copper coloured pyramid roof, attracted a storm of protest, from English Heritage, the Thirties Society, SAVE Britain's Heritage, Lord St Levens of Michael's Mount – from which a clear view of the pool may be had – and from the National Trust, which owns the Mount.

In its own response, the Royal Fine Arts Commission stated, in July 1989, 'This is not the site for a major building'. The proposal, it added, 'constitutes a major architectural blot on the landscape in one of the most beautiful cities of the United Kingdom.'

Penzance Town Council also objected, as did nearly 600 local signatories to a petition.

At the same time, however, an attempt to have the pool listed was turned down.

Enter John Clarke, a retired architect and resident of Penzance since 1956.

'Up until that point,' he recalls, 'I had probably swum in the pool only once. But as an architect, I felt it would be a great shame to lose the pool. I thought perhaps I could do something for Penzance and the people of Penzance.

'There was also the social side. The pool was the only real place in Penzance for youngsters to let off steam, and it was a good place to learn to swim. It would have been a great tragedy had it closed.'

Clarke duly appeared as an objector at the subsequent public inquiry in 1991. In his evidence, he described the pool as a 'rich reminder of the development of architecture in the inter war period,' and argued that the proposed pyramid or any raised structure would ruin views across Mount's Bay to St Michael's Mount. 'An essential part of the charm of the town would be lost by the dominating effect of any building on the site,' he said.

For their part Penwith District Council made clear its view that the Jubilee Pool had 'come to the end of its useful life' and would have to be 'at the centre of consideration for new visitor attractions.'

It also declined to give an undertaking that the pool would be retained, even if the leisure centre were built elsewhere. At that stage, it was estimated, it would cost £500,000 simply to stabilise the structure and carry out modest improvements.

In the end, the inspector's findings came down in favour of the Council. Crucially, however, he added that any redevelopment of the site 'should be of exceptional quality which will preserve and enhance the character of the Conservation Area.'

By focusing on this one specific point, Clarke and his fellow objectors finally succeeded in persuading the Council to abandon its plans.

On 2 July 1991, the Planning and Development Committee undertook to retain the Jubilee

The Jubilee Pool and St Michael's Mount in this seductive British Railways poster by artist Harry Riley in 1952.

Hello sailors! Two joined images from July 1949 show the scene when the Western Union fleet, consisting of vessels from the Dutch, French and British navies, paid a visit to Penzance. Among the events staged for their amusement was a water polo match. Water polo tournaments are still held at the pool and continue to attract large crowds. The sport originated in England in 1876 when 'aquatic handball' was played for the first time in Bournemouth.

Pool and to invest in it to enhance it as a tourist attraction.

The crisis was over.

But there still remained much work to do.

The following year, the Jubilee Pool Association was formed with John Clarke as its first President. In the same year, the Council set up the Jubilee Pool Steering Group, involving the Association as well as councillors in the decision-making process.

Also, in 1993, the Department of the Environment granted the pool a Grade II listing at the second time of asking.

Thereafter nearly £1 million in funding flowed in from a variety of sources: the Heritage Lottery Fund, the European Regional Development Fund, the Shell Better Britain Campaign, Penzance Town Council and Penwith District Council, who contributed more than £300,000 of ratepayers' money.

The Jubilee Pool Association made its own contribution by carrying out small improvements on a voluntary basis and by raising funds through special events.

When the Jubilee Pool re-opened in 1994 after a year's closure, its refurbishment was greeted with widespread national acclaim.

As one council officer was to concede, 'We've had excellent publicity out of it. The big articles we've had in national newspapers would have cost us thousands in advertising.' He also admitted that there were plenty of people around at the time who just wished the pool 'would fall into the sea.'

Major structural repairs were carried out in two stages, in 1993 and in 1998. These included re-concreting the floor of the pool (which had first been concreted in the late 1940s) and reinforcing its inner walls. In effect, an inner retaining box was inserted into

the site, making the pool slightly smaller today than its original 330 x 240 feet.

Two levels of terracing were also created in 1993; the lower one for sunbathers, the upper one offering breathtaking views across Mount's Bay to St Michael's Mount.

In the 1930s the revenue from spectators at open air pools often far exceeded that from bathers.

Today, the Jubilee Pool is one of the few remaining pools that still encourages that. In 2004 the entry fee for non-bathers was just 70p, plus £1 for the hire of a deckchair.

Also in the tradition of the 1930s, water polo matches continue to be an attraction at Penzance. Certainly the pool's arena-like layout makes it ideal for such events.

Among the spectators one might encounter there is Sheila Richards, a member of the Penzance Swimming Club, which is based at the pool, and a former

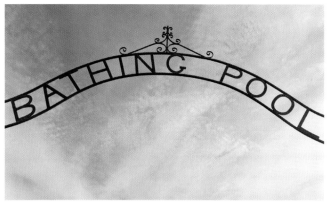

▲ The minimalist lines, pastel blues, stainless steel railings and uncluttered roughcast surfaces of the **Jubilee Pool** in **Penzance** are not to everyone's taste. Roger Deakin, in his epic book, *Waterlog* (*see Links*) admitted that when he first paid a visit he found the pool 'more Fascist than anything I had ever seen'. Then, gradually, he warmed to its charms.

As the saying goes, 'less is more'.

County Butterfly Champion. Now aged 67 her enthusiasm for the place remains undimmed.

'Swimming here is a way of life. Come rain or shine, this is where we are,' she says, and then adds thoughtfully, 'It was the place where I learnt to swim. It was our growing-up ground, our courting ground, our children's playground, our absolute delight.'

In 2005, however, the pool's future once again came under scrutiny. Penwith District Council, it was revealed, subsidises every swim to the tune of £16.

Clearly this is a burden that they are unwilling to shoulder indefinitely. And so in Penzance, as in so many locations around Britain, the Jubilee Pool's fight for survival shows no sign of abating.

▲ Whether viewed as a functional swimming pool or as an ornamental water work, only by slipping into its depths can the sheer size of the **Jubilee Pool** in **Penzance** be truly appreciated. Measuring 330 x 240 feet (100 x 73 metres) on its longest axes, the Jubilee Pool is Britain's largest surviving lido.

By comparison, Tooting Bec Lido in London (*see page 52*), which appears vast, is 300 feet long and 100 feet wide, while Plymouth's Tinside Lido (*page 108*), which in common with the Jubilee Pool protrudes into the sea, measures a mere 180 feet on its longest axis.

The Jubilee Pool is also unusually deep, measuring 15 feet (4.6m) at its deepest point – a depth once common for the diving pits of lidos built before 1939, but now extremely rare.

In the foreground, a shallower pool in the north-east corner has been set aside for children.

Although a seawater pool, the water is now changed not with each tide but when its quality demands.

▲ Jutting out into Mount's Bay, the **Jubilee Pool** is one of Penzance's finest attractions, and one of the great engineering wonders of the outdoor swimming world.

Commenting on its construction, the *Cornishman and Cornish Telegraph* of June 5 1935 reported that 'jutting out into the sea, exposed to the full violence of the south-easterly and southerly gales, it was necessary to take advantage not only of every natural asset, but of every other idea that modern engineering science could devise.'

Not only was the interior of the pool a fine piece of engineering by Frank Latham, but it was also a work of art in itself.

'The monotony of straight walls and right angles – the domain of the compass and ruler – has been entirely and utterly avoided.

'Instead, there are graceful curves and pleasing lines – an adaption of cubism to the terraces and diving platforms which enhances the effect and makes the whole so pleasing to the eye.'

And so it remains.

Case Study

Purley Way Lido, Croydon 1935–79

Architects CE Boast
Cost £15,600
Size 200' x 70' and 100' x 60'
Water freshwater, 650,000g
Opened 20 July 1935
Closed 1979
On site now Garden centre

Drive down the Purley Way section of the A23 today and there seems little to arouse the imagination. Just another anonymous arterial route, leading from Croydon's curious cluster of postwar high-rise office blocks to the distant delights of Brighton and the south coast.

Yet seventy years ago there was hardly a road in Britain to match it for sheer excitement.

For Purley Way was a gateway to the world – and the modern world at that.

Completed as one of the country's earliest bypasses in 1925, the road's major landmark was Croydon Aerodrome, London's first airport, originally laid out in 1920. In 1928 the airport's growing stature was confirmed by the construction of a substantial passenger terminal, backing onto Purley Way, where it was joined by the Aerodrome Hotel.

Here at the 'Gateway to the Continent' gathered the privileged few for Imperial Airways flights to Paris, Berlin and beyond. Here came the curious in their thousands to see Charles

Lindbergh land from America, and Amy Johnson take off for Australia.

Purley Way soon became Britain's first main road to be lit by newly developed sodium lighting, suspended on cables down the centre of the highway. When the entire route was lit in 1936 the BBC staged a special broadcast to mark the occasion.

Meanwhile modern factories sprang up on nearby estates with roads called Commerce Way, Progress Way and Trojan Way. They manufactured aircraft and car parts, electrical components, adding machines, and a sparkling new drink called Tizer.

To add to the airport terminal and hotel, the Bowater corrugated box company built on Purley Way one of London's most finely articulated Art Deco factories.

Such was the hotbed of modernity into which the Purley Way Lido arrived, directly across from the airport, in July 1935.

As the Croydon Borough Council's motto had it, 'Sanitate Crescamus'. By Health We Progress.

But this was no ordinary London lido. Hailed by the local press as a 'Masterpiece of Science and Skill', it was quite different from its understated brick counterparts being built north of the River Wandle by the London County Council.

Above all, dominating the parkland setting was its main 200 foot long service building, a crisp Modernist block faced in white concrete with extensive metal framed windows and skylights.

In common with its hi-tech neighbours, Purley Way Lido brimmed with innovation, soon becoming billed as 'the electric pool'.

Lighting was installed all over; under the water, amid the swaying palms planted in the shingle beach areas (*see page 22*), and within the pool's two stunning Art Deco fountains (*see left*), whose lights changed colour at regular intervals, creating a memorable tonal effect on its green 'Cullamix' cast stone surfaces.

Unusually, but predictably in the circumstances, the water was heated, by an electric boiler. 》

▲ Of all the London area's lidos built during the 1930s, **Purley Way** came closest to the scale and grandeur found at such coastal resorts as Morecambe, New Brighton and Weston.

Photographed here in 1935 is the lido's two-storey main block on Waddon Way, and (*left*) its first floor café area with stairs leading up to the roof terrace.

Both the exterior and interior detailing showed distinct stylistic similarities with the Croydon Airport terminal built across Purley Way seven years earlier.

▲ Viewed here from the south, in 1969, **Purley Way Lido** was accessed from Waddon Way and formed part of an extensive open space otherwise used as playing fields. Directly across Waddon Way can be seen the freestanding Waddon Waterworks, which presumably supplied the lido.

Set in the midst of a 4.5 acre site offering ample room for sunbathing, the pool was cruciform in plan, with a 15 foot deep diving pit forming one end of the shorter axis, octagonal fountains at each end and a children's paddling pool.

Architect CE Boast's original plans provided for a separate café on the south side, but in the event the 200 foot long block on the north side proved sufficient.

Croydon Airport (not shown) lay a few hundred yards to the west, so that the drone of aircraft taking off and coming in to land must have been a regular accompaniment to this otherwise parkland setting.

» It was purified, moreover, not with the usual chlorine, but with ozone, described at the time as 'the most up-to-date method in existence'.

The ozone – a condensed form of oxygen – was created by subjecting dry air to electrical stress. It was then introduced into the water through rows of jets ranged along the floor of the pool.

Apart from recreating the smell and spray of seawater, one advantage was that, unlike chlorine, ozone did not sting bathers' eyes.

All these modern features, plus the lido's generous 200 x 70 foot main pool area, convinced local councillors that Purley Way would soon be on the international swimming map.

'Within five minutes of leaving their aeroplane,' they pointed out, 'members of a foreign water polo team could be in their dressing-rooms, preparing to take part in a contest in one of the best equipped water pools in the country.'

Their hopes were not realised. But at its peak before the Second World War, Purley Way was nonetheless considered one of the leading pools of its time, able to cater for 3,000 bathers a day.

But like the adjoining airport – eclipsed by Heathrow during the 1950s – its star gradually waned. The heating system was switched off. Chlorine replaced ozone when the latter was found to damage the skin.

By 1979, the lido's final season, the total for the whole summer had dropped to 28,000.

Two years later the pool was no more. In its place, as at Mill Hill and Durnsford Road in north London, a garden centre opened.

As seen opposite, however, not all was lost.

▲ There really is no other lido relic like it in Britain today.

Seventy years after two American Olympic gold medallists – Pete Desjardins (the 'Little Bronze Statue') and Harold 'Dutch' Smith – put on a daredevil display from its heights 'to stun and thrill the crowds' at the lido's opening, the diving stage of the **Purley Way Lido** remains instantly recognisable on the local skyline.

Yet how different its setting. Stranded amid the potted plants and shrubs of a typical suburban garden centre, the concrete diving stage, with its three, five and ten metre boards, now serves as an advertisement hoarding.

Closer inspection of the garden centre's main block (*above in the background*) also provides a clear idea of the lido's former scale and sophistication. Indeed it is almost as if both surviving structures are merely biding their time until a new outdoor pool is recreated in their midst.

Case Study

Hilsea Lido, Portsmouth 1935

Architect Joseph Parkin with additions by Adrien Sharpe
Size 220' x 60' (main pool)
Water Originally seawater, now freshwater, 190,500g
Opened 24 July 1935

On land and on sea the people of Portsmouth have been defending the nation for centuries.

But amid the Georgian and Victorian ramparts to the north of the dockyards another prolonged defensive action has been waged to keep the city's Hilsea Lido open against all the odds.

It is a campaign which continues until today.

Hilsea was designed in the very latest International Modern style by the Portsmouth City Engineer's department under Joe Parkin, in 1933, in part to serve the thousands of residents rehoused in the area from the city's slums.

Opened in 1935 it was a lido in the true sense of the word; a resort for recreation and relaxation, with a putting green, tennis courts, an open air dance floor, a miniature railway and two pools.

Swimmers, revellers and romantics alike were drawn to its stylised concrete portal, added in 1938. Bus conductors called out 'Hollywood!' as the Hilsea stop approached. On summer evenings floodlights and music added a daring allure.

Britain's Olympic swimmers came here to train for the 1936 Games in Berlin. The Women's League of Health and Beauty held classes on its terraces. During the Second World War American troops stationed at the nearby Hilsea Barracks dreamed of home from its saltwater depths.

And yet the Lido's long term future has been the subject of re-development proposals for nearly five decades.

As long ago as 1958 councillors considered roofing over the main pool to make it more viable. A few years later they considered

installing a removable floor to cater for off-season use. Another scheme called for the construction of a leisure complex alongside.

By 1987 Portsmouth City Council decided that the only way forward was to redevelop the site completely, and invited tenders for a range of leisure, recreation and entertainment facilities. Of 13 schemes submitted, three went forward for public consultation, each of them centred around a multi-screen cinema complex and extensive car-parking.

But Hilsea's modern day defenders stood firm.

City Architect Adrien Sharpe's splended gateway to Hilsea Lido was added in 1938 but demolished only 30 years later as part of a road widening scheme.

After the Council received over 700 letters in opposition, all three proposals were dropped the following year. The campaigners wanted improved swimming and paddling facilities, not an intrusive entertainment mall.

Conservationists were also concerned about the aesthetic impact any new buildings would have upon the surrounding landscape, and particularly the historic Hilsea Lines (*see right*).

Next came a proposal, in 1991, to demolish the 1930s structures and build an indoor heated pool on the site. But this too failed for lack of matched funding from private sources. (Around the same time Portsmouth Football Club were hoping to build their own new stadium nearby in Farlington, only to fail because of the need to add so much commerical development to the package.)

But Hilsea's defenders knew that this would not be the last threat to their beloved pools, and in 1994 attempted to have the lido listed. This however was turned down on the grounds that Hilsea was not 'of comparable architectural quality' with others of its type; for example the Jubilee Pool in Penzance, Saltdean Lido in Brighton or Peterborough Lido, all of which were Grade II listed (and featured elsewhere in this book).

Local historian and lido enthusiast, Jane Smith, argued that 'as a genuine 1930s' Lido, Hilsea is a valuable part of Portsmouth's heritage. The Council supports Southsea Castle and the Mary Rose – neither of which serves their original purpose – so why not the Lido, too?'

Support for this stance arrived in 2002, when The Twentieth Century Society (formerly the Thirties Society) made a second »

▲ For centuries military and civil engineers, and more recently motorway builders, have sought to tame and traverse the former marshland around Ports Creek, the waterway that separates Portsea Island (on which Portsmouth is built) from the mainland.

As seen above, looking west in the early 1970s, **Hilsea Lido** is located on the north western corner of the island, between the Creek and a moat, the latter forming part of the Hilsea Lines, defensive lines constructed in phases between 1757 and 1871 to repel foreign invaders, and now scheduled as an ancient monument.

The lido itself has two pools; the lozenge-shaped children's pool nearer the camera, and the main pool on the tip of the promontory – not to be confused with that part of the Creek forming a basin in the centre of the adjacent roundabout (*lower right*).

On the far bank of the Creek is Horsea Island, along which the M275 motorway now follows the bend of the Creek heading south towards the city.

To the left are the inter war housing estates of Hilsea, whose residents found their recreational needs catered for not only by the Lido but also by the provision of playing fields and allotments (*centre*) and by the Portsmouth Greyhound Stadium (*just out of the picture, top left*) which opened in 1931. Close by is the Mountbatten Centre for cycling and athletics.

THE CHILDREN'S PADDLING POOL, HILSEA LIDO.

Built by Portsmouth Corporation, this fine pool measures 150 ft x 60 ft. The Cafe has an excellent dance floor. Immediately behind the Cafe is the main swimming pool.

Seen here in the late 1940s, Hilsea's paddling pool is still open and remains free of charge to children under eight. As is the modern way, however, it is now referred to as the Splash Pool.

▲ Pictured in a 1969 Portsmouth City Council tourist brochure, **Hilsea Lido** consciously celebrated the city's nautical links.

This was most evident in its flat roofed sun terrace above the main entrance block (*right*), with its strong horizontal lines and polished handrails, accessed via open steps from the pool surrounds.

Behind the far end stood the Blue Lagoon Café, and beyond that the children's paddling pool (*left*) where low level toilets created an impression of being below decks.

Also distinctive at Hilsea was the provision of shallow ends at both ends of the pool, with a diving pit, 15 feet deep, in the centre.

This allowed the gantry-like diving stage – its topmost board, 32 feet high – to provide a perfect focal point for daredevil divers,

eager to impress. (Apparently in the 1930s a one legged man was seen to scale the top, set alight his wooden leg and then dive into the water to all round astonishment.)

Perhaps uniquely the diving pit was also flanked by shallow sections, each 2' 6" deep, separated from the main pool by booms. These variations in levels were eradicated in 1973, when as a cost-cutting measure the pool was made shallower. Nevertheless, the 'deep end' remains in the centre, which is rare indeed.

One feature of the above scene that is also no longer possible is that of the young lad, playing in the fountain in the foreground. As seen opposite, neither of Hilsea's fountains remain in use, the victim of increased concerns over health and safety.

» attempt to get the pool listed. But, once again, it was turned down by the Department for Culture, Media and Sport.

Meanwhile in 1998 the Council drew up a further planning brief to reduce the length of the main pool to 25 metres and heat both the pool and the children's splash pool. Once again these measures and the running of the pools were to be financed by commercial developments.

Marlborough Leisure Ltd., which had carried out similar refurbishment work at Saltdean Lido, were all set to carry out these works in 1999, until it was realised that their proposed commercial add-ons (including a health and fitness club, 40 bed hotel and a pub and restaurant) would fail to satisfy the intended brief.

And so followed a lull in the action, forcing lido users to face each summer with trepidation.

In 1999 the pool was closed temporarily because of algae growth. Ticket sales that summer were down to little more than 7,000. In 2001 the pool did not open at all and in the summers since then it has opened for a short season only.

Yet on occasions, such is its attraction, that the public have had to be turned away at the gates when capacity has been reached.

In July 2004, as part of the Portsmouth City Local Plan, the council gave an assurance that: 'Hilsea Lido and its environs will be retained for community use and public open space.'

But with plans for new indoor pools in the city still under discussion – at the Mounbatten Centre in particular – and with no listing to protect the building, at the time of writing Hilsea Lido remains in grave danger.

▲ Negative equity – the diving boards have gone. Both shallow sections on either side of the pit have been infilled. The fountains lie idle and overgrown. The floodlights have been removed, and the café has been boarded up.

'No diving' is writ large on one side of the main block. Other signs warn: 'No pushing. No bombing. No running. Look before you jump or dive.' And in case none of these warnings sinks in, another advises 'First Aid Upstairs'.

Hilsea Lido, pictured here in 2004, clings on to life in the modern era of prohibition and budget restraints.

The writing on the wall seems to indicate 'No Future'.

But Hilsea's battle-weary defenders fight on.

Case Study

Uxbridge Lido 1935–98

Grade II Listed (1998)
Architect G Percy Trentham
Cost £24,500
Size 220 x 72' 6" x 90' x 75'
Water 480,000 g
Opened 31 August 1935
Closed 1983
Reopened 1984
Closed 1998

A fanfare of trumpets from the band of the Royal Air Force signalled the opening of Uxbridge Lido in the late summer of 1935. And sure enough airmen from the nearby RAF station would number among its regular users.

But now the lido is well and truly grounded. Unused, vandalised, weed-infested and strewn with graffiti, it currently awaits a decision by Hillingdon Borough Council as to whether sufficient funds can be raised for the site's transformation into a modern sports and leisure complex.

In most instances plans of this nature automatically assume the demolition of the lido.

But in the scheme for Uxbridge, drawn up by architects Faulkner Brown and approved by the Council in June 2005 (*illustrated right*), the outdoor pool, its two fountains, grandstand and entrance block – all of which were listed separately when the pool last closed in 1998 – would be restored to use, while being supplemented by, and integrated with, an indoor pool and other sporting, fitness and leisure facilities to be constructed on either side of the lido. Changing rooms and a café would, for example, be shared.

Uxbridge Lido has experienced mixed fortunes since it was built on the slopes of the Hillingdon House Farm Estate, on the edge of this outer London suburb.

It was immediately popular and in good years attracted up to 300,000 visitors. But in 1983, despite a petition signed by 6,500 protestors, it remained closed for a year in order to save £62,000 from Hillingdon's leisure budget.

For the following five years the lido's management was leased out to the Uxbridge Pool and Leisure Club Ltd (formed by members of the Uxbridge Pool Action Group), in an early attempt at a public-private partnership.

Aided by a £148,000 grant from the Greater London Council – shades of the good old days of lido support from the LCC – the new operators started promisingly, cleaning up the lido with voluntary labour and raising funds for a new system of solar heating panels.

A model showing how a restored Uxbridge Lido might look should redevelopment proposals for the site proceed. The unusually shaped 12-sided outdoor pool is to be split into three; one section of 50m and, at each end, two smaller children's areas. Heated water from these will flow into the main pool.

The first panel tried out raised the temperature of the children's pool from 70-90° in ten minutes.

But the group could not control the weather, or afford ongoing repairs, and after yet one more plea for additional subsidies, they were relieved of control by Hillingdon in 1989.

Following this, another group, the Yiewsley Pool Development Trust, had a brief spell as operators, before the Council finally closed the lido in 1998.

Since then, seven years of talks and planning have finally resulted in a ray of hope for this now forlorn and beleaguered lido.

Whether that hope is justified now hinges on applications for funding from the Heritage Lottery Fund (for works to the lido), and from Sport England (for the new facilities). In the latter case the hope is to raise sufficient capital to make the indoor pool an Olympic sized 50m length.

Hillingdon Borough Council will also be a major contributor, aided, it is envisaged, by an enabling residential development to the south of the site.

The aim, according to the Council, is to revive 'the original health, fitness and well-being ethos of the 1935 Lido.'

A date of 2007 has been given for completion. Plenty of time to rehearse those trumpets.

Moderne marvels – Uxbridge Lido in happier days. The reinforced concrete grandstand (*top*) which offers stunning views to the south, would be retained as part of the new development, as would the main entrance and brick archway (*centre*) and the two octagonal fountains at either end of the main pool (*right*).

Case Study

Tinside Lido, Plymouth 1935

Grade II Listed (1998)
Architect JS Wibberley
Size 180' diameter x 2'-9'
Water filtered seawater, 500,000g
Opened 2 October 1935
Closed 1992
Re-opened 15 August 2003

For an open air pool that has in recent years become a byword in swimming circles for beauty and hope – following its stunning £3.4 million refurbishment in 2003 – Plymouth's Tinside Lido owes its title to a rather prosaic structure.

Tinside Beach, where the lido was created below the famous Plymouth Hoe in 1935, was named, it is thought, after a tin shed used by women who bathed in the rock pool there.

In fact this whole stretch of coastline facing the Plymouth Sound has a long tradition of open air bathing.

All along the foreshore are to be found rocky coves and inlets where local people have swum for centuries. One or two can still be seen today, for example, Piskey's Pool, just to the west of the lido.

Of course it was expected for modesty's sake that men and women would use separate pools, at least until 1922 when mixed bathing was officially sanctioned by Plymouth City Council.

Development of Tinside Beach and its neighbouring inlets

Tinside's three fountains may not have achieved quite the same repute as Rome's *Tre Fontane*, but they were once a regular feature of postcards on sale in Plymouth. In the background is Plymouth Hoe's pier pavilion, added in 1890 to Eugenius Birch's original design of 1884, and demolished in 1953 after suffering bomb damage in World War Two.

actually began a little earlier than this, in 1902, when cubicles were provided and concrete used to line the bases of several of the pools.

But in 1925 the Borough Engineer, JS Wibberley, was instructed to prepare more elaborate plans for the foreshore.

Included in these plans were two small outdoor pools at Mount Wise, completed in 1934 to the west of the Hoe. One of them is still in use today and remains free of charge.

Meanwhile on the Hoe itself, Wibberley and the contractors Nuttall & Sons and John Mowlem and Co., combined on two major pieces of construction.

The first was the Tinside Colonnade, a promenade and sun terrace, with a cantilevered section to support Hoe Road as it skirted the clifftops.

The second, immediately below the Hoe Road, was the Tinside Pool. (Only later would it be known as the lido.)

It is not known whether Wibberley paid any heed to the design of the Jubilee Pool, being built in Penzance at the same time. But there were obvious similarities in their designs; both protruding into the sea and therefore subject to powerful tidal forces.

But whereas his counterpart in Penzance chose a triangular plan for the Jubilee Pool, Wibberley opted for a more classical semi-circular design, not dissimilar to the South Bay at Scarborough.

Tinside Colonnade was completed in 1935. But poor weather hampered efforts down on the shoreline, so that not only was the new pool's opening delayed until the very tail end of the season, in October 1935 – four months later than Penzance – but the work could not be fully completed for a further two years.

Unlike at many seaside lidos, there was little attempt at Tinside to create a bold architectural statement.

THE BATHING POOL, PLYMOUTH

Arguably there was no need. The setting was dramatic enough in itself.

Even so, photographs of the main pool building in its early years show it to have been a relatively plain and functional structure – indeed much less attractive than it looks today since its recent makeover. In any other situation it might easily have been a school or a warehouse.

Bathers and spectators entered at first floor level, and then made their way, via a prominent stair tower at the side of the block, to the lower level dressing rooms and pool. A roof terrace lined with railings added a nautical flavour.

But it was the pool itself, with its three fountains and wide expanse jutting out into the Sound that grabbed all the attention, and the views looking out to sea which provided much of its allure.

Over the next fifty years Tinside Pool's fortunes mirrored those of most lidos around the country.

Healthy attendances in the early years gradually diminished. Maintenance struggled to keep pace with wear and tear. And although in 1989 the pool successfully withstood the might of Force 12 gales, in 1992, faced with growing repair bills and annual costs of £120,000 – set against ticket income from only 12,000 bathers in 1991 – Plymouth City Council pulled the plug.

For the next ten years Tinside lay empty, gathering rust and disparaging looks, while local councillors debated its future.

To demolish it altogether, according to one estimate, would have cost up to £2 million.

Meanwhile the newly formed Tinside Action Group made sure the issue was never dropped from the political agenda.

TAG's co-ordinator was Kelvin Kelway, a lifelong Plymouth resident whose parents first met at the lido as teenage sweethearts.

What counted most, Kelway later recalled, was the support of bodies such as English Heritage, The Twentieth Century Society and SAVE Britain's Heritage.

With their help Tinside was listed Grade II in November 1998.

'We also organised two petitions and collected 72,000 signatures on the streets. We took both petitions to London and delivered them to the Queen and to number 10 Downing Street.'

Kelway also made contact with John Clarke, the saviour of the Jubilee Pool in Penzance, further along the coast. 'John gave me a wonderful action plan and advised me to be terribly vocal to get the message across. And believe me, we were loud!'

Meanwhile in the town hall a split formed largely along party lines. The Labour group strongly opposed diverting funds to the pool, while their Conservative opponents made a commitment to restore it part of their manifesto for the local government elections in 2000.

Fortunately for supporters of the lido, it was the Tories who won, and who, moreover, stuck to their word.

Thus, after years of debate and campaigning, the revival of Tinside began in earnest in 2002.

Plymouth City Council's Engineering Department under John Williams led the project, with Interserve Project Services (formerly known as Tilbury Douglas) acting as contractors.

As he would later admit, Interserve's Steve Radcliffe had certain reservations when the project began.

PLYMOUTH
DELIGHTFUL CENTRE FOR HOLIDAYS
Guide free from Publicity Manager (Dept. B.R.)
TRAVEL BY TRAIN BRITISH RAILWAYS

Harry Riley's 1950s idealised poster for British Railways shows off the winding terraces and promenades built along the Plymouth Hoe foreshore as part of the programme of works which also delivered the Tinside Pool in the mid 1930s. For the same view today, see page 111.

'When I first saw this project, I perceived a very tricky job, purely because of the sea. People underestimate its power. I was particularly worried that the water would come through and completely blow the old floor of the pool. We would then have been worse off than when we started.'

Plymouth Hoe's topography also set a challenge, requiring a tower crane to lift heavy materials and plant down from the road level to the pool level below.

A third issue concerned the conservation of the listed structures – a process closely monitored by English Heritage – balanced by the need to meet modern standards for pool management and access. This meant that while the main pool building's exterior could not be altered, the interior had to be virtually gutted and redesigned (for example to allow for a lift to be inserted into the stair tower for disabled access).

Fortunately no serious obstacles were encountered, however, and after little more than twelve month's work, Tinside Lido, as it was now to be known, was unveiled to an expectant public.

Performing the official re-opening ceremony, on 15 August 2003, was 88 year old Councillor Claude Miller, whose father, also a Plymouth councillor, had been involved in the construction of the original pool.

'Tinside Pool,' he recalled, 'was the playground for most Plymouth children. There was no going away in motor cars or going abroad. You spent your holidays either at Tinside or at Devil's Point.

'The lido was also a place of entertainment – mannequin parades, fashion shows, swimming galas and water polo matches.'

Kelvin Kelway was equally misty eyed. Looking down from the upper terrace at children swimming in the pool, he said, 'I'm proud of all that Tinside Action Group did – the publicity, the demonstrations, the heckling at council meetings. It was well worth five years of my life.'

But was it worth over £3 million of ratepayers' money?

'Yes,' he insisted, 'it was money well spent. It will generate hopefully millions of pounds in years to come. And just look at the media interest Tinside has generated. Suddenly people are talking about Plymouth again.'

But there were reservations too.

Peter Smith, head of Sports, Leisure and Culture at Plymouth City Council pointed out that five children's playgrounds could have been provided for the money.

By the time the lido was re-opened, moreover, the Labour group, which had strongly opposed the project from the start, were back in power, and having to build into their budget the lido's running costs of £250,000-£300,000 per year.

Not that the lido's many supporters were complaining.

Tinside Lido today is a prime example of how sensitive conservation methods allied to modern materials and advanced water management processes can bring a tired and neglected open air pool back to life.

Indeed for many people who remembered how it was in the past, it might well be said that Tinside has never looked so good.

While for those who wait in hope, at Hilsea, Uxbridge, Broomhill, Droitwich and elsewhere, Tinside is a jewel whose lustre shines out far beyond the shores of Plymouth Sound.

Things are looking up at the rejuvenated Tinside Lido.

TINSIDE LIDO

▲ The original and replacement octagonal fountains, before and after the superb restoration of **Tinside Lido** in 2003 – a graphic illustration of how modern materials and finishes can transform the appearance of an open air pool and add visual appeal to modern users.

Meanwhile Harry Riley's palm trees are nowhere to be seen (*left*) but the view from the Hoe remains as dramatic as ever.

▲ Restoring **Tinside Lido** required the complete reconstruction of the pool basin, a technically complex feat which won Plymouth City's Engineering Department a merit award from the Institution of Civil Engineers in 2004.

Made of 2,500 cubic metres of reinforced concrete, the basin is anchored to the rockbed by 167 piles, driven to a depth of 18m.

To add visual impact, the pool's floor has been painted with dark blue stripes, while two of the original fountains have been replicated and the central fountain replaced by a 10m high water jet.

Underwater lights have also been fitted, as part of a general lighting scheme which revives the tradition of late night illuminations, once a common attraction at Tinside.

Unlike the old days, however, the changing rooms are now uni-sex, while the windows have been replaced by glazed bricks, as also used in the stair tower.

Seen hovering above the pool building is the cantilevered section of Hoe Road, another JS Wibberley construction from the 1930s, and the red and white bands of Smeaton Tower.

▲ Plymouth Hoe from the south, with **Tinside Lido** a startling presence on the foreshore. As can be imagined, even with the raised sea walls, cold winds can whip in from Plymouth Sound.

To the immediate left of the lido is a sunbathing terrace, built on the site of the original Tinside women's bathing pool. To the left of this are two smaller rock pools. Just visible in front of the first one – Piskey's Pool – is an old diving stage.

To the right of the lido is the Tinside Colonnade, now Grade II listed, while immediately above it is the cantilevered section of Hoe Road. The oval building is the Plymouth Dome visitor attraction.

Easiest of all to spot is Smeaton's Tower, which started life in 1789 as a lighthouse on the Eddystone Rocks and was moved to its present position in 1884.

No-one knows the exact point where Sir Francis Drake was supposedly playing bowls when the Spanish fleet sailed into view, but in the top left corner of the Hoe, to the left of the obelisk (the Naval War Memorial) lies a modern bowling green, thus maintaining the Hoe's sporting tradition.

Case Study

Victoria Park Lido, London 1936–89

Architects HA Rowbotham and TL Smithson
Cost £26,000
Size 200' x 90' x 2' 6"-9' 9"
Water 650,000 g
Opened 16 May 1936
Closed 1989
Demolished 1990
On site now car park

Open air bathing was a popular pursuit in Victoria Park long before the London County Council resolved to build a lido there.

As stated earlier (*see page 27*), a bathing lake had been created in the park as early as 1847, followed by a second, massive one, 20 years later. Both were hugely popular.

By the early 1930s, however, neither lake was found to meet new health standards, and in 1933 they were finally closed.

One might imagine that the completion of a brand new open air pool at London Fields (*see page 169*), opened in 1932 and barely a mile from Victoria Park, might have been deemed an adequate replacement. Nevertheless, in November 1934 the LCC drew up plans for a new super lido in the park, fully expecting that the three boroughs whose boundaries bordered Victoria Park – Hackney, Bethnal Green and Poplar – would contribute to the costs.

As it transpired Poplar refused, only for the LCC to go ahead regardless, after having made a few adjustments to the plans to pare down costs.

But then the LCC chairman, Herbert Morrison, did also happen to be the MP for South Hackney, in whose boundaries parts of Victoria Park lay.

At its opening in May 1936 Morrison declared, 'This is more than a swimming bath. It is East London's Lido.'

That he used the term lido at all shows how it had crept into usage since the christening of the Serpentine Lido in 1931. But his pride was well founded.

Measuring a massive 200 x 90 feet – compared with the then typical size of 165 x 65 feet, as at London Fields – it was the largest modern pool to have been built in the capital. It was also the most expensive, at £26,000 (compared with a reported £10,000 for London Fields).

Stylistically, however, it clearly came from the same design team as London Fields; that is, the

LCC Parks Department under Harry Arnold Rowbotham and TL Smithson, who were also working on a similar design for Brockwell Park (*see page 138*).

Compared with its counterparts in the likes of Croydon and New Brighton, Victoria Park was an exercise in municipal restraint. Faced in handmade multi-bricks which blended comfortably with its park setting, the lido consisted of a single-storey compound with metal-framed windows and white stone trimmings.

But if it displayed little of the brashness of several of its provincial contemporaries, nor was it expressly Modern. For while its entrance block on Grove Road was characterised by a flat roof, the café on the park side featured a pitched roof topped by a traditional clock tower.

The pool floor, meanwhile, was painted an enticing shade of blue.

The Grove Road entrance to the Victoria Park Lido sports a new concrete cantilevered canopy in 1952, erected as part of the building's restoration following a V1 bomb attack during the Second World War.

One visitor described it 'as blue as the Mediterranean'.

The lay out, it was also said, ensured that no shadow would ever be cast on the bathing-area, except by human beings.

Richard Coppock, chairman of the LCC's Parks Committee, told the *Daily Herald*, 'This summer we shall bring the seaside to East London. Why, this is as good as Margate!'

It was cheaper too. On weekdays entrance was free for children. For men there were two free bathing days, though for women only one.

Up to 1,000 bathers were able to use the pool at the same time.

But their enjoyment was short-lived. During the Second World War the pool was used as a water supply by the National Fire Service. It was then severely damaged by a VI flying bomb. Repairs completed in June 1952, including re-building the entrance block, cost £30,000.

By the 1980s the passing of its ownership from the abolished GLC to the Borough of Tower Hamlets signalled its death knell.

According to one councillor, every 50p swim was subsidised to the tune of £37. Another jibed that it would be cheaper to pay swimmers to attend a private health club.

The axe finally fell in 1989.

There was a bid for Sports Lottery funding to re-open the lido. But as elsewhere, Sport England proved unwilling to allocate money to open-air pools that were only open in summer.

Victoria Park Lido was demolished in 1990, and the site turned into a car park.

All local hopes now focus on the proposed restoration of London Fields (*page 169*) which itself closed in 1988 but somehow escaped demolition.

Victoria Park at the time of its opening in May 1936, before the flower beds had been planted. Note the classic Wicksteed diving platform, boards and chutes. The café building (*left*) served lido users on one side and park visitors on the other. Later LCC lido cafes would offer more curves.

Case Study

Peterborough Lido 1936

Grade II Listed (1992)
Architects S Dodson and SE Dodson, AW Ruddle, WP Hack, AW Wilson and HJ Wilson, and Traylen, Lenton and Warwick
Cost £21,000 (including adjacent bus terminal)
Size 165' x 60' x 3'-9'
Water freshwater, c.388,000g
Opened 28 May 1936

How many architects does it take to design a swimming pool? Usually one, sometimes two. But in the case of the Peterborough Open Air Pool, no fewer than five separate practices were involved.

The City Engineer had a hand in it too, as did a consulting engineer.

This apparent over staffing was the result not of municipal indecision, however, but of an extraordinary collaboration between the architects themselves.

In 1933 Peterborough City Council launched a competition to find a suitable designer to work on the project in collaboration with the City Engineer, FJ Smith.

In response, the town's leading architects combined to suggest that in the best interests of the community they would be prepared to work together on a scheme.

Moreover, as to any fees being offered, they wrote, no thanks, they were quite prepared to carry out the work for nothing.

As the *Peterborough Standard* would later record, 'The Council at once accepted that remarkably fine public-spirited offer.'

The question was, would too many cooks spoil the broth?

In July 1935, a year before the pool was scheduled to open, a graphic description of the building process appeared in the *Peterborough Advertiser*.

'...upwards of a hundred men... are steadily attacking the soil. Here is a group of shovellers, unloading the lorries which are bringing the consignments of gravel for the concrete and the surrounding paths. There, in the deep end of the pool, another squad is excavating with pick and shovel for the foundations...

'Other men are at work on the steel reinforcement for the concrete walls, bending the long rods and planting them in an intricate pattern... A vast heap of woodwork, made up into moulds, takes the eye. These moulds are the shutters for the concrete sides of the bath.

'Nearby, in the carpenter's shop, a temporary shed erection, have been installed labour-saving machinery, saws, mortise-cutting devices and the like.'

Finally the lido was ready in May 1936. Peterborough Mayor, Councillor AH Mellows, performed the official opening, for what was, it transpired, a design quite different from that of most preceding lidos, or indeed from any other subsequently built during the late 1930s.

Unlike its contemporaries in London or in Britain's seaside resorts, Peterborough lido's chief characteristic was its Mediterranean styling.

In plan, it resembled a semi-enclosed Spanish hacienda, or even a Roman army camp, with two corner pavilions resembling look out towers – perhaps an allusion to the presence of Roman settlements in the area.

Peterbrough Lido is a unique surviving example of a style which, in the mid 1930s, bucked the trend for open air pools in the Modernist guise. This recent image was taken from the rooftop terrace which overlooks the pool on three sides. The open fourth side is bordered by a children's pool.

The main pavilion, on the west side of the site, dominated the compound, with three arched doorways leading into an entrance lobby where there was a small area of mosaic flooring. Crowning the pavilion was a square tapered clock tower, with dials on all four sides, topped by a pyramidal copper roof.

But what set the building apart from the usual run-of-the-mill municipal fare of the period was its colour scheme. Though constructed in brick, the walls were rendered and painted in a rich shade of cream, itself offset by the green pantiles of the hipped roofs.

Inside the enclosure, two staircases from the pavilion led to a first floor viewing level, from which – again in the manner of a Roman camp – it was possible to walk around three sides of the pool. From this level a fine view could be had, to the north-west, of the city's most famous landmark, Peterborough Cathedral.

And so the view remains today, from a lido which, since its last refurbishment in 2002 – the same year that a Grade II listing was granted – appears to be in fine fettle. The fountain, no longer in use, has been planted with flowers. The changing rooms have been refitted and the exterior repainted in the original colour.

Peterborough Lido is now a hub of activity. A local sub aqua club is based there, and it remains popular with early morning swimmers during the summer. But to extend its use further the City Council is considering plans for a demountable roof to make it a year-round facility.

The question is, how many architects will be necessary to drawn up the plans?

▲ For convenience, location and especially for the views to be enjoyed from its sun terraces, **Peterborough Lido**, just a few hundred yards from the city's 12th century cathedral – resting place of Katherine of Aragon – can hardly be bettered.

Set in the midst of a large expanse of playing fields on the banks of the River Nene, on two acres of land purchased by the Corporation from the Ecclesiastical Commissioners in 1927, the lido forms part of a cluster of public amenities. These include the Key Theatre to the south and, to the north and east, the Wirrina indoor arena, a running track, and the Regional Fitness and Swimming Centre, where there is a 25m indoor pool.

▲ Reminiscent of a Spanish hacienda, **Peterborough Lido** retains many of its original features, not least its cream rendered concrete exterior, refurbished in 2002 and a perfect complement to the green pantiled roofing.

On 8 June 1940 the lido's north west corner pavilion (*on the left*) was badly damaged by German bombs. Russell Coe, now 76 and still a regular swimmer at the pool, remembers the day well. 'I was only a schoolboy at the time,' he says. 'I went along for a swim as usual and couldn't believe it when I was told I couldn't go in. "The pool's alright" I said. But they weren't having it.'

After the war the building was restored. But it has since faced further damage from vandals, as a result of which, regrettably, the original metal casement windows and fanlights over the entrance arches have been infilled and painted to look like windows.

But is it impregnable? In 1973, a suspicious looking tunnel was discovered by the boundary walls, leading to speculation that it had been dug by children intending to sneak into the lido for free.

▲ This view of **Peterborough Lido**, taken since its refurbishment in 2002, shows the arrangement of changing rooms located under the rooftop terrace, which encloses three sides of the pool.

The terrace was designed so that, in addition to the viewing area within the main pavilion on the far side, temporary seating could be added for galas and events.

When the lido opened in 1935, the pool was unheated. However the designers had the foresight to provide pipework for a later installation, and this is now in use.

The lido also originally featured a 5m high diving stage, with springboards at one and three metres. But, as elsewhere, these have been dismantled for safety reasons, as has a water chute.

Until the 1960s children aged under 12 had to be accompanied by an adult. But when a seven year old boy drowned in the nearby River Nene, the coroner urged that all children should be allowed into the lido, regardless (though not via a tunnel). Certainly the lido caters well for their needs. There is both a pool for children and a small paddling pool, a rare combination.

Case Study

Portobello Bathing Pool, Edinburgh 1936–79

Architects Ian Warner and WA
Macartney
Cost £70-90,000
Size 330' x 150' x 1'-6' 2"
Water Seawater, heated, 1.25m g
Opened 30 May 1936
Closed 1979
Demolished 1988
On site now Indoor bowling centre

Visiting 'Edinburgh's seaside resort' at Portobello today it is hard to picture the place as a busy holiday destination.

A quiet, somewhat windblown community of terraced streets and seafront villas, it serves well for a bracing walk along the front and perhaps a bag of chips.

And yet there was a time when this eastern outpost of Edinburgh drew huge crowds for horse racing and entertainments on its beach; to its pier and Marine Gardens. So much so that its station had reputedly the longest suburban railway platform in Scotland to cope with the influx of daytrippers.

Nowadays, for people wanting to swim, Portobello is best known for its beautifully restored indoor baths on the Promenade, built in 1901 and still with its original Turkish Baths.

But the Portobello Bathing Pool which used to stand a few hundred yards down the seafront, that was different. That was special.

And for all kinds of reasons.

When the idea for an open air pool was first mooted by Edinburgh Town Council in 1928, and again in 1930, and once more in 1933 – to restore Portobello's place on 'the pleasure seeker's map' – doubters cited the Scottish weather as the main obstacle. Others argued that funds should be directed towards the construction of a new pier instead (the old one having been dismantled in 1917).

Then someone hit upon a cunning plan.

Dominating one end of the seafront was the Portobello Power Station, its tall chimney belching out smoke across the Firth of Forth. Next to the power station, which had opened in 1923, was the now rundown site of the Rosebank Potteries (one of several in the area dating back to the 18th century).

One of the main by-products of a coal-powered power station is hot water.

And so the objectors were silenced.

Designed by Ian Warner and the City Engineer William Macartney, the 'Porty Pool' or even 'Pond' as it was often known, took two years to build and, at a cost of around £70-90,000, according to which source one reads, it proved to be one of the most technically advanced lidos of the 1930s.

Apart from its highly unusual water heating system (*described opposite*), it had several noteworthy features.

The first was its revolutionary wave-making machinery.

According to unverified sources, Britain's first wave-maker had been built in Kilmarnock, before the First World War, by shipyard apprentices.

A more advanced system was installed at the Empire Pool at Wembley (opened in 1934).

Portobello's machine, which cost £7,000, was, however, the first at any outdoor pool. »

Engineers from Brown Brothers test out their new wave-making machinery, shortly before the Portobello Bathing Pool's opening in 1936. Although a common feature at today's waterparks, this was the first at an outdoor pool in Britain.

▲ 'What about the smell?' begged the *Edinburgh Evening Dispatch* when the City Council proposed building Portobello's new open air pool next door to the power station.

But there was method in their madness. As explained at the time by the pool's engineer, William Macartney, 'The water supply is taken from the tubes discharging the condenser water from the electric power station adjoining. The water is salt water from the Firth of Forth, and when received (at the pool) it is about 78 degrees Fahrenheit. It passes through settling tanks before reaching the filters and is finally chlorinated.'

A heated open air pool in the 1930s was a rare luxury. One that cost the council no extra money seemed like a miracle.

In fact, despite claims that the water would be maintained at an average temperature of 68° F, at times it could be freezing.

Cecilia Cavaye, whose father was a manager at the power station, recalled, 'He would always tell me when the next lot of hot water was due to be released so that my friends and I could be sure of catching warm water in the pool.'

The grandstand at Portobello was by any standards – British or Continental – an accomplished and advanced piece of engineering, with a streamlined canopy, 320 feet long and cantilevering nearly 33 feet forward from the rear columns. Integrated lights under the canopy can just be discerned, as can the underwater pool lighting along the sides of the tank. In any other sporting context this stand would have been acclaimed. Yet somehow its merits were never fully recognised.

》 Manufactured by the firm of Brown Brothers of Edinburgh, it was operated by four, 24 foot long steel plungers, moved up and down by connecting rods driven by a 140 hp motor.

According to the power setting the effect could vary from 'the merest ripple' to waves of three to six feet in height, before breaking at the 'beach' or shallow end 'with all the naturalness of sea waves'.

The machine definitely worked, 'It was absolutely fantastic,' recalled Ruth Couper. 'The waves would roll down from the deep end and had an incredibly strong back-draw, which could knock you off your feet. But you knew it was coming because they would always announce it was about to be switched on.'

But unfortunately for Brown Brothers the machine failed to make any waves in the business, as it were, and only in recent decades have wave-makers become regular features at pools and waterparks. Coincidentally, one of the world's biggest supplies of equipment today is based in Glasgow.

Another aspect of the Porty Pool was its remarkable grandstand.

As we have seen in many previous case studies, lidos of the inter war period were designed as places for viewing and entertainment as much as for swimming. In most locations during the 1930s, in fact, the revenue from spectators far outstripped that from bathing.

Even so, the grandstand at Portobello was engineered to a surprising level of sophistication, certainly far in advance of any stand then belonging to a professional sports club.

Consisting of a single tier on the west side of the pool – so that it faced the diving board – with the changing rooms incorporated into the space below, the stand was covered by reinforced concrete, its roof supported on 12 columns at the rear and cantilevered forward over the 2,000 seats.

On the Continent concrete cantilevered stands of this ilk were becoming increasingly common, in France and Italy especially. But in Britain, stadium design remained faithful to the steel-framed, column supported method seen at all major football, rugby and cricket grounds (at Wembley Stadium too).

Indeed the Portobello grandstand is thought to be only the second of its kind built in Britain; the first claimant being at Northolt Racecourse in 1927.

But this was not the only area of spectator accommodation. Opposite the stand was an open terrace lined with teak bench seats, able to hold an estimated 4,000.

If these two banks of seating gave the baths the distinct appearance of a stadium so too was it managed rather like a sporting arena.

There were, for example, separate entrances for bathers and spectators. Once inside the building, circulation routes were also kept quite separate, with all 'wet' areas at ground level, and 'dry' areas at first floor level.

The main entrance was on the west side, providing access to the dressing rooms; approximately 133 cubicles and 642 lockers each for men and women. (The locker system, it was argued,

PORTOBELLO OPEN AIR BATHING POND

Total Cost (approx.) £90,000

Length 330 ft.   Width 150 ft.   Area 1·13 Acres.   Five Diving Stages from 12 ft. to 32 ft. 8 ins. high.
Accommodation for 6000 Spectators.   Lockers for 1284 Bathers   Artificial Wave up to 3 ft. high can be developed.

required larger dressing rooms, but fewer staff than, for example, the wire basket system of clothes storage, which would later become common, at Weston for example.)

Apart from the grandstand, the other major structure at the baths was the two-storey pavilion at the north, or seaward end.

This was the most lavishly appointed part of the baths, housing a pool level café (looking out over the 'beach' area – and a first floor restaurant, which also doubled as a ballroom and was available for hire all year round. This was accessed from the lobby by a staircase adorned with a Dalzo steel balustrade.

The flooring was in oak parquet and the skirting in teak. Over the central lounge hung a suspended ceiling, pierced with a skylight glazed in amber-coloured glass.

From this room a cantilevered balcony with wrought iron railings provided diners with views across the pool.

In elevation the block was perfectly symmetrical, with a central projecting bay – crowned by a fetching Art Deco clockface – and two side bays, each stepped back from the other, all with metal framed windows.

The exterior walls were rendered, as were all the pool's facings, in cement applied in 'cottage texture', presumably to soften the appearance. This render was then painted cream, offset by jade green tiles forming a band across the upper part of the elevations.

At ground floor or pool level was a café, first aid room, offices and kitchens.

At the opposite end of the pool was a narrow spectator area and snack bar, under which the wave making plant was installed.

According to the local press, the first people to see the Portobello pool found it 'finer than anything they could possibly have imagined.'

Charles McKean, in his book The Scottish Thirties (see Links) was less enthusiastic. 'The architecture was, for its date,' he wrote dismissively, 'way behind the engineering.'

But one thing was for sure. The Porty Pool was an extraordinary success in its early years.

It was opened by the Lord Provost, Sir Louis Gumley, on 30 May 1936, in front of an estimated crowd of 6,000 spectators (though one account claims 10,000). As

was customary, the ceremony was followed by a variety of aquatic entertainments: swimming races, a display by the Women's League of Health and Beauty, and an exhibition of high and fancy diving.

Among the spectators that day was 12 year old Peter Heatly, who was totally mesmerised by the diving. 'I remember thinking 'I want to do that,' he later recalled. 'I had never seen anything like it before. It really inspired me.'

It certainly did. Sir Peter, as he now is, went on to take part in the London Olympics in 1948 and to win three Commonwealth Gold Medals for high diving (in 1950, 1954 and 1958). During the 1940s and 1950s he became a regular performer at open air pools, including at Portobello itself. (Maybe that is him on the cover of this book?)

By the end of its first season, 290,000 bathers and nearly 500,000 spectators had used the bathing pool, bringing in receipts of just over £15,000. But thereafter the numbers started to decline, and by 1938 the revenue was little more than a third of what it had been in the first year.

With the outbreak of war, Porty Pool required a major cover up; its bright blue 'pond' being so visible from the air and therefore making it easy for German bombers to target the neighbouring power station. So, for the duration, turf was laid on the pool floor, so that for a while it must have looked even more like a sports stadium.

Finally the pool was re-opened in 1946, and on 8 June that year, a sizzling 80° F was recorded, attracting 4,000 people to the pool in a single day. In his daily logbook the pool manager, or Pondmaster as he was officially known, RP

The Porty Pool's much altered noticeboard was last amended for 1978, the final season of its operation. The board is now in the collection of the Portobello History Society.

Yeoman, jotted down jauntily 'Best Friday for years'.

But the trend was downward all the same, and in the summer of 1971, according to records kept by James Thomson, the pool's engineer from 1946-72, only 39,282 bathers attended. On some days there were as few as four admissions.

A further blow was the closure of the power station in March 1977. This meant an end to the supply of free heated water.

Not that it could always be counted upon.

James Thomson later recalled, 'The most memorable aspect of the pool was its coldness. I once dived in and my nose started to bleed with the shock! The metal grilles at the deep end covered the wave-making machinery . But I'm sure they also concealed a refrigeration plant!'

By then there was also the rival attraction of the new heated indoor pool in Edinburgh, built for the 1970 Commonwealth Games.

By 1972, Edinburgh District Council were already considering closing the pool and replacing it with either an indoor leisure centre, a variety club, a conference centre or even a dolphinarium.

The dithering continued for most of the rest of the decade, until the Council finally voted to close the pool in March 1979.

Four years later they offered it for lease or for sale, but not a single offer was received.

So it was that throughout the 1980s, the Porty Pool stood abandoned, exposed to vandals and the weather, until finally the bulldozers arrived in the spring of 1988.

An indoor bowling centre and five-a-side football pitches now occupy the site.

◀ In 1946 **Portobello Baths** in **Edinburgh** started a tradition that was guaranteed to bring press photographers to its doors on an annual basis.

Quite simply the first boy and first girl in the queue for the opening of the baths at the start of each summer season would be awarded a free ticket for the rest of the summer.

Some youngsters would start queuing the night before to make sure that they were the lucky ones.

In this instance, from the 1970s, the first pair into the water were siblings, Alex and June Fairbairn, watched as ever by the avuncular pool manager, or Pondmaster, as he was referred to at Portobello.

To mark the end of the season, another tradition was the staging of a treasure hunt, in which, rather bizarrely, the lifeguards would throw dozens of cans of food into the water. On a given signal, eager bathers would dive in to retrieve what they could.

In the 1950s one of those lifeguards was an aspiring young Scottish actor, Sean Connery.

Shown left are the somewhat austere changing rooms, underneath the grandstand. The designers had intended to include a gymnasium in part of this area, but were forced to add extra cubicles when the level of demand took everyone by surprise.

Case Study

Super Swimming Stadium, Morecambe 1936–75

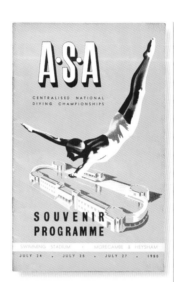

Architects Kenneth MB Cross and Cecil Sutton
Cost £130,000
Size 396' x 110' x 0-6' 6"
Water Seawater, 1.25m g
Opened 27 July 1936
Closed 1975
Demolished 1976
On site now Open space

By 1936 a clear pattern had emerged in lidos designed for seaside resorts.

Following on from the classically inspired open air pools of the previous decades – as seen at the more established destinations of Scarborough, Blackpool and Southport – a second wave of more linear, structurally defined lidos inspired by Modernist thinking, characterised the designs chosen by those towns who now, in the wake of the Depression, were desperate to capitalise upon the growing domestic holiday market.

Hastings (see page 80) paved the way in 1933, followed by New Brighton (page 86) a year later. In 1936, as we learnt in the previous chapter, the opening of the Portobello Bathing Pool in Edinburgh signalled a further stage in the process.

Each of these designs advanced the notion of the open air pool as a focus for entertainment and events as much as a place for swimming and sunbathing.

Morecambe's effort, also opened in 1936, took that concept one stage further.

If the pools at Hastings, New Brighton and Portobello may be described as aqua-arenas – in effect, mini-stadiums with water in the middle rather than turf – then Morecambe represented one further leap forward.

For here was no ordinary lido. Here was an unashamed swimming stadium, and a Super Swimming Stadium at that.

Forever in the shadow of the mighty Blackpool, 20 or so miles south along the Fylde coast, Morecambe had embarked upon a major redevelopment of its seafront in the early 1930s.

Until then the town's front had been dominated by its Old Harbour, which had, since the turn of the 20th century, been occupied by a ship breakers' yard belonging to a firm called TW Ward Ltd.

Based alongside the Stone Jetty, Ward's yard, ironically, formed something of an attraction in itself, as old ocean liners and warships, such as the SS Majestic and the torpedo ship Northampton, were broken up in full view of the town. Tourists would pay 3d to climb aboard the hulks, the money being donated to the local cottage hospital.

But while Ward's offered a major source of employment in the town, for many local people its presence was no more than 'a blot on Morecambe's fair face'.

For years the two factions – the company and its workforce on one side and the modernisers, headed by the Corporation and urged on by the *Morecambe Visitor* newspaper on the other – argued over the Old Harbour's future. In 1928 a Parliamentary Bill seeking the purchase of the harbour by the Corporation formed the focus of a heated public meeting and a spate of pamphleteering.

But as the *Visitor* would later declare, 'Progress won'.

The ship breakers' yard was cleared, and a £120,000 revamp of the harbour area begun.

A further boost came in 1932, when the London, Midland and Scottish Railway decided to replace its existing hotel in Morecambe. In its place arose what was to be described, for example by *Country Life* magazine, as 'the most beautiful building in this country.'

Designed by Oliver Hill, the Midland Hotel – now Grade II* listed and subject to a major restoration by Urban Splash – was, and remains, an iconic example of 1930s Modernism; a building whose very presence transformed Morecambe's profile.

But while the hotel's appeal was firmly upmarket, Morecambe Corporation recognised that the town would need other attractions if its fortunes were to prosper.

'Every ratepayer with any knowledge of the holiday making public,' reported the *Visitor*, 'knows that the lack of bathing facilities has lost the town each year thousands of visitors – particularly the young, freespending types.'

And so the die was cast.

Apart from its obvious scale, one crucial factor that set the Super Swimming Stadium apart from all its counterparts was that its design was not by the Borough Engineer but by two architects.

Kenneth MB Cross and Cecil Sutton, in 1931, designed Morecambe's Town Hall. Cross, moreover, was a specialist in pool design, as was his father Alfred. »

Morecambe's aptly named Super Swimming Stadium formed an impressive counterpoint to Oliver Hill's superb Midland Hotel, whose circular café can be seen in the far right of this 1950s view. Both the hotel and the Winter Gardens, opened in 1897 (*top left*) are now Grade II* listed. Had it survived, the open air pool would surely have merited similar recognition.

THE COLONNADE, NEW BATH, MORECAMBE.   G.4910.

>> As we learnt earlier (*see page 32*), Cross, who would become president of RIBA in the 1950s, was a fierce critic of local authorities who tried to save money by using their own in-house engineers rather than employing experienced architects, like himself.

Construction of the pool did require the Borough Engineer to pave the way, however. Before work on the foundations could begin 10,000 tons of concrete, 500 tons of steel reinforcement and 50,000 cubic yards of infill were needed to secure the sea walls.

Morecambe's big day arrived on 27 July 1936. The queue to attend, it was said, stretched for a mile.

Performing the official ceremony was Sir Josiah Stamp, Governor of the Bank of England and President of the London, Midland and Scottish Railway, owners of the Midland Hotel.

Praising the Corporation for putting the 'More' into 'Morecambe', the giant pool, he said, was a great leveller.

'Bathing reduces rich and poor, high and low, to a common standard of enjoyment and health. When we get down to swimming, we get down to democracy.'

Over the ensuing years, the Super Swimming Stadium richly fulfilled its promise. In addition to the usual fare of lido

Holidaymakers gather outside the Super Swimming Stadium's main entrance (*top*) where neon signs and posters trumpeted its heated water in preference to the 'chilly plunge' to be had in the bay. Spectators paid 6d to enjoy a range of sitting areas, either on the sun terraces above or in the shaded colonnades below (*left*).

entertainments, after 1945 it also became synonymous with the Miss Great Britain beauty contest.

Heats were held weekly, and the winners presented with their prizes by whoever was top-of-the-bill at the Winter Gardens, which could mean Laurel and Hardy, Tommy Trinder or George Formby.

By the 1970s, however, the crowds and the stars had drifted away, both from the beauty contests and from the pool. The Winter Gardens closed in 1977.

Worse, the pool was flooding at high tide and leaking at low tide, a problem that, despite regular grouting, apparently plagued the building throughout its life.

Meanwhile, rather as was happening over the road at the equally troubled Midland Hotel, the concrete started to crumble and the steel reinforcements to corrode. Allegations were made that the original concrete had been of poor quality, but this was strenuously denied.

Compared with other pools, the end was early, and quick. Morecambe Council closed the stadium in 1975, and within a year it had been demolished – this, in the days before the fate of 1930s buildings enjoyed any support within the public realm.

In its place, appeared a smaller, circular open air pool with an indoor pool adjacent, the two being operated privately as the Bubbles complex. But even this venture struggled before finally being closed in 2001.

So while across Marine Road work continues on the £7 million, long awaited restoration of the Midland Hotel, and the Winter Gardens welcomes visitors after its own restoration programme in the late 1990s, an aching void fills the site of the Super Swimming Stadium.

Overleaf, the scale of that loss may be fully appreciated.

The so-called 'Kiddies Korner' at the Super Swimming Stadium in the late 1930s. As the Morecambe Corporation motto declared, 'Beauty surrounds. Health abounds'.

▶ Behold the mighty **Super Swimming Stadium** of Morecambe!

As an architectural statement, Kenneth Cross and Cecil Sutton's colossal creation dwarfed any of its contemporaries, and might even be considered the greatest of them all.

It was also, at a total cost of £130,000, the most expensive.

And yet its sheer mass, allied to its location on reclaimed land, may partly have contributed to its relatively early demise.

Built by the contractors Sir Lindsay Parkinson & Co., the building measured 396 x 110 feet and appeared to have been constructed entirely in reinforced concrete. In fact, that applied only to the foundations, frame and roofing. The remainder was brick, rendered with 'Brizolit' cement.

Later investigations by the Council into the leakages which eventually undermined its operation revealed a series of problems. Reinforcements had allegedly been inadequately covered. High concentrations of calcium chloride rendered the concrete vulnerable to moisture and corrosion.

Such problems were by no means unique to Morecambe, and might well have been cured by modern techniques. But the Super Swimming Stadium was denied a second chance.

It was in business for just 39 years.

Case Study

Larkswood Pool, Chingford 1936–87

Architect SJ Hellier
Cost £23,400
Size: 220' x 90' and 165' x 60'
(cruciform) x 2'-10'
Water Freshwater, 765 000g
Opened 28 July 1936
Closed 6 September 1987
On site now Larkswood indoor
leisure centre

Open air swimming pools and lidos were designed in all shapes and sizes: rectangular, semi-circular, elliptical, star-shaped, and L-shaped.

One of the few cruciform lidos was Larkswood Pool at Chingford, east London.

The design, also seen at Croydon, had various benefits.

It allowed the provision of a shallow area for children and non-swimmers, without the need to build a separate paddling pool.

The two shorter axes could also be roped off and used at the same time as the main swimming pool.

Having seen Larkswood in operation, the *Municipal Journal* of 27 August 1937 strongly advocated the design. Based on the calculation that 12 per cent of users were swimmers, 8 per cent divers and 80 per cent 'waders and players,' the journal argued that only the cruciform shape catered for all groups at the same time.

The formalised layout and landscaping of Larkswood's site was similarly symmetrical, as the aerial view (*opposite*) shows. From New Road, a centre line

ran from the car park, through the main entrance (*left*) along the shorter axis of the pool, through the spectators' terraces and up to the splendid Art Deco café on the highest point of the site.

Appropriately for a swimming pool built in the form of a cross, at the official opening ceremony in July 1936, a prayer was said for its future success:

'O Lord God, we bless Thy Holy Name that it hath pleased Thee by Thy good Spirit, to put into the hearts of Thy people in this District the desire to build this Swimming Pool, and grant, we beseech Thee, that all who shall enjoy the benefit of this good work, may show forth their thankfulness by making a right use thereof...'

Despite the torrential rain that came close to spoiling that first day, the prayer seems to have been answered. By September 1936, some 70,000 visitors had tried out the new pool. In 1959 Larkswood

recorded what may well have been a London record of 290,400 users in a single year, and by the time that Chingford Urban District Council was absorbed into the new London Borough of Waltham Forest six years later an estimated total of 3.8 million swims had been taken at the pool, an average of about 33,000 every month.

In the vanguard of Larkswood swimmers was local historian Len Davis. As a teenager in the late 1930s he would regularly take a dip before breakfast.

'It was all quite informal,' he remembers. 'We used to throw our clothes down in heaps on the side and just get into the pool. It was mostly young men at that time of day – the ladies swam later – and nobody cared about being naked.'

In the early post-war period, as at many other lidos around Britain, lavish entertainments – or Aqua Revues – were staged at the pool, featuring The Gorgeous

Larkswood's cruciform plan was picked out by a series of concrete lighting masts, thus adding vertical emphasis to the clean horizontal lines of the entrance block. The diving stage overhung a diving pit just ten feet deep.

Aquabelles, The Aquabats, The Awkward Bats ('the world's craziest diving team'), and Roy Fransen, who would close the show with a death-defying dive in flames from a height of 60 feet.

In the 1970s, Larkswood was also one of many lidos that played host to BBC Television's hugely popular *It's a Knock Out* series.

But this wider exposure had no effect on attendances, and by the 1980s the numbers had fallen so steeply that a Larkswood Action Group, formed to save the lido, proved unable to stop its closure.

After 51 years in use, Larkswood finally closed in 1987.

At first the lido was replaced by a joint council and private venture, a white-tented themed swimming attraction called FantaSeas. This lasted only two years before sinking under £6 million worth of debt.

For the next decade the site lay derelict, until finally in 2001 Waltham Forest built an indoor leisure centre and pool on the site (now operated by Greenwich Leisure Ltd), combined with a private fitness club.

▲ For a suburban pool, **Larkswood** enjoyed a surprisingly rural setting. Located a short distance west of Epping Forest, in 7.5 acres of woodland (Larks Wood) acquired by Chingford Urban District Council in 1931, it was built on sloping ground, so that on a clear day visitors could see Alexandra Palace and the dome of St Paul's.

The pool itself faced westwards, offering protection from the wind and ensuring maximum sunshine on the water well into the evening.

Architecturally, Larkswood was typical of its era, with an especially fine clock tower over the entrance and a detached Art Deco café in the elevated south east corner of the site (*shown above in 1966, backing onto the woods*). Its fully glazed rounded frontage offered excellent views down onto the pool.

An original 1936 menu from the café offers a useful guide to the tastes of the day, ranging from a single slice of white bread for one penny, up to the most expensive dish, two fried eggs and bacon, costing 1s 2d (6p). Also on offer was Welsh Rarebit at 6d (3p) or Buck Rarebit at 9d (4p).

Case Study

Bathing Pool, Weston-Super-Mare 1937–2000

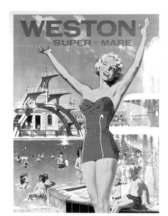

WESTON
SUPER - MARE

The Smile in Smiling Somerset

Guide free from A. R. Turner, Town Hall, Weston-super-Mare

TRAVEL BY TRAIN BRITISH RAILWAYS

Architect HA Brown
Cost £60,000
Size 220' x 140' x 0-15'
Water Seawater, 850,000g
Opened 1 July 1937
Closed 1982
Re-opened 28 May 1983
as Tropicana Pleasure Beach
Closed 3 September 2000

The most striking feature of the Bathing Pool at Weston-Super-Mare, on the north Somerset coast facing the Bristol Channel, was neither the extra large swimming pool, nor even its ancillary buildings, but its magnificent diving stage, dominating the west side of the pool.

Described from the outset as 'the finest diving platform in Europe', it immediately became synonymous with the town, just like the Tower at Blackpool or the Pavilion at Brighton. (The British Railways poster by the artist Merville, shown left, being but one example of its depiction.)

If it were standing today, Weston's diving stage would be considered one of Britain's most important concrete structures from the 1930s.

But alas, it has gone, its much lamented demolition by Woodspring District Council in February 1982 signalling a low point in the troubled life of Britain's classic lidos. If the iconic Weston diving stage could be taken down, went the feeling, then surely no lido was safe.

Both the diving stage and pool were designed by the office of the Borough Engineer, HA Brown.

Weston-Super-Mare was, at the time, going through a boom period. Having established its credentials as a select resort in the 19th century – during which time the Knightstone Baths were opened in 1820 – a Winter Gardens had been built in 1927, followed six years later by the unveiling of Britain's largest end-of-pier pavilion, housing an amusement arcade and funfair. In 1936 the newly built Weston Airfield started welcoming the first generation of airborne British holidaymakers.

With its catchline 'Air Like Wine', all Weston needed now to complete the very picture of a modern tourist destination was a lido.

The location chosen for the pool was on the foreshore; attractive enough perhaps, but not an ideal spot for a major structure, as it turned out. Shifting sands

and underground water courses required the contractors – Bolton and Lakin of Birmingham (who built several other lidos during the period) – to drill piles across the entire 120,000 square feet site.

'I think you have done a great thing for the inhabitants and visitors of Weston-super-Mare by providing such a swimming pool,' the MP, Sir Edward Campbell, told Weston's councillors at the opening ceremony in July 1937.

A private secretary in the Ministry of Health, Campbell had flown in especially for the occasion to deliver his government's message.

'Any money which may have been expended upon (the pool) will come back a hundredfold,' he predicted, 'not necessarily in cash, but in health, which is better than wealth.'

As soon as the speeches were over the assembled crowd of 4,000 spectators watched in awe as a local swimmer, Marwood Bailey,

Weston Pool's main entrance viewed from the promenade in the early 1980s, shortly before the pool was transformed into the Tropicana Pleasure Beach.

led a team of diving club members in a spectacular 'Grand Opening Dive', a sequence of synchronised diving 'from the dizzy height of the top stage'.

This breathtaking curtain raiser was followed by a 'mannequin parade of bathing fashions for 1937' (*see page 42*) and a demonstration of 'physical culture' by the Women's League of Health and Beauty in their trademark black and white silk costumes.

Throughout the afternoon, the Municipal Orchestra provided musical accompaniment, and in the evening a repeat performance of the afternoon programme ended with a water polo match; Somerset Police v. Weston Amateur Swimming Club.

At a celebration ball held at the Winter Gardens that night, Sir Edward was presented with two mementoes: an engraved cigarette box and a chromium plated scale replica of the diving platform. (How wonderful it would be to track that down now!)

As to the pool itself, the main building was a stately two storey pavilion, with single-storey wings containing changing rooms and roof terraces. Dressed in Bath stone, the pavilion was quite different in style from the gracefully arched and cantilevered diving stage which faced it across the pool. Indeed it is hard to believe the two structures were designed by the same individual.

But behind the scenes the pool was modern throughout.

Thanks to the use of the new 'Hyg-Gard-All' system of wire clothes baskets – which freed up cubicles for a regular turnover of bathers (*see page 44*) – 1,440 bathers could be accommodated in the pool at any one time. »

In stark contrast to the modernity of the diving stage, Weston's main pavilion was a relatively unadventurous exercise in neo-classical styling. Compare, for example, its windows, detailing and café interior (*left*) with those built at Croydon (*see page 99*), two years earlier.

▲ July 1937 and a 4,000 crowd gathers to see the spectacular inauguration of the unique diving stage at **Weston-Super-Mare**.

Whatever one's views on 20th century architecture, this artfully proportioned piece of modern engineering surely cannot fail to strike a chord.

Built by Messrs George Pollard of Taunton, with reinforced concrete steelwork by Messrs Coignet of London, we do not know how much input the Borough Engineer, HA Brown, had in the actual design.

But whoever was responsible clearly decided to depart from the linear forms seen at other lidos.

The structure consisted of two parallel reinforced concrete arches, 26 feet high, faced with a band of coloured tiles, from which seven boards were cantilevered, each one accessed by steps from the rear.

The boards were set at heights of 3, 5, 7 and 10 metres, the highest being suitable for national high diving championships.

Specifications for diving boards were always given in metres, rather than in Imperial measures, in order to comply with international swimming regulations.

» A state-of-the-art filtration system, meanwhile, offered 'the cleanest, purest and most inviting swimming pool in this country.' (The manufacturers of the plant went further by claiming that one might happily drink the water.)

In common with all Britain's seaside resorts, Weston suffered greatly from the advent of cheap continental holidays from the 1960s onwards. As the Bathing Pool's fortunes waned, the local authority responsible for its upkeep, Woodspring District Council, pondered how it might be adapted to modern tastes.

Their own tastes, it seemed, did not include the diving stage.

Initially it was cordoned off on safety grounds, in 1976. There had been no serious accidents, but the Council stated that 'authorative bodies' no longer recommended having diving boards over areas where swimming took place.

Early discussions concerning its fate followed in March 1978, when it was estimated that to repair the diving stage's structure – which clearly was exposed to salty sea air and deteriorating as a result – would cost £4,800. Another £4,000 would be needed, said the Council, to fund an extra lifeguard to monitor the diving area.

Demolition, it was added, would cost £10,000.

Alerted to the threat, The Thirties Society lobbied hard for its preservation, and were rewarded in November 1981 when an inspector from the Department of the Environment – no doubt mindful of the controversy caused by the sudden demolition of the Firestone factory in west London in August 1980 – chose to spot-list the diving stage (this, at a time when buildings of the 1930s were far less valued than today).

But the battle was by no means won. A month later Woodspring District Council countered with its own view in *Concrete* magazine.

The writer, who had previously criticised the decision to demolish the diving stage, said that he had now been made aware 'that the Council have very technically-plausible, financially-proper and socially-beneficial reasons for wishing to lay it all low.'

Accordingly, the Council applied to the DoE for listed building consent – in effect, permission to demolish.

A second inspector called, and the consent was granted.

Weeks later, in February 1982, Weston's iconic treasure was duly sledge-hammered into oblivion.

Over the next year the Bathing Pool was transformed into a £1 million water theme park, featuring a re-shaped swimming pool, water slides, a fibreglass elephant and a giant pineapple.

Described as 'fun, fruity, wet and wild', the Tropicana Pleasure Beach opened for the first time in 1983. And for the last, in 2000.

Ever since the site has been boarded up, its future awaiting a decision by North Somerset Council. Along with two other former tourist attractions in the town, Birnbeck Pier and Knightstone Island, it has become part of what one councillor has called 'the town's tatty trinity'.

All that is set to change, as part of a major urban redevelopment plan drawn up for the whole town.

No doubt somewhere within those plans there will be a prominent piece of public art.

If so, should the artist commissioned be looking for inspiration, he or she might study the image opposite. Weston will never find a more potent symbol.

▲ Clive Landen's haunting photo at the **Bathing Pool** in **Weston** in February 1982 was described by Marcus Binney in *Taking the Plunge* (*see Links*) as like 'a modern day Calvary out of the imagination of Fellini'.

No less an image is conjured up by the 1960s aerial view above, in which the diving board sits like a high altar watching over the flock.

Case Study

Brockwell Park Lido, London 1937

Grade II Listed (2003)
Architects HA Rowbotham and TL Smithson
Cost £26,150
Size 165' x 90' x 2'6"- 9'6"
Water Freshwater, 600,000g
Opened July 1937

Lidos attract a wide cross-section of swimmers, but Brockwell Park Lido – often referred to locally as 'Brixton Beach' – has perhaps the broadest social mix of all: from middle-class families to hip Brixton teenagers, from gay couples to a peer of the realm.

A blackboard propped by the entrance in the summer of 2004 read: 'Come in, chill out, dudes!'

Inside, another notice announced, 'Temp: Nice!'

Brockwell Lido was one of four, or possibly six lidos designed by Harry Rowbotham and TL Smithson of the London County Council Parks' Department.

Opened to the public in July 1937 it was an almost identical twin to Victoria Park Lido (*see page 114*), opened a year earlier, consisting of the then standard hand-made multi brick LCC compound, but at Brockwell with flat rather than pitched roofs.

Also in common with Victoria Park the lido was designed to replace a Victorian swimming lake (also located in Brockwell Park), that failed to meet newly introduced health standards.

Perhaps with that in mind the *Municipal Journal and Public Works Engineer* noted that the new lido was fitted with a new feature called a 'scum trough',

This, an end-of-pool tiled and recessed channel that would soon become standard, ensured the continuous withdrawal of surface water, to a depth of 12 inches – this layer being where most pollutants, or, as the journal put it, 'objectionable floating matter' gathers.

Otherwise, Brockwell Park was a workmanlike, unspectacular, but highly valued new lido on the south London circuit.

So highly valued over the years, in fact, that unlike other LCC lidos in south London – such as Peckham, Southwark, Kennington and Eltham – the Brixton Beach has proved a hardy survivor.

The story begins in 1990 when the lido was mothballed as part of cost-saving measures forced upon Lambeth Borough Council.

Accordingly a Brockwell Lido Users (BLU) group formed and maintained the pressure until, four years later, Lambeth put out the lido's management to competitive tender.

Two former Council employees, Patrick Castledine and Casey McGlue, managed to beat off 14 other competitors to win the contract, and were given a £39,000 start-up grant and a seven-year lease to show what they could do.

To start with the two go-ahead young managers introduced a wide variety of poolside activities, including yoga, tai chi, aerobics and salsa classes. Indoor rooms were made available to a pre-school children's group.

Brockwell Park in 1937 – looking towards the café side on Dulwich Road – was a standard Rowbotham and Smithson LCC brick compound with hexagonal aerators, flower beds, concrete paving and Wicksteed diving boards and chutes.

At the same time they decorated the café in vibrant colours and hired it out for parties, jazz evenings and even a highly publicised lesbian 'wedding'.

Castledine and McGlue attracted a fairy godmother too, when in 2001, Evian, the mineral water company, agreed to sponsor the lido for £100,000. This money went towards repairs, new changing rooms, poolside furniture and a facelift to the bar.

In return, the pool was renamed the Evian Lido and the company's name painted in large red letters on the floor of the pool.

Castledine and McGlue looked forward to a long term relationship with Evian. But it was not to be. In 2002 the company reduced its sponsorship to just £10,000, while grants from other potential funders proved impossible to attract with a lease of only seven years' duration.

By now Brockwell was reported to be losing £2,500 a day.

On some days barely a handful of swimmers turned up. Clearly the demand was there, for on good days the lido would be packed to capacity. »

The Brixton Beach, 1938 style. The social mix, haircuts and swimwear may be different today, but a similar ethos prevails. As has often been said, lidos exist not merely to swim, but to see, and to be seen.

▲ **Brockwell Park**'s 'Blue Period', starting in 1994, saw the unashamed use of vibrant murals, inside and out, to grab attention and liven up a building that would otherwise merge unobtrusively into the landscape (as, no doubt, was intention of the LCC Parks Department).

Inside the Brixton Beach (*right*) a similar rebranding exercise took place, with the mineral water company, Evian, having its name painted on the pool floor.

Although the sponsorship, eventually worth £110,000, lasted only two years, similar deals may yet be an option for other struggling pools to consider.

>> But how to ride out the bad times, and at the same time maintain the historic building?

Thus in 2003 Lambeth began talks with a new management company, called Fusion Lifestyle.

Set up in 2000 by more former council employees, from both Lambeth and Southwark Borough Councils, Fusion is, in its own words, 'a not-for-profit, community-oriented organisation' aimed at providing facilities and services in south London.

Meanwhile, in August 2003 the lido was listed Grade II.

Bolstered by the listing, and by the offer of a 25 year lease from Lambeth, Fusion then set up lengthy consultations with the BLU, the Friends of Brockwell Park and the Herne Hill Forum in conjunction with their appointed architects, Pollard Thomas Edwards (PTEa).

This resulted in a decision, approved by English Heritage, to extend the lido's southern range of buildings to accommodate a wider number of community activities.

Planning consent for this was granted in March 2004, allowing Castledine and McGlue – who had been asked to stay on in the interim – to withdraw gracefully as Fusion took over in 2005.

By that stage £500,000 had also been secured from the Heritage Lottery Fund.

Once the works are completed in 2006, Fusion's fortunes will be closely followed by lido operators all over Britain.

Their goal, like Fusion's, is to find viable ways and means of maintaining much loved lidos, while extending their role in the wider community beyond the summer months.

By extending the lido itself, Fusion hope to do just that.

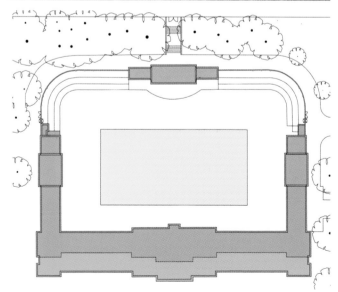

▲ Classic modernism will prevail at **Brockwell Park Lido** as part of a £2.5 million revamp by architects PTEa and Qudos interior designers, to be financed by Fusion Lifestyle and the Heritage Lottery Fund.

In addition to the creation of a new glazed entrance on the north side of the lido, accessed from Dulwich Road, and the upgrading of the café, the refurbishment will see the extension (marked in pink) of the southern wing by 6.5 metres.

To maintain the building's integrity this extension will, as far as possible, match the existing materials and styling of the 1937 original building.

The added space will house a health and fitness suite, spa pool, sauna and community rooms, designed to create 'a democratic, inclusive and laid back place'.

A Brixton Beach resort, no less.

Case Study

Broomhill Pool, Ipswich 1938–2002

Grade II Listed (2001)
Architect E McLauchlan
Cost £17,000
Size 165' x 60'
Water Freshwater, 464,000g inc children's pool
Opened April 1938
Closed 2002

Broomhill Pool is one of two 1930s listed lidos whose fate hangs in the balance as of mid 2005 (the other being Uxbridge).

Closed at the end of the 2002 season after Ipswich Borough Council had calculated that it was losing £60,000 a year, the pool's future depends on detailed studies being carried out to assess the magnitude and cost of its long overdue refurbishment.

An independent survey in 1998 uncovered serious problems. The pool's tank was leaking. There were signs of subsidence – not surprisingly, given that during construction in 1938 the engineers had encountered problems with sand and naturally occurring springs – and steel reinforcement rods in the concrete were rusting.

Following the survey, the council calculated that a patched-up pool would be good for only another five years.

To effect a more long term refurbishment would cost no less than £1.5 million, perhaps double.

So is Broomhill Pool worthy of all the effort that will be undoubtedly be required?

Set on the edge of a suburban park in a quiet and comfortable residential district of the city, it is certainly well placed for local families. Describing its location in *The Independent* in April 2003 Jay Merrick noted that Sir Alf Ramsey, the former Ipswich and England manager, had retired to a house nearby. 'And the vibe here is just like Ramsey: ordered, taciturn.'

Merrick considered the pool 'unremarkable' architecturally.

Others disagree. As shown by the image opposite, taken shortly before the opening in 1938 – and it has changed little in essence since – it is a classic of the genre, characterised by its symmetry, coherence and sense of enclosure, and not dissimilar to contemporary designs seen in Italy or Germany during the inter-war period.

Certainly nothing else like it survives in Britain.

When listed Grade II in 2001 Broomhill was described as a 'well-detailed and carefully integrated example of an urban lido which remains little altered in its principal features.'

The listing also noted its 'Moderne style' buildings of reinforced concrete with flat roofs, its original tubular steel four-stage diving-boards, and its striking 700 seat grandstand. This, and the sloped sunbathing terraces opposite, lends it the character of a small stadium.

As Eva Branscome of The Twentieth Century Society noted, here is a pool not only of 'great historic interest, but also a fine building in its own right'.

It is also deceptively large, having a tank that measures just over 50m in length – that is, Olympic sized – the only such swimming facility in East Anglia.

Broomhill may therefore lack the national profile accorded to Saltdean, Tinside or Penzance. But it is arguably their equal in architectural significance.

It has numerous supporters too.

In 2002 the Friends of Broomhill Pool formed to campaign for its restoration. A year later they became the Broomhill Pool Trust and registered as a charity.

Also in 2003, a council survey showed that 88% of respondents

in Ipswich favoured saving the pool. A Trust petition gleaned more than 18,000 signatures.

These initiatives were followed in late 2003 by the setting up of a Steering Group, composed of Councillors, Council officers and the local MP, as well as members of the Trust and local residents.

Their deliberations led to the Council allocating £67,000 towards the costs of drawing up a bid for Heritage Lottery funding.

A change in control at the council soon after led to a nervous five month hiatus, finally ended in March 2005 when the Council pledged £1 million towards the pool, provided that the balance required for renovations – which could reach as much as £2-3 million – is raised from other sources, and that the Trust draws up a workable business plan for the pool's future operation.

If those hurdles can be overcome, ownership of the pool will be transferred to the trust.

But raising the funds will be a mammoth task within the two year timescale set by the Council.

Broomhill Pool is not out of the water yet.

A feast of angles, levels and concrete detailing – Broomhill Pool awaits filling in 1938. Note the position of the aerator, unusually screened off from the pools. The original 5m diving board is still in place – a rarity nowadays – and this, together with the pool's deep end, also measuring 5m, makes Broomhill ideal for training and for sub-aqua divers.

▲ The Sherrington Road entrance to **Broomhill Pool**, as seen in 1938 and 2001 (*right*). The clocktower. most regrettably, was demolished in 1965.

Also since removed are the pool's floodlights (*illustrated in full glory on page 35*).

Designed by the Ipswich Borough Engineer, Broomhill is apparently similar in design to another, slightly smaller open air pool built on the other side of Ipswich in 1937, at Pipers Vale, but closed during the 1970s.

▲ Back to nature – **Broomhill Pool** in 2005, awaiting its fate.

The grandstand originally housed the ladies' dressing rooms and the filtration plant, but was designed, according to one source, to be used as a decontamination centre in the event of war.

That did not happen. But, alas for swimmers, the war did result in the decommissioning of the water heating system, which was never re-installed.

Shown left is the former aerator, now serving as a flower bed.

Case Study

Saltdean Lido, Brighton 1938

Grade II Listed (1987)
Architect RWH Jones
Cost not known
Size 140' x 50' x 4'-7' 6"
Water Filtered seawater, unheated (originally), c. 200,000 g
Opened July 1938
Re-opened 4 July 1964
Closed 1995
Re-opened 23 May 1998

For those readers who like to be beside the seaside, but who are also susceptible to the clean cut charms of the international Modern school of 20th century architecture, Saltdean, on the outskirts of Brighton, is a haven.

In its midst, moreover, lies one of the finest lidos to have emerged from the 1930s; a lido that is unique both in its design – it was the first operating lido in Britain to be listed, in 1987 – and in its somewhat unusual history.

Opened in 1938, it has been closed not once, but twice since, for periods totalling 26 years.

And as we shall discover, it is by no means secure today.

As told by local historian, Douglas d'Enno, the suburb of Saltdean was essentially the product of one property developer's business acumen between the wars.

Charles Neville, who had established his wealth in Canada before returning to England, had first spotted the then largely rural area's potential before the First World War, while on holiday in Bexhill.

A wily businessman who used prize draws and stunts to attract buyers to what would later be described as 'the Coming Resort', he started by developing the new residential district of Peacehaven

in 1915. After 1922 his holdings spread steadily westwards, towards Brighton, to include most of Saltdean and parts of Rottingdean by the mid 1930s.

Neville's Saltdean Estate

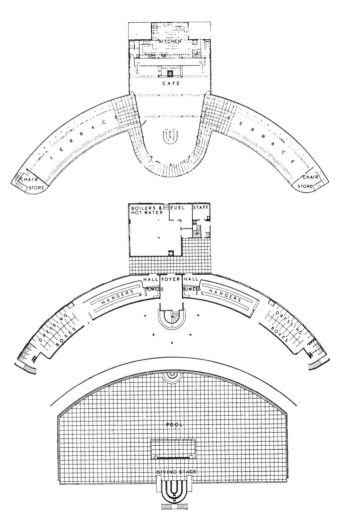

Saltdean Lido – its plans published in the *Architect and Building News* of 18 August 1938 – represented a startling break from all previous lido designs. Its upper storey (*top*) housed the café and terrace, with dressing rooms and the foyer on the ground floor (*centre*), curved to embrace the 140 feet wide pool.

Company offered incomers a wide range of house and bungalow styles, from Tudoresque to Spanish, Italian and, ultimately, Cubist. In the latter style the respected firm of Connell, Ward and Lucas designed three houses within the estate, one of which, in Wicklands Avenue, survives and is, along with the lido, a magnet for architectural historians and enthusiasts.

Saltdean Lido was not the first open air pool on this popular stretch of the south coast.

Preceding it, and barely a mile or two distant, was one on the front at Rottingdean, and another, a tidal pool at Black Rock, close to the Brighton Marina (*see page 38*). Both were designed by D Edwards and opened in 1935.

There was also a small pool at the Tudor House Hotel in Rottingdean, where guests such as Cary Grant and Bette Davis would bring a touch of Hollywood glamour to Neville's domain.

Meanwhile, on Brighton's seafront, Embassy Court, a stunning Art Deco block of luxury flats by Wells Coates, opened in 1936. In Saltdean this was echoed by Teynham House (named after Lord Teynam, an associate of Charles Neville) and Curzon House, both designed by RWH Jones, an architect who had previously worked for FW Woolworth in Liverpool.

Jones gained two further commissions in Saltdean.

One was for the Ocean Hotel, a £200,000, 426 bed Art Deco development on Longridge Avenue, in the centre of the Saltdean estate.

This had its own open air pool, sunk into the chalk hillside and overlooked by the hotel room balconies.

The other commission, a few hundred yards to the west, was for Saltdean Lido.

Both were completed in July 1938, and both were determinedly Modern in style and ambience.

But if the Ocean Hotel was a conscious echo of that other great Art Deco hotel of the 1930s, the Midland Hotel in Morecambe, by Oliver Hill (opened in 1933), in the case of the lido, Jones's prime architectural influence was rather closer to hand.

The De La Warr Pavilion, designed by Eric Mendelsohn and Serge Chermayeff (a German escapee from Nazism and an anglicised Russian), had been completed at nearby Bexhill-on-Sea, three years earlier.

Built of reinforced concrete, the pavilion's striking blend of horizontal lines and curves, glazed walls, cantilevered balconies and flat roof terraces, made it arguably the first truly Modernist building in Britain, and certainly the most talked about and revered.

Saltdean Lido, with its similarly projecting curved central feature, like the bridge of an ocean liner, might well have emerged from the same drawing board. »

Shades of Bexhill's De La Warr Pavilion – Saltdean Lido, captured by photographer John Maltby shortly after its opening in July 1938.

▲ Three miles east of Brighton's Palace Pier and nestling from the sea breezes in a natural hollow, **Saltdean Lido**, shown in 1965, occupies a segment of the Oval, an open expanse containing at various times tennis courts, a boating pond and a riding school.

In the foreground, the 1934 subway linking Saltdean to the beach, can be seen passing under Marine Drive.

》 'This is a remarkably restrained design,' waxed *Building* magazine of Saltdean in October 1938.

'It has a well-shaped curvilinear plan form, and in the treatment of the elevations there is a sensitive appreciation of line and massing which is unusual in buildings of this character...

'It is certainly one of the few really first-class designs of its type in the country.'

It might also have been the first of a whole new generation of Modernist lidos.

Instead of which Saltdean Lido's acclaimed reception was to prove but a brief interlude.

The outbreak of war in September 1939 saw it closed to the public after just two summer seasons in use.

As at other lidos around the country, in moved the Auxiliary Fire Service, using the pool itself as a water tank. The lido grounds were taken over for training and exercise drills. The Ocean Hotel, meanwhile, became a fire service college for senior officers, opened in 1941 by Herbert Morrison, who was now Home Secretary.

Saltdean Lido performed one other, less expected use during the war.

Charles Neville's Saltdean had developed in such a commercial flurry that by 1939 the area was still without basic communal facilities. No schools, no police station, no library or public hall, not even a pub. Thus the lido's male dressing rooms were turned into a temporary church, while the ladies' section served as a Sunday School.

When the Fire Service finally vacated the premises in 1945, this once pristine Modernist pool was said to be 'a mass of broken concrete and weeds'.

But worse, it would remain in that state – closed to the public and completely untended – for the next 19 years.

During that prolonged period of uncertainty, Brighton Town Council made repeated attempts to buy the land from the Saltdean Estate Company, but the two parties failed to agree on a price.

The company then went into voluntary liquidation, leaving the lido in the hands of the Mutual Building Society.

Had it been sold then, that might well have been the end.

Instead, two public enquiries were held into various proposals for the site. One set, put forward by the Council, was for a park and flats. Another, from a subsidiary of Butlins, was for the lido to be turned into a licensed roadhouse. (Butlins had already taken over the lease of the Ocean Hotel, itself also in a neglected state, in 1953).

Had the latter proposal been successful Butlins would have filled in the pool, built an indoor one in its place, and added a tenpin bowling alley, the craze of the day. Very un-Saltdean. »

A swimmer's eye view of Saltdean Lido before its refurbishment in 1998. Compared with most 1930s lidos, Saltdean was built on a modest scale, with space for only 500 bathers. A spiral staircase led from the glazed café in the centre to the solarium roof terrace.

▼ Graceful curves and rusting railings at the ever problematic **Saltdean Lido**, on yet another quiet summer's weekday in 2005.

In the 1950s, Butlins proposed running a cable car from the pool's upper terrace to the nearby Ocean Hotel (now the Grand Ocean Hotel) which they had just taken over.

In the distance, to the right, can be seen the white heights of another RWH design, Curzon House, and the former Saltdean Estate Office, now Marine View.

Also visible are the Tudoresque homes built by Charles Neville's Saltdean Estate Company.

But where are all the swimmers?

》 At both enquiries, however, the government minister responsible turned down the applications.

This impasse eventually ended in 1962 – two years after the death of Charles Neville – when the Council issued a compulsory purchase order.

For a mere £20,000 – rather less than they had offered in 1955 – the lido and the land behind it (known as The Oval) were now in public ownership.

Some councillors were still keen to see the site turned into a park for local residents.

Others made the case for refurbishing the lido.

'Saltdean is a growing community,' argued Councillor Watson-Miller, 'and I think they are going to ask for something more than walks and parks. A bathing pool there will be a great attraction not only for Saltdean people but for an ever-growing number of visitors who dislike the hurly-burly of Brighton and decide to spend their holidays on the outskirts of the town.'

Accordingly, refurbishment plans costed at £86,000 were drawn up, to include the addition of a library and community centre at the rear of the lido.

Thus on 4 July 1964 began only the lido's third summer season in 27 years.

For the next twenty years or so Saltdean Lido once again became a focal point for the area, which had by now had its own schools, church and pub.

But by the 1990s attendances had fallen and the structures were again in desperate need of attention.

Brighton and Hove Council declined to carry out the work, so in 1995 the lido was closed for a second, indefinite period.

For a couple of years the prospects looked grim until in 1997 a former Saltdean resident, Mark Bunting, decided the building had to be saved.

Combining with two businessmen – Phillip Graves, who had learnt to swim there as a boy, and his business partner, Cliff Collins – Bunting persuaded Brighton and Hove Council to grant them a 125 year lease to run the lido at a peppercorn rent.

At the same time, repairs to the pool would be financed by the sale of land behind the lido to Allied Domecq Leisure, who built a family pub and restaurant

Thus began the third phase in the eventful life of Saltdean Lido.

Re-opened on 23 May 1998, Saltdean Lido was all set to become a model for other struggling lidos, with part of the original buildings converted into a health club which operates all year round, and another part rented out to the local community association, who hold regular events in the former café area.

It would be comforting to report that all has gone well since, and that Saltdean Lido is now safe for the forseeable future.

Regrettably, this is not the case.

Messrs Graves and Collins sold on the lease to health club operator Dennis Audley in 1999, but like them, he has struggled to make the enterprise pay.

Given a long hot summer, when up to 25,000 people might attend, the lido can just about break even. But in the dull summer of 2004 attendances barely reached 3,000.

Indeed over four of the five years that Audley has managed the site, he reveals, annual losses have averaged £40,000.

Of equal concern is the continuing deterioration of the main building's fabric.

Behind the repainted exterior, rusting steel reinforcement rods and leakages have to be addressed, at great expense, if the building is to remain useable.

It is a scenario that will be familiar to anyone who has ever had to maintain a 1930s concrete building, particularly one so exposed to the salty sea air.

Saltdean Lido is a building of national importance. It is being run by individuals who care for it deeply and have no desire to see the pool closed for a fourth time.

But as we have read so many times before, elsewhere in this book, without either public subsidies or commercial enabling development, its future must remain a cause of great concern.

Along the coast at Bexhill, the De La Warr Pavilion has been beautifully restored to its original glory at a cost of £8 million.

Saltdean Lido's restitution would cost only a fraction of that.

In the meantime, a bit of sun would not go amiss.

▲ Since its partial refurbishment in 1997 the pool at **Saltdean Lido** has been divided into two, with a children's pool on the left, and a snaking path in between.

A tall mast in the centre has also been erected to take a canvas sail, to add further to the lido's nautical appearance.

In the foreground can be seen the pathway that leads to the beach, via the subway under the coast road.

Case Study

Parliament Hill Fields Lido, London 1938

Grade II Listed (1999)
Architects HA Rowbotham and TL Smithson
Cost £34,000
Size 200' x 90' x 2'6"-9'6"
Water Freshwater, 650,000g
Opened 20 August 1938

We finish our round of case studies with the last of the great showcase lidos to be completed before World War Two.

Located in the south eastern corner of Hampstead Heath – where open air swimming may also be enjoyed in three Victorian swimming lakes a short distance to the north (*see page 171*) – the lido at Parliament Hill Fields was the twelfth of thirteen outdoor pools in whose construction the London County Council was involved during the period 1906-39.

The thirteenth, at Charlton (*see page 30*) which opened a year later, was more compact, while plans for three others at Battersea Park, Clissold Park and Ladywell Recreation Ground had to be abandoned because of the war.

Costing £34,000, Parliament Hill Fields Lido was also the most expensive outdoor pool financed by the LCC, even though it was almost identical in design to those at Victoria Park (opened in 1936) – which had the same sized pool as Parliament Hill Fields – and the smaller Brockwell Park (1937), both of which had cost £26,000.

All three were, of course, the work of Harry Rowbotham and TL Smithson, chief designers at the LCC Parks Department, and followed the standard LCC pattern of a rectangular, brick compound.

The only significant differences concerned the elevations.

As shown on these pages, Parliament Hill Fields had flat roofs all round, a more defined entrance block (*shown opposite*), a café with a gently curved frontage, and rectangular openings throughout, whereas Victoria Park featured several arched ones (and a café with a pitched roof).

Parliament Hill Fields Lido was opened in August 1938, for reasons which even he was unable to explain, by the Secretary of the Football Association, Stanley Rous. (Perhaps the LCC's preferred celebrity had cried off at the last minute.)

According to the *Hampstead and Highgate Express*, Rous admitted in his speech that he was a little bemused to be there, as he could see no connection between football and swimming – this was in the days before 'diving' gained

a footballing connotation – apart from the fact that each sport was concerned with 'figures and form'.

'A great deal of money has been spent here, however,' he went on, 'and I for one feel that if 34,000 people learn to swim here in the next few years, it will have been money well spent.'

(This was no mere platitude. Today we take it for granted that the majority can swim. In 1938 that was by no means the case.)

Councillor John Perni, the Mayor of St Pancras, in whose boundaries the lido then fell, made a rather fuller speech to the 500 guests gathered around the pool side (*pictured on page 4*).

'As a member of the architectural profession,' he said, 'I can look around this lido and truthfully say it is a fine piece of work and a credit to all...

'St Pancras would have been proud to provide an amenity such as this, but our finances are more restricted than those of the LCC.'

He was therefore delighted that the lido had been built, 'especially as the LCC are paying the bill for it and are going to maintain it.' »

Rowbotham and Smithson's early drawings for Parliament Hill Fields showed arched rather than square openings on all its elevations. The amended front elevation from 1938 (*below right*) is otherwise unchanged today, apart from a ramp, added as part of a major refurbishment in 2005. Part of those works also saw the welcome removal of noticeboards that had for years concealed the three slit windows flanking the entrance (*shown in 1938, above right*). It is to be hoped that during the second phase of works, being considered for 2006 or after, the original form of serif signage above the door will replace the unsympathetic lettering added in the 1990s.

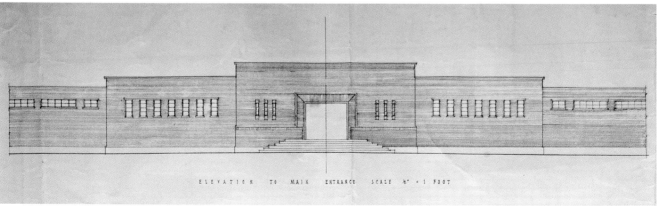

ELEVATION TO MAIN ENTRANCE   SCALE ⅜" = 1 FOOT

》 No doubt to polite laughter he added, 'This aquatic generosity of the LCC is much appreciated, but we hope it will not be too severely expressed in the next LCC precept.'

The speeches over, the pool was then officially opened by a diving display from members of the Mermaid Swimming Club and the Highgate Diving Club.

As reported by the *Hampstead and Highate Express*, 'an hilarious mock life-saving episode' then concluded the proceedings.

Of all London's lidos, Parliament Hill Fields has probably encountered the fewest obstacles during its lifetime.

It stayed open throughout the war, and in the 1950s and 1960s regularly clocked up aggregate attendances of over 100,000.

Even so, in common with its fellow London lidos, after its ownership was transferred to the LCC's successor body, the Greater London Council, in 1965, budget cuts led to a gradual decline.

This culminated in the death of a young man, Enrico Sidoli, in 1976, in a diving related accident.

As a foretaste of things to come nationwide, all but one of the lido's diving boards were removed.

Parliament Hill Fields might have succumbed four years later when a motion for its closure was defeated at County Hall.

Those were dark days in the capital. Between 1980 and 1990 eight other former LCC lidos were closed, including Victoria Park,

The 1937-38 drawings for Parliament Hill Fields shown on these pages and now held by the Corporation of London, are thought to be the only original LCC lido plans surviving. A graphic version appears on page 29.

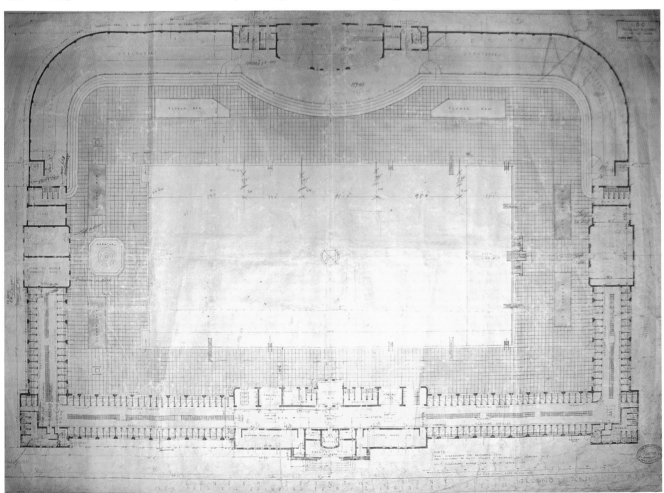

and a ninth, Brockwell Park, was about to be mothballed for the next four years.

Yet Parliament Hill Fields continued to lead a charmed life.

Because of its location within the boundaries of Hampstead Heath, instead of being transferred into the ownership of Camden Borough Council (into which St Pancras had been absorbed in 1965), when the GLC was abolished by the Conservative government under Margaret Thatcher in 1986 it was passed instead to the temporary control of the London Residuary Body.

As the LRB had been established to pick up the pieces left over from the abolition of the GLC, and was tasked specifically with the sale of former GLC properties, the lido's future seemed more uncertain than ever. And yet instead of closing the lido, almost miraculously it seemed, the LRB actually invested in its upkeep.

This charmed existence took a further turn in 1989 when control of Hampstead Heath, and therefore the lido, passed to the Corporation of London (Britain's oldest and most affluent local authority, which administers not only the City of London but a number of open spaces beyond its boundaries).

Then in 1999 the pool's future was yet further secured by the granting of Grade II listed status, making it the first Rowbotham and Smithson lido to gain statutory protection. (Brockwell Park would follow in 2003.)

But for the many active and well connected users of the lido – Hampstead being one of the heartlands of London's 'chattering classes' – not all of the Corporation's stewardship of the pool was well received.

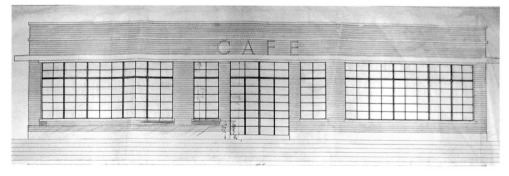

For example, in November 2003 the Corporation was granted listed building consent to remove the last remaining springboard, a decision which elicited vehement protests from the United Swimmers Association of Hampstead.

The springboard, they argued, the pool's last surviving original Wicksteed board (other than the 3m diving stage, part of which was now used as a lifeguard's tower), was part of the lido's heritage.

For their part, the Corporation cited Amateur Swimming Association guidelines that recommend a minimum water depth of 3.2m for a 1m board, whereas the pool was actually only 2.6m at the deep end.

Outside London, other lido campaigners were baffled that such an apparently small detail should arouse so much passion.

'They should get real,' said one. 'At least the Corporation is spending money to keep the pool open.'

In fact, the Corporation was about to spend no less than £2.8 million on the lido. »

The curved café frontage at Parliament Hill Fields Lido as seen in 2004 (*top*) and in the original LCC plans (*above*).

» Once again, it appeared, Parliament Hill Fields had eluded the fate of other London pools.

On the other hand, this is no ordinary struggling lido. In 2004 attendances totalled around 50,000, a fraction of the glory days perhaps, but by today's standards still remarkably healthy.

Carried out by the Corporation's Technical Services department in 2004-05, the refurbishment works consisted of improving the pool's accessibility, by installing ramps to the entrance and café, and the replacement of the paddling pool.

Improvements were also made to the filtration system – still with its original Permutit filter vessels – which had been struggling to turn over the water in thirteen hours, compared with the five hours claimed in 1938. (This required new pipes to be imported from the USA, the only remaining source of Imperial sized fittings.)

But by far the most radical, and costly element of the works concerned the lining of the tank.

In common with most ageing pools, the tank at Parliament Hill Fields had been leaking for some time. In the past the only solution to this was to patch up the concrete lining every year, a tedious and expensive process.

Rather than continue this cycle, the Corporation opted for a novel approach; the complete relining of the tank in stainless steel.

It is a method that has become increasingly popular in indoor pools, but has never been applied at an outdoor one in Britain, least of all one as large as Parliament Hill Fields, where the tank measures 61 x 27.4m.

At the same time the decision was made to reduce the overall depth of the pool, from a maximum of 2.6m to 2m, with an increase in the proportion of the pool measuring 1m or less.

The aim of this was twofold.

Firstly, it would reduce the volume of water by a third, so that it can be turned over more quickly, thereby also counteracting the clouding effects of sun tan oil in the water (a problem at all outdoor pools since greater awareness of the risks of skin cancer).

Secondly, a shallower pool was felt to be more appropriate for children and families.

Once again the decision infuriated the users group. They argued that by reducing the depth, and by removing the springboard, the pool was being 'dumbed down' for mere leisure use.

But their protests were to no avail, and in late May 2005, the new look stainless steel tank was unveiled to a curious public.

▲ **Parliament Hill Fields Lido** in 2005, with its new stainless steel tank lining appearing surprisingly blue, even on a grey day.

Note also that the new tank is filled to 'deck level' (that is, flush with the paving); a now common practice which helps to skim off the top level of water, where most pollutants settle, more efficiently.

Another part of the filtration system improved in 2005 was the fountain (*right*). Still the original 1938 wedding cake design, it is now framed by a clear glass screen, replacing an opaque one that had masked its splendour before.

Hardly a murmur of disapproval was heard. Indeed when more than 5,000 bathers packed the lido over one of the following weekends, many hardly noticed the new tank at all, apart from a few who were aware that the floor has small dimples in its surface.

Not all is sweetness and light, however. Since the revamp, a long tradition at Parliament Hill Fields has been brought to an end by the Corporation of London.

Since the lido opened in 1938 entry before 9.30am had always been free. Indeed in the early years all LCC open air pools were free of charge all the time.

But in 2005 that custom ended and early birds must now pay £2 (albeit half the entry fee charged after 10.00am).

Even more controversially, the Corporation also decided to introduce charges at the swimming lakes on the other side of Hampstead Heath (*see page 171*), where, historically, admission fees have never been charged.

These genuine concerns apart, Parliament Hill Fields Lido would appear to be the very model of a well restored historic lido.

Moreover, the Corporation has agreed in principle to a second phase of works, concentrating, it is hoped, on restoring the general fabric of the buildings.

Added to the revamp of Brockwell Park and the proposed re-opening of London Fields Lido, all this spending offers hope that what little remains of the unique legacy bequeathed by the LCC will be protected, and enhanced, in the years to come.

To borrow that expression used by the St Pancras Mayor in 1938, the capital's liquid assets can only benefit from such acts of 'aqua generosity'.

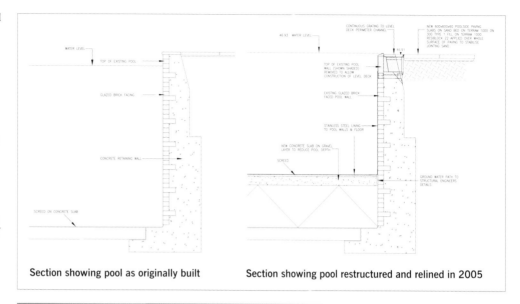

Section showing pool as originally built   Section showing pool restructured and relined in 2005

▲ Could the stainless steel tank lining at **Parliament Hill Fields**, the first of its kind to be fitted at an outdoor pool in Britain, offer the lidos of the 21st century a leak-free future? Time will no doubt tell.

The lining, a mere 2mm thick, was supplied by the Swedish firm Invarmex, has a dimpled surface and is said to be more hygienic, as well as eliminating the need for maintenance and grouting.

Seen left is the new tank's 'deck level' effect, with the white grills to the side drawing off the top surface more efficiently than was the case with the old scum troughs.

One aspect of deck level pools is that in order to ensure they do not overflow onto the paved surrounds when large numbers of swimmers are in the water, a ballast tank has to be provided to accommodate the excess.

As Parliament Hill Fields Lido can attract as many as 3,000 visitors on a good day, the ballast tank's 40 cubic metres should be well used.

Chapter Seven

Community

Ingleton Swimming Pool, Yorkshire – one of many small open air pools thrown a lifebelt by local campaigners and now operated by a charitable trust. Over the last two decades this scenario has occurred at around 25-30 locations, meaning that approximately one quarter of Britain's surviving lidos and open air pools (*see pages 182-83*) are run largely by volunteers.

For many people in Britain today, an interest in sport remains a largely passive matter.

They may watch televised football, rugby, cricket or tennis, but never actually play. They may pay to be a spectator at a ground and hugely enjoy the experience.

But they are unlikely to feel the same passion, the same sense of attachment for their sporting arenas, as open air swimmers do for theirs.

For swimmers are both supporters and active participants, both spectators and performers.

Swimming itself is only a part of the appeal.

All lidos and open air pools, even the larger urban ones, seem to inspire a strong sense of community. As one swimmer at Parliament Hill Fields in London put it, 'When people swim together on a regular basis, a bond develops. They share things when they are at the pool, and are concerned for each other when the pool closes.'

That sense of a support network becomes even stronger should the pool be threatened with closure.

In the previous chapter we learnt how lidos were saved by concerted community action in Guildford, Penzance, Cheltenham, Stonehaven and Plymouth.

In this chapter we highlight the many vociferous campaigns to keep lidos open in several smaller communities; in villages, suburbs and towns such as Lewes, Chagford, Cirencester, Hampton, Hathersage and Arundel.

Current, and as yet unresolved campaigns in Reading and Droitwich complete the survey.

A common outcome of these campaigns is that the local authority responsible for the pool has handed over its operation to a charitable trust, formed specifically for that purpose by the campaigners.

In other words the users become, if not the owners, then at least the operators.

As is the case with so many of Britain's community sports clubs and grounds, none of this would be remotely possible without the efforts of an army of volunteers.

Among them are those running the Weardale Open Air Swimming

Pool in Bishop Auckland, County Durham, who in 2004 were rewarded by a Queen's Award for Voluntary Service.

But the work of dozens of other local groups carries on, year after year, largely unrecognised. The *Played in Britain* series, is, in that respect, dedicated to their efforts.

As might be expected, funding is by far the most challenging issue they have to face.

Trusts generally receive a small subsidy of a few thousand pounds from the pool's owner (usually the local council). Other funding, invariably hard won, comes from grants and foundations that are not open to local authorities, such as The Big Lottery Fund, and in certain locations, the SITA Environmental Trust.

The rest has to be raised by the usual round of fundraising events.

As one volunteer put it, 'We stagger from crisis to crisis'. There is never any letting up.

The cost of running even a modestly-sized pool can be up to £30,000 a year.

At the very least a pool manager is usually employed, and although at a going rate of less than £10 per hour for only a couple of months' work during the summer, it is a role that requires total dedication.

At Petersfield Open Air Pool in Hampshire, for example, Vivien Mays has served as the pool manager for 33 years. Her counterpart at Woburn Pool in Bedfordshire, Pauline Dehaan, has been in post for nearly 20 years.

Both speak of the enormous satisfaction gained from seeing different generations of children enjoying themselves as they grow up, and then returning as adults with their own families.

Lifeguards can be another cost. No pool can open without at least one qualified lifeguard on duty. If no qualified volunteers are available, at rates of between £5-8 an hour, this too can place a heavy toll on annual budgets.

Changes in legislation have also added to the burden.

The Part-Time Workers Regulations 2000, for instance, give part-time staff the same rights as full-time employees.

The Disability Discrimination Act 1995 requires that even small pools install ramps or sloping steps and, where possible, a hoist.

The cost of public liability insurance is another burden. One charity-run pool in the south of England found its premium doubled within four years to £4,300. For a typical twelve week summer season that amounts to nearly £360 per week.

And yet despite all these growing challenges, Britain's community-run pools continue to battle for survival with dogged determination.

Such is the allure, and so great are the social benefits, that the simple act of swimming in the open air would appear to possess.

▲ The **Pells Pool**, in **Lewes**, East Sussex, is Britain's oldest operational public outdoor pool.

Built by subscription in 1860, there were originally two pools on site; one subscription, the other free. But the latter, hardly more than a communal bath for the poorest people of the town, gained a reputation for dirty water and was infilled during the 1920s.

Since then the main pool has been modernised, though it is still fed by natural spring water.

The Pells Pool is a lido in the pure sense, surrounded by lawns and flower beds, with a paddling pool, refreshment kiosk and an occasional bouncy castle.

That it survives at all, however, is a testament to local campaigners.

Threats to its survival first emerged in 1989 when Lewes District Council resolved to build an indoor leisure centre nearby.

The Council had, however, overlooked the fact that the pool had been built on land – the Pells – given to the people of Lewes in 1602 for purposes of recreation and 'in perpetuity'. Indeed the land was held on behalf of the people by the Town's Brooks Trust, of which all District Councillors were automatically trustees.

In other words, they were unable to dispose of the land because they did not actually own it.

In 1990 a group of alarmed residents formed the Save the Pells Pool Campaign and after two public inquiries managed not only to save the pool but to make it part of the town's Conservation Area.

Still, responsibility for financing the pool swung between the District Council and Town Council, neither of which wanted to meet the costs. For the year 1996-97 these amounted to nearly £65,000.

With receipts from the pool and a subsidy from the Town Council amounting to some £40,000, this left a shortfall of about £25,000.

Despite this funding gap, the campaigners never lost faith and in 2000 formed themselves into the Pells Pool Community Association, a not-for-profit charity. Soon after they took over the running of the pool from Lewes District Council.

At the same time Lewes Town Council offered an annual grant of £10,000, an arrangement that continues today. Further funds are raised through grants, sponsorship and events.

Conrad Ryle, a schoolteacher and chairman of the Association now looks forward to the pool's 150th anniversary as a local asset.

'It's affordable, provides healthy, supervised recreation for the town's youth and is a great place for families on a summer's day.'

▲ Reached via a short stroll from the town centre, along a millstream and over a small stone bridge, **Cirencester's Open Air Pool** in **Gloucestershire** appears relatively modern, set against the splendidly castellated barracks looming in the background.

And yet only thirteen years separates the two.

The barracks were completed in 1857, while the original pool, set up by eight local businessmen, opened in 1870. The pool is thus the second oldest open air pool operating in Britain, after the Pells Pool, Lewes (see previous page).

Cirencester was also the first open air pool to be run by local activists, back in 1973.

When first opened the water was pumped in from a nearby well and was often extremely cold. When Cirencester Urban District Council took it over in 1896 they therefore reduced the depth and filled it with warmer water from the mill stream.

Winifred Waites first started using the pool in the mid 1920s:

'There was no chlorination or water circulation. Instead it was filled every Sunday morning and emptied every Saturday evening. At the beginning of the week the water would be clean, but the temperature painfully low.

'By the end of the week, the water might have warmed up a little, but it had also got so dirty that by Saturday afternoon, covered with a green slime and full of leaves, bathing was free, though it was confined to those males who were not quite so fastidious.'

As a local grammar school girl, Winifred learnt to swim in the pool.

'Plunging into the icy water was an ordeal. We stayed in about 15-20 minutes, then, wet and shivering, endeavoured to dry ourselves in the ten minutes we were allowed. I can still feel the damp of my partially dried body and the numbness of my posterior as we marched back to school.

'We were not allowed to run, which might have warmed us up, as that was not considered ladylike.'

Finally in 1931 the water was heated and chlorinated, and dressing rooms added.

In 1970 the pool's centenary celebrations were muted by the discovery of several potentially serious problems.

Gallons of water were being lost every day, while the heating system was struggling. The Council, meanwhile, were keen to close it.

That it still operates today is thanks to a group of volunteers who formed themselves into the Open Air Swimming Pool Association, and in 1973 took over the pool's running from the local council.

Early indications were not positive. Season ticket sales were disappointing, and it needed the emergence of a fairy godmother, in the person of an ardent outdoor bather from a nearby village, to save the day by offering to stand surety for the running of the pool.

Thanks to her belief and the continuing efforts of volunteers, enough money has been raised since to install a new heating system, replace the changing-cubicles and carry out repairs.

As Winifred Waites says, 'Cirencester still has a fine outdoor pool, built in 1870 by private enterprise and kept going by private enterprise a hundred years later.'

▲ Not far from Glastonbury in the small Somerset town of **Street** lies an unexpected treasure.

The Grade II listed **Greenbank Swimming Pool** was a gift to the townspeople from Alice Clark, one of the Clark family firm of shoemakers, whose factory – which grew from humble beginnings in 1825 – brought the town its wealth and whose headquarters are still based there.

Much of Street's housing was built by Clarks for its workers, as was the pub and other public buildings. But there was no public pool, which meant that the menfolk were often to be seen skinny dipping in the local River Brue.

Alice, a firm believer in equal rights, decided that Street's women should be able to swim too, and so bequeathed in her will sufficient funds to build an open air pool.

Opened three years after her death in May 1937, the credit for the design is attributed to Bancroft Clark (son of the company chairman and later chairman himself) and Jack Stock.

Two adjoining pools were provided; a rectangular one for adults and a smaller semi-circular one for children. The former was for many years heated by cooling water piped in from the Clarks factory. (Since shoe production moved elsewhere in 1992 an independent heating system has been put in place.)

But it is the main entrance block (*above*) which earned the pool its listing. With its white rendered concrete walls, multi-pane metal frame windows and flat roofs, it is very much in the international Modern style – a complete contrast to its stone-dressed, gabled and tiled semi-detached neighbours (*see right*) and all the more elegant for it.

Flanking the central entrance block are two gently curved and unadorned white walls which screen the pools and turfed sunbathing areas from the road.

Either side of the main entrance are carved stone tablets by Henry Parr, one of which (*above right*) commemorates 'Alice Clark of Somerset, born Aug 1874, died May 1934'.

Run by a charitable trust and partly funded by Street Parish Council, Greenbank Pool enjoys an unusually long season, from early May to mid September.

▲ The fight for small lidos and open air pools is not confined to the shires and villages of Britain.

In London's outer suburbs a defiant reaction from swimmers saved the **Hampton Pool**, Middlesex, from demolition by Richmond Borough Council in 1984.

The pool, situated in the rustic setting of Bushy Park, opened in 1922, was modernised in 1939 and again in 1961, but in 1981 was closed after it was reckoned to be losing £40,000 a year. Two years later, the Council passed a resolution for its demolition.

Marshal Lees, a senior manager in a firm of chartered accountants and father of four, who lived opposite the pool, was incensed and promptly launched a fight back under the banner of 'Sink or Swim'.

'I gradually started accumulating information and then people,' he recalls. 'That was in September 1983.'

As it transpired he would remain active in the campaign for the next twelve years.

First, in 1984, Lees and his allies set up the Hampton Pool Ltd., a not-for-profit company and registered charity, and started talks with the Council, which at the time was a hung council.

This effort yielded an agreement that the Council would delay its own application for planning permission to bulldoze the site.

Shortly after, a by-election in Hampton Wick unexpectedly delivered the Council into the hands of the Liberal Democrats, who strongly supported the re-opening of the pool. They then examined a detailed report from Hampton Pool Ltd and agreed to offer a grant of £20,000, but only if the campaigners could match it with a similar sum.

In fact, £60,000 was raised and the pool – now heated – re-opened in the summer of 1985.

Twenty years later, Hampton Pool remains hugely popular, with about 100,000 admissions a year.

It has not all been plain sailing, however. In early 2001 a bid for Sports Lottery funding to repair the tank and add a diving-pit was rejected. Sport England admitted that although outdoor pools were 'technically eligible' for lottery aid they were 'extremely unlikely to receive any because seasonal factors significantly reduce their value for money'.

And yet the pool stays open all year round.

Since then plans have been scaled down, and further improvements funded by Richmond Council and Hampton Fuel Charity.

The pool has been re-lined and re-tiled and old pipework replaced. The next stage of works includes a new gym and upgraded changing facilities. The total for both phases is around £600,000, of which £500,000 has already been raised.

▼ Grandstands and a bandstand at two of Britain's most attractive community pools – the **Hathersage Open Air Pool**, on the edge of the Derbyshire Peak District (*below*) and **Ingleton Swimming Pool** in the Yorkshire Dales (*right*).

Opened in 1934, Hathersage is managed by the parish council, with support from the Derbyshire Dales Council and the High Peak Borough Council (which subsidises season tickets for local residents).

So popular is this heated pool, with its handsome timber stand and adjoining Victorian bandstand, that during the hot summer months the pool manager has to operate a strict 'one in, one out' policy.

Ingleton's tree-lined pool was built in 1933 by striking miners, assisted by workmen who were building a bridge over the adjoining River Greta.

Such was their haste to complete the task during that particularly

long hot summer that no-one remembered to seek permission from the landowner – an omission which had to be rectified later.

Originally filled from the river and emptied after a week's use, the pool was upgraded (and heated) during the 1970s, when a charitable trust was set up to run the pool and other recreational facilities in the village.

Since then further funding has been secured from donations, the National Lottery and from the EU's Structural Fund (Objective 5b) for rural communities.

Ingleton Pool is patently much cherished.

At the entrance a pristine kiosk offers drinks, snacks and ice-creams, as well as hiring out swimming costumes, hats and towels; a level of service usually found at only much grander lidos.

Also in common with much larger lidos of old, Ingleton offers

spectator accommodation, in the form of a terraced stand overlooking the pool. In 2004 tickets for these seats were priced at just 40p.

In the changing rooms, meanwhile, a polite but firm notice reminds visitors of how much

graft goes into the running of a community pool.

'These benches were funded by the work of Jackie and Jeni Rowe, and local children, who put a lot of effort into raising the money. Please take care of them.'

▲ Not all Britain's open air pools predate the Second World War.

Arundel Lido in **West Sussex**, was completed in 1960 on land donated three years earlier by the 16th Duke of Norfolk – whose family seat at Arundel Castle (*seen above in the distance, beyond the paddling pool*) dominates the town – to mark the 21st birthday of his eldest daughter, Lady Anne.

The Duke attached one condition to his gift; that the land be used for the construction of a public swimming-pool.

Arundel Council duly built a heated open air pool, 30m x 10m, plus a paddling pool for children.

Set in a rolling green meadow, both pools were opened in July 1960 by Lady Anne herself.

In 1999, however, Arun District Council, which had been running the pool for 25 years, decided that its operational costs were too high and attendances were too low. It thus transferred the site to Arun Town Council, who promptly invited bids from developers. There was even talk of a hotel on the site.

Rather as happened across the county border at the Pells Pool in Lewes (*see page 159*), as soon as this news emerged, residents quickly rallied round. This was, after all, the last surviving open air pool in West Sussex.

Besides which, there was also the original covenant to consider.

It was at this point that the Duke of Norfolk's four daughters stepped into the fray.

'When we realised that most people in Arundel were keen to keep the pool,' says Lady Mary Mumford, a younger sister of Lady Anne, 'we wanted to support them. We were thrilled to be asked.'

Their intervention undoubtedly had the desired effect. 'The Girls saved the pool!' is how many local people remember it.

The Friends of Arundel Lido also played a major part, raising some £35,000 through sponsorship, donations and special events.

For their part, Arun District Council and Arun Town Council then agreed to provide grants amounting to £212,000.

In the meantime, the Arundel and Downland Community Leisure Trust was established to operate the pool.

Arundel Lido was re-opened in June 2004, by Lady Mary.

Its main pool has been reduced in depth, partly to save money. The paddling-pool is now separated from the main pool by a barrier with two spray fountains, and both pools have been re-lined.

If its first season is anything to go by, Arundel Lido looks set to be another glowing example of a community run pool.

More than 10,000 visitors attended during the ten week summer period, as a result of which in 2005 both the season and opening hours were extended by popular demand.

▲ Chagford Pool, in the **Dartmoor National Park**, may have been modernised since this postcard was issued some 70 years ago, but the pool's rural setting remains still clearly recognisable.

What has changed is how the pool is managed.

Advertised as 'the largest outdoor freshwater swimming pool in Devon,' Chagford Pool was built in 1934 on a site made available by a local landowner, George Hayter-Hames, between a river and a mill-stream, from which the pool draws its water.

George's daughter Belinda remembers it well. 'The water was always freezing, even in summer,' she says, from the safe distance of Edinburgh. 'It comes straight off Dartmoor. Absolutely freezing.'

But the water temperature was not the only problem. By the mid-1990s conditions at the pool had fallen well short of Health and Safety requirements.

Says Marion Symes, who galvanised the village into action, 'I realised that if we didn't do something, we would lose the pool. I am absolutely passionate about it; for its unusualness and its simplicity.'

An action committee was formed, which in turn led to the pool coming under the aegis of the Chagford Recreational Trust.

This enabled the committee to access grants from such funding bodies as the Foundation for Sport & the Arts, South-West Regional Development Agency and Shell Better Britain.

For a year a local woman was also hired specifically to make funding applications. Other donations have come from local firms and individuals.

The first phase of restoration work, which began in 1998, cost around £120,000, a substantial sum for a village of only 2,000 residents. This paid for a new water filtration system, a children's paddling pool and, to huge relief, solar covers, which cover the pool at night to retain the daytime heat.

The pool itself is open only in the afternoons and early evenings. Two lifeguards have to be on duty at any one time – the biggest headache for any community pool – but they are at least paid through a grant from Chagford Parish Council.

The Trust meanwhile ensures that training is provided and basic life-saving skills taught to children.

▲ Just outside the boundaries of the Duke of Bedford's Woburn Estate in Bedfordshire are two outdoor village pools, both now run by trusts, but originally built by the 11th Duke, it is said, after a child had drowned in his lake.

Eversholt Swimming Pool (*above*), opened in 1910 but completely modernised in recent years, is in a village of just 300 residents, and is run by a committee of ten trustees.

Six miles away lies the second pool, at Woburn, opened in 1911.

There was a third village pool built by the Duke, at nearby Husborne Crawley, but this now lies derelict (*see page 172*).

▶ We finish this chapter with summaries of two pool campaigns which are yet to be resolved.

The **King's Meadow Swimming Baths** in **Reading** takes us back to the 19th century.

Reading Corporation were pioneers of open air pool provision when they funded a large, if basic outdoor pool for men, fed by water from the River Thames, on whose banks it was built in 1879.

A few yards from that pool a second, more substantial pool was built in 1902 – designed by the Borough Engineer, John Bowen – specifically for women.

That alone made it fairly rare. But a century later the King's Meadow Baths has an even wider significance.

Several examples of Edwardian indoor pools survive, for example in Liverpool, Manchester, Birmingham and even Reading, in the form of the Arthur Hill Pool, opened in 1911. But as a surviving example of a municipal open air pool of the early 20th century, King's Meadow may well be unique.

It is also a rather remarkable building in its own right.

As can be seen, with its ironwork loggia surrounding the 120 x 45 foot pool, it bears similarities to the much earlier Clifton Pool in Bristol (*see page 14*). But unlike Clifton, King's Meadow is a fully detached compound, set in parkland.

Its exterior walls – windowless on three sides – are in orange brick with white bands above. The fourth, south side has an octagonal entrance bearing a shield with the date 1902 (although it was not opened until the year after).

Patently it was designed with absolute privacy in mind.

Once mixed bathing became socially acceptable, King's Meadow opened its doors to

men, and operated as a normal, if characterful outdoor pool, popular with families. Its water supply, originally piped in from the Thames, was converted to the mains during the 1950s.

It was finally closed in 1974.

Since then King's Meadow has been used only as meeting place for a diving club, and has, as result, fallen into considerable disrepair.

Eventually Reading Borough Council decided to invite tenders to redevelop the site. Given its riverside location, close to the city centre, the pool seemed destined to be replaced by a hotel, sports pavilion and retail outlets.

Those plans were already in an advanced stage when, quite unexpectedly, the Department for Culture, Media and Sport decided to list the pool in August 2004.

A cause that had seemed dead and buried suddenly revived.

At the time of writing Reading Borough Council is considering its options, including talking to community groups as well as possibly undertaking a marketing exercise to explore potential uses for the pool.

But supporters of the King's Meadow Campaign are adamant that the pool should remain in public use.

Its chairman, Bob O'Neill, who swam there in his youth, points out there are no cafés serving the surrounding meadow, no public toilets, that the neighbouring playing fields would benefit from changing rooms and that commercial development would compromise what could, with imagination, become an attractive open space for tourists and walkers.

Naturally he hopes also to see the pool restored, perhaps with an option for ice skating in winter.

A lengthy and vigorous debate, in which English Heritage will be actively involved, along with other conservation interest groups, is fully expected.

▶ Another ongoing campaign of recent years concerns **Droitwich Spa Lido**, one of the few brine water pools to have operated in inland Britain. (Nantwich is now the only remaining example.)

Droitwich first developed as a spa in the mid 19th century, taking advantage of the presence of a large underground brine lake.

As the town struggled to attract visitors by the 1930s, however, the directors of the Norbury Hotel decided that a saltwater lido would prove the ideal draw for tourists.

To design the new lido in 1934 they secured the services of one of Britain's leading firms of landscape architects, Thomas H Mawson & Sons, which had earlier been responsible for Droitwich's Winter Gardens (as well as Blackpool's Stanley Park and the Hill Garden in Hampstead), and who would, in 1936, design Ruislip Lido for the Grand Union Canal Company.

The legendary Thomas Mawson himself was not involved – he died in 1933 – although it is possible his architect son, EP Mawson, had a hand in the design.

Its principal building, overlooking one end of the pool, is a detached Art Deco pavilion with an unusual projecting Crittall window on its upper storey.

But it was the quality of the pool's water – a mix of one part of brine to nine of freshwater – that won most praise.

As one dignitary announced at the lido's opening on 10 June 1935, 'The sea with all its health-giving properties has been brought to the heart of the Midlands.'

The pool, measuring 132 x 66 feet, was also heated, thus offering 'the exhilaration of open-air bathing with bathroom comfort.'

After 20 years in private hands, Droitwich Borough Council purchased the lido in 1953 for £15,000, which soon proved to be money well spent. Such were the profits earned during the hot summer of 1959 that the Council was able to reduce local rates by sixpence in the pound.

But as recounted in the lido's history (*see Links*), throughout the 1980s, as elsewhere, attendances went into decline.

In 1996, the current owners, Wychavon District Council, developed plans to convert the lido into a partially covered leisure and health centre. However failure to attract lottery funding led them to abandon the scheme, and in 2000 the lido was closed.

Ever since, local campaigners – under the apt banner of SALT (Save a Lido Today) – have fought for its re-opening.

In 2002, their attempt to get the lido listed was turned down, despite the endorsement of The Twentieth Century Society, which described it as 'an exceptionally interesting and well-preserved example of inter-war leisure architecture… of unusual quality and completeness'.

SALT followed this in November 2004 with a plan to erect an 'air-dome' over the pool, to allow it to stay open all year round. But this proposal met with rejection also, by the Council, who then voted to demolish the lido and incorporate the site into the adjoining park.

Once again SALT responded, this time with a renewed campaign in the media, and in April 2005 they were rewarded by the results of a specially convened parish poll to assess public opinion.

Over 4,000 votes were cast overall – a quarter of the electorate – resulting in a resounding majority for the restoration of the lido 'to its former splendour'.

SALT's aim is persuade the Council to form a charitable trust that, as we have seen in several earlier examples, appears to be a growing model for Britain's threatened community pools.

But with a second attempt to have the lido listed failing once again in June 2005, the campaign group faces an uphill task to retain the structures in their original form.

Droitwich Lido, before its much lamented closure in 2000, and again in 2004, in a forlorn state of abandonment. In the background stands the Mawson designed Art Deco pavilion, with its unusual projecting central window and flat roof.

Chapter Eight

Future

Plunging towards extinction or about to enter a sparkling new era? For historic lidos and open air pools such as Broomhill (*above*), Cleveland, King's Meadow and Uxbridge, the future remains uncertain, as it does for a number of lesser known pools. But as events elsewhere demonstrate, where investment has flowed, Britain's liquid assets have brimmed with renewed vigour. All it takes is a leap of the imagination.

When the authors of the aptly named Thirties Society publication *Farewell My Lido* concluded their study in 1991 (*see Links*), the future prospects for Britain's lidos looked grim.

Over the previous two decades closure after closure had virtually halved the number of open air pools left operating since the end of the Second World War.

In 1991 Britain's lidos appeared to be neglected, underfunded, and unappreciated at every level of government and within the realms of the sporting establishment.

As the authors noted ruefully, had the historic Piscine Molitor in Paris been in Britain, it too would probably have been demolished.

'Now is the time,' was the report's conclusion, 'to bring lidos back out of the cold and into the floodlight of publicity.'

Fourteen years after *Farewell My Lido* did just that, how might *Liquid Assets* maintain that exposure?

In this concluding chapter we summarise the main issues and challenges which look set to face Britain's lidos and open air pools in the years ahead.

Closures

Since 1991 the rate of closures has barely slowed. Between 2000 and 2005 ten more have closed: at Banbury and Carterton (Oxfordshire), Bulwell (Nottingham), Compton Leisure Centre (Northolt), Cumnock (Ayrshire), Droitwich Spa (Worcestershire), Hendy (Carmarthen), Broomhill (Ipswich), Malmesbury (Wiltshire) and St Neots (Cambridgeshire).

Another, Royston in Hertfordshire, is scheduled to close at the end of 2005.

As of mid 2005 this leaves just under 100 public open air pools remaining in use.

But still this total is expected to fall further. On the danger list as this book went to press were Abingdon (Oxfordshire), Beccles and Halesworth (Suffolk), Hilsea Lido (Portsmouth), and Letchworth (Hertfordshire).

If the present rate of closure continues, therefore, it is possible to predict that some time between 2030 and 2040 there will be few, if any open air pools still operating in this country.

The need for vigilance and public awareness has therefore barely receded at all since 1991.

Conservation and protection

Of immediate concern is the fate of three historic survivors; namely the Cleveland Pool (Bath), King's Meadow (Reading) and Broomhill Pool (Ipswich). (A fourth, the Clifton Pool in Bristol, is currently being refurbished.)

All three are disused and in danger of further deterioration. They are, however, all listed.

In fact, as *Farewell My Lido* fervently hoped would be the case, the level of statutory protection has increased substantially.

In 1991, just three open air pools – Cleveland Pool, Worthing and Saltdean – were listed, of which only the latter was still operating. As noted on page 25, a further eleven open air pools and lidos have been listed since.

Are there any remaining locations which might yet be considered for listing?

That can only be a matter for further investigation. But if there are potential candidates, we hope that *Liquid Assets* will offer a useful resource in any subsequent evaluation.

Best Value

Without radical and imaginative changes in the way our open air pools and lidos are operated, we must expect more to fall victim to the 'Best Value' system of reckoning, introduced under the Local Government Act 1999.

Local authorities are required under this system to measure the 'economy, efficiency and effectiveness' of all their facilities and services.

It was exactly such a review that led to the closure of Bulwell Lido by Nottingham City Council in 2003. Every swim at the lido, it was calculated, was costing the Council £5-6.

As a follow-up to that report, consultants recommended that the Council rationalise its existing pools and invest more in the remaining facilities.

In February 2005, the Bulwell site was therefore sold, for £1.2 million, money which, the Council has stated will go towards improving the Ken Martin Leisure Centre 'to meet the needs and expectations of today's customers... and better promote sport, active lifestyles, health and well-being.'

The Ken Martin Leisure Centre is, of course, indoors.

Funding

As we learnt in Chapters Six and Seven, both public and private funds have been ploughed into historic lidos to an extent that would have seemed unimaginable in the 1980s and early 1990s.

Plymouth City Council invested £3.7 million in the refurbishment of Tinside Lido in 2003. »

▲ Crumbling and overgrown, in 2005 **London Fields Lido**, in London's east end – the earliest surviving example of what is thought to be a Rowbotham and Smithson design for the LCC, opened in 1932 – looked to be beyond redemption.

But Hackney's swimmers are hardened campaigners. The nearby Edwardian baths at Haggerston closed in 2000, while a brand new £7.5 million pool at Clissold Park ended up costing £32 million in 2001, only to be closed for repairs after just 20 months in use.

But the London Fields saga at least looks set to have a rather happier outcome.

After the lido closed in 1988, campaigners fought first to prevent its demolition, and then spent years lobbying, before, in 2004, Hackney Borough Council finally decided to restore it to its former glory.

The £2.5m scheme, drawn up by S&P Architects, will see the tank relined to create a 50 x 17m deck level pool, with a reduced maximum depth of 2m, together with the complete overhaul of the original buildings. The pool will also be heated, using solar energy, and designed to allow for a 'bubble' (or air-supported dome) to be installed for use during the winter months.

As in south London at Brockwell Park, when the restoration is completed in 2006 the lido's operation will be handed over to a not-for-profit organisation.

By then, 18 years will have passed since London Fields was last in use. As campaigners elsewhere will no doubt note, where there is still a building, there will always be hope.

Life after lidos – Worthing Lido (*top*) is now an entertainment centre, Husborne Crawley (*above*) became a fish farm, while in Wallasey the Derby Pool is a pub.

» In 2005 the Corporation of London spent £2.8 million on Parliament Hill Fields Lido, and may add to this spending in future years. Other big spenders have been Guildford (£1.6m) and Wandsworth Borough Council, at Tooting Bec Lido (£600,000).

Current spending plans include £2.5 million at Brockwell Park Lido in south London, and a similar sum at London Fields Lido in east London (*see previous page*).

At Hillingdon, meanwhile, funding is also being sought for the restoration of Uxbridge Lido, as part of a larger sports complex.

In short, the rapid and inexorable decline that seemed almost inevitable in 1991 appears to have been partially arrested, in southern Britain at least.

But despite these significant capital sums, the ongoing costs of operating open air pools and lidos cannot be lightly dismissed.

For example, Penwith District Council received £295,000 from the Heritage Lottery Fund for refurbishing its Jubilee Pool, in Penzance, in 1994. To this the Council added a similar sum from its own coffers, and won deserved acclaim in the process.

Yet a decade later Penwith now calculates that every swim at the Jubilee Pool is costing local ratepayers between £16-18. Put another way, the pool costs £120,000 a year to run, yet is open only for three or four months.

Heartening though it is therefore to see such an injection of Lottery and other public funds, the ongoing costs remain an appreciable burden.

Multi-functionality

In order to meet these routine costs, a major priority for operators of open air pools, and for their would-be designers, is to find ways to cater for, and attract as many additional sources of revenue as possible.

Diversification has assumed particular importance since the publication in March 2005 of the government's *Choosing Activity* consultation paper (part of its public health White Paper, *Choosing Health*).

Its main aim is to increase participation in sport as a means of improving the nation's health, in much the same spirit as the campaign for fitness launched in 1937 under the Physical Training and Recreation Act.

In support of this policy, Sport England, which administers the Sports Lottery Fund, has pledged to give priority to 'multi-use, multi-activity' projects.

The message is clear. Even if they survive scrutiny under Best Value, single-use, seasonal outdoor pools are still unlikely to receive funding via Sport England.

But how can pools be adapted to achieve multi-functionality?

Simply because the majority of our lidos were built during the first half of the 20th century does not mean that the building form itself is somehow preserved in aspic.

Clearly the form must evolve.

Triathletes, sub-aqua divers and canoeists are all regulars at Hampton, Stroud and Tooting Bec, for instance. At Saltdean, Sandford Parks and Guildford, fully equipped poolside gyms generate an income, all year round. Other increasingly popular activities are yoga, tai chi and aerobics.

But many of these activities depend on the availability and suitability of ancillary buildings, not on the pools themselves.

In this respect the extension of Brockwell Park's facilities »

▶ There exists in Britain a hardy minority for whom swimming pool water, indoor or outdoor, remains an abomination, a clinically dead concoction of chemicals.

For these 'open swimmers', paradise is no urban beach, but a natural lake or river or flooded quarry in the middle of nowhere.

Before creeping urbanisation, London used to offer many such wet and wild opportunities.

Now, apart from certain stretches of the Thames, only the ponds on Hampstead Heath fit the bill.

Of the Heath's 23 ponds, three are set aside for swimming. In the chain visible here – known as the Highgate Ponds – is the Ladies Pond, second from bottom (and in public use since 1925), with the much older Men's Pond the most distant. To the far right, hidden amongst trees, is the Mixed Pond.

Just visible also, as a sliver of blue in the top left corner, lies Parliament Hill Fields Lido, with its hard edges and chlorinated water.

In fact, the ponds are almost as man-made as the lido, having been dug as reservoirs in the 17th and 18th centuries. They were later cleaned up by the LCC in 1893, and improved a second time in 1905 after 600 swimmers protested at the 'accumulation of mud and broken glass'.

But for all their Arcadian charms, in recent years the Heath ponds have become a battleground for what open swimmers would consider to be two ancient rights.

The first concerns the right to swim on early mornings in winter, a tradition that the Corporation of London – which took over management of the Heath in 1989 – wished to curtail in order to save costs on lifeguards.

So grave was this assault on custom that the ponds' numerous

interest groups took the matter to the High Court in April 2005, where, to their delight, and that of all free spirits, Mr Justice Stanley Burnton judged that so long as individuals took responsibility for their own actions, they could swim without lifeguards present, and that, just as importantly, the Corporation of London would be immune from prosecution under

health and safety legislation should an accident occur.

But if this was one landmark victory, on a second front, also bitterly contested, the pond users were to suffer defeat.

For over 250 years swimmers had enjoyed the ponds without charge. In June 2005, however, the Corporation introduced a £2 entry fee, payable via an honesty box.

The swimming community was scandalised. An ancient right had been breeched. Civil disobedience was threatened. Pay machines were ignored, or even vandalised.

From the air all appears tranquil. Yet down below, rebellion ripples across the water. Whether defending a lido or a lake, it would seem, Britain's swimmers always always always shall make waves.

▲ **Wotton Pool**, run by Stroud District Council, was one of the first public outdoor pools to be fitted with a sliding roof. Consisting of four 10m telescopic sections, the polycarbonate roof cost £60,000 to install in 1999. A larger version today would cost £250-300,000.

Problems with heating the interior prevent the pool opening in midwinter, but the roof does allow daily use from May to September, whatever the weather.

》 in south London (*see page 141*) might provide a telling model for the future.

Where pools are located within parks or close to playing fields, there might also be potential for changing rooms to be adapted for use by teams and athletes other than in the summer season.

Extending the season

According to figures from the Meteorological Office, the hottest August on record was that of 2003. Moreover, researchers at the University of Berne predict that every second summer in the 21st century will be at least as hot as it was in 2003.

For better or worse therefore, climate change could offer British lidos an extended lease of life.

Of the hundred or so operating in Britain as of 2005 (*see page 182*), only four remain open all year round. These are at Tooting Bec, Parliament Hill Fields, the Oasis and Hampton

Hampton is heated, as are 80 per cent of all open air pools currently operating. And as Tracey Emin pointed out in her foreword, there is something quite special about swimming in a heated outdoor pool in winter.

It would therefore be wonderful if more heated pools stayed open for longer periods.

Nor should we forget the success of those community pools, such as Stonehaven (*see page 84*), where night-time swimming sessions have been re-introduced.

One possible means of extending useage is the use of retractable pool covers, such as the one installed at Wotton Pool in Stroud (*see left*), and at Waterside Pool, Ryde, on the Isle of Wight.

There are plans for similar installations at Highworth Recreation Centre (Wiltshire) and Arundel Lido (West Sussex).

Sliding roofs are also to be found at several lidos in Paris.

For existing pools, such roofs are only likely to be practical where the tank is relatively narrow. But at larger sites air-supported domes may offer an option, while for new build, the technology is forever improving. The All England Club at Wimbledon, for example, is to have a sliding roof over its new Centre Court by 2009, using a form of folding lightweight and translucent fabric.

A purpose-built modern lido could benefit similarly.

Pooling research

Innovations such as sliding roofs require careful planning.

For this reason, *Played in Britain* endorses existing efforts to bring together lido operators, designers, commercial providers and user groups to share knowledge.

A model for this could be the Football Stadia Advisory Design Council, which from 1990-93 encouraged parties from within football and the stadium sector to share best practice and develop research.

There already exist strong lobbying organisations formed by community groups and pool users, such as the London Pools Campaign. Parties on the other side of the table, as it were, should be encouraged to pool their experience too.

Clearly there is much to be gained from such a process.

Already thermal covers, such as at Chagford (*see page 165*), are routinely used to retain daytime heat overnight. Advances in solar powered heating units also hold the promise of sustainable energy and lower fuel bills. 》

There are no rules to say that lidos cannot be built in city centres, just as they were in Roman times.

Hidden away behind an eleven storey office block and a housing estate, the 27 x 10m open air pool at the **Oasis Sports Centre** in Endell Street, London – owned by Camden Council but managed by Holmes Place – is hugely popular amongst office workers, local residents and tourists in the know.

For swimming or for posing it has no rival in Britain.

The site itself has an interesting past. A bagnio operated in the vicinity from c.1730 to 1851, to be replaced by the Bloomsbury Baths and Washhouses in 1852, then Holborn Baths in 1902.

When work on the current pool started in 1937 it was intended as an indoor facility. Then war broke out, and the half-finished pool was commandeered as a water tank – hence its tag, the Oasis – before being finally opened, but as an uncovered facility, in June 1946.

It was central London's first outdoor baths since the Peerless Pool (*see page 12*) closed in 1850.

The complex as it appears today dates from 1960, when, in an early example of a public-private partnership, an indoor pool – 25 x 9m, designed by the Holborn Borough architect Sidney Cook – was built alongside the outdoor pool by the developers of the office block which now conceals the pool from the West End bustle outside.

Oasis by name, oasis by nature. Why can't every city have one?

▲ Floating swimming pools are hardly new. The French built one on the River Seine in 1786, followed by the Victorians with an iron and glass structure by London's Hungerford Bridge in 1875 (of which more in *Great Lengths*, a future *Played in Britain* book on indoor swimming pools).

Architect Alex Lifschutz, of Lifschutz Davidson, designed this modern marvel for a mooring by the South Bank in 1998.

Although never built it provides a tantalising glimpse of how lido design might develop.

Measuring 50 x 16m, the pool itself occupies the upper deck of the hull, with changing rooms in the basement, below the river water level, and cafés and sun decks occupying the mid level.

Encasing the upper storey is a crystalline glass roof, allowing swimmers a 360 degree view out across the Thames. The central roof section slides to one side to provide the benefits of open air swimming, while integrated solar panels heat the water all year round.

Until such a pool is built in Britain the nearest modern equivalent is a £9 million, 90 x 20m floating pool with retractable roof, designed by Robert de Busny and moored on the River Seine in Paris, opposite the Bibliotethèque Nationale.

》 In the 1930s lidos were built to meet the demand for sunbathing. How appropriate it would be therefore for the lidos of the 21st century to become solar powered themselves.

But where to start? Which system to use? There needs to be a co-ordinated approach as to how this and other technological opportunities might be met, if lido operators, and therefore the public, are to gain the maximum benefit.

Health and safety

Like all public amenities, outdoor swimming pools are duty bound to meet standards set by the Health and Safety Executive.

Most of these standards are not legal requirements but 'best practice' guidelines, intended to minimise risk. But in an age of 'blame and claim', pool operators naturally err on the side of caution.

So for example the Atlantis Water Park in Scarborough (the former North Bay lido) failed to open at the start of the 2005 season simply because the floor of the pool had been painted in the wrong shade of blue. This was not just a matter of aesthetics. The darker shade, it was said, would prevent a lifeguard from spotting a body in the water.

The question is, will today's already onerous health and safety regime become ever stricter?

Few can argue with the decision not to allow diving in areas where others are swimming. But many fear that a recent move to discourage the use of large goggles, on the grounds that they could harm both the wearer and other swimmers, is a step too far.

In this respect the High Court struck a notable blow for risk-takers in April 2005 when it ruled in favour of unsupervised winter swimming at the Highate ponds in north west London (*see page 171*).

But even if no further controls are imposed, there are still concerns that ever higher insurance premiums will place an untenable burden, particularly on smaller community-run pools.

Health benefits

Finally, we return to the social and health benefits of open air swimming.

In the late Victorian and early 20th century most of Britain's publicly funded open air pools were free of charge.

At a time when so many concerns are being voiced about the health of the nation, what better way to spend health promotion budgets than to encouraging free visits to lidos?

In Wales, after all, the Welsh Assembly has introduced a free swimming scheme for all people aged under 16 and over 60. Glasgow City Council operates a similar scheme, as does Plymouth at its Mountwise Pools.

In his seminal 1930 book *Modern Public Baths*, Kenneth MB Cross, architect of the Super Swimming Stadium in Morecambe, wrote, 'Fresh air, sunlight, exercise and companionship are essential to the fullness of life, and the provision of the necessary facilities is not a luxury; it is an urgent and ever insistent national need if the standard of physique and morale of our people is not to be allowed to deteriorate.'

Supporters of lidos would argue that 75 years later, nothing has changed to challenge that view.

The purpose of this book has been to celebrate Britain's open air pools and lidos; to record what we have lost and to bolster efforts to save what we can.

We hope also to have shown that this should not be the end of the story; that there remain powerful arguments for building new and improved open air pools for the very same reasons expounded by Kenneth Cross and his fellow pioneers of the early 20th century.

In short, we believe in increasing, not diminishing our nation's liquid assets.

There is value, and there is life in the British lido yet.

A fountain to the gods – fresh air, sunlight and sparkling water bathe nature in glorious colour at Sandford Parks Lido in Cheltenham. In 2005 the pool celebrated its 70th anniversary. The gods must know paradise when they see it.

Defunct lidos and open air pools

The defunct lidos and open air pools in this directory are included on the basis of two main criteria; that they were open to the public for at least part of the 20th century, and that the lido, pool or its related buildings were designed structures. Private lidos and pools, and naturally formed tidal pools are not included. A directory of lidos and open air pools currently operating (as of June 2005) follows on page 182.

Both parts of the directory have been compiled from the author's own researches, from data kindly supplied by Dr Ian Gordon (author of our forthcoming book on indoor swimming pools, *Great Lengths*), and from a variety of other web-based sources, including Oliver Merrington's excellent www.lidos.org.uk (*see* Links). *Played in Britain* welcomes additions and amendments to the directory, which will be updated and available to view at our website: www.playedinbritain.co.uk.

Measurements are given in feet, except for more recently built pools where m = metres.
Locations are listed under either counties, towns or cities
* indicates location is subject of a case study in this book

England

Location	Name and Address	Opened	Size	Architect	Outcome
Bath	Cleveland Pleasure Baths, Hampton Row, Bathwick	1815	137 x 38	–	Closed c.1985 (listed Grade II)
Barnsley	Barnsley Bathing Pool, Cudworth, Carlton Road	1926	–	–	Indoor 1971
Beds	Bedford Outdoor Pool, Commercial Road	1936	165 x 60	CH Blakeway	Demolished 1980s
	Dunstable Lido, Whipsnade Road	1935	110 x 45	J Blake	Closed 1973
	Husborne Crawley Outdoor Pool, Mill Road	c.1910	–	–	Closed, now fish farm
	Stewartby Outdoor Pool	–	–	–	–
	Wardown Swimming Centre, Bath Rd, Luton	1935	165 x 90	JW Tomlinson	Closed 1990s
Berks	East Street, Maidenhead	1909	100 x 40	Mr Johns	Demolished c.1937
	Showboat Lido, Maidenhead	–	–	N Bailey / DC Wadhwa	–
Birmingham	Bournville Open Air Bath, Oak Farm Rd, Rowheath	1937	100 x 50	E Stanley Hall et al	Now housing
	Brookvale Park, Erdington	1909	–	–	Closed 1926
	Cannon Hill Park Open Air Pool, Edgbaston	1873	216 x 100	–	Closed 1939, Midland Arts Centre.
	Keepers Pool, Sutton Park, Sutton Coldfield	1887	75 x 20	Borough surveyor	Closed 2002 after fire
	Shirley Sports Lido, Sansome Rd, Shirley	1936	–	–	Closed 1939, now printworks
	Small Heath Park Open Air Pool, Tennyson Road	1883	138 x 85	–	Closed 1939
Blackpool	South Shore Baths*	1923	376 x 172	JC Robinson & F Wood	Closed 1981
Bradford	Lister Park Swimming Bath	1915	150 x 60	W Dawson & W Williamson	Closed 1983
Brighton	Black Rock Baths	1935	165 x 60	D Edwards	Demolished 1978
	Rottingdean Lido, Undercliff Walk, Rottingdean	1935	100 x 35	D Edwards	Closed 1990s
Bristol	Ashton Park Swimming Bath	c.1906	–	–	–
	Clifton Pool, Victoria Park	1850	–	–	Closed c 1990, listed Grade II
	Eastville Park Swimming Bath	1904	120 x 35	–	Bombed WW2, garden
	Greville Smyth Park	1905	120 x 35	–	–
	Shirehampton Park Road	1935	75 x 30	CW Denning	–
	Victoria Park Swimming Bath	c.1904	120 x 35	–	–
Bucks	Buckingham Open Air Pool, London Road	1955/1977	–	–	–
	Burnham Sea Bathing Lake	1931	Semi-circular	G Pimm	Demolished 1991
	Vale Park Swimming Pool, Park Street, Aylesbury	1935	132 x 48	WH Taylor	Closed c 1998
Cambs	Ely Open Air Pool, Angle Grove	1934	82 x 33	AE King	Closed 1980
	St Neots Open Air Pool, Huntingdon Street	1962	50m	–	Closed 2003
	Wisbech Open Air Pool, Osborne Road	1911	132 x 30	Borough surveyor	–
Cheshire	Congleton Pool, Park Road	1936	105 x 45	J Hood	–
	Ellesmere Port Pool, Rivacre Valley	1934	165 x 60	C Davis	Closed 1980
Cornwall	St Ives	1913	–	HJ Softley	Closed c1940
Coventry	Gosford Park Open Air Pool, Walls Grave Road	1934	–	A Ling	Closed, now car park
Cumbria	Grange-over-Sands Open Air Pool, The Seafront	1932	165 x 105	B Smith	Closed c.1993
Derbyshire	Alfreton Open Air Pool, Alfreton Park	1964	–	–	Closed 2002
	Inkerman Pool, Ashgate Rd, Chesterfield	1910	180 x 150	–	Demolished 1950s
	Martham Open Air Pool, Chasworth Road, Chesterfield	1936	75 x 30	–	–

Location	Name and Address	Opened	Size	Architect	Outcome
	Wittington Moor Open Air Pool, Chesterfield	1936	75 x 25	WS Wilson	–
	Ilkeston Open Air Pool, Wharncliffe Road, Victoria	1921	60 x 30	HJ Hilford	Demolished 1974
	Long Eaton Open Air Pool, Grange Park, Station Road	1935	150 x 50	H Haven	Closed c.1977
	Matlock Lido, Imperial Road	1938	125 x 50	–	Roofed over 1974
Devon	Barnstaple Open Air Pool, Rock Park	1930	100 x 30	–	Demolished 1975
	Buckfastleigh Open Air Pool, Plymouth Road	1906	70 x 30	–	–
	Exmouth Open Air Pool, The Esplanade	c.1930	150 x 30	–	–
	Okehampton Pool, Simmonds Park	–	–	–	Closed c.1989, now covered
	Mountwise Baths, Plymouth	1934	150 x 54	–	Re-designed as 3 pools
	Penn Inn, Newton Abbott	1935	–	–	Demolished 1987, supermarket.
Dorset	The Swimming Pool, Blandford Forum	1922	–	–	Closed c.1994
	Shaftesbury Pool, Shaftesbury	–	–	–	Closed 2004, future uncertain
	Poole Open Air Pool, Lake Park Road	1929	–	–	Demolished 1975, car park
Co Durham	Ryton Open Air Pool, Ferndene Park, Gateshead	1958	–	–	–
	Hartlepool Bathing Pool, Albion Terrace, Hartlepool	1923	–	–	Closed 1950s
	Murton Pool, Murton Colliery, Seaham	1962	50m	–	–
Essex	Braintree Open Air Pool, Rose Hill	1914	–	–	Demolished 1987
	Brentwood Pool, North Road	1935	120 x 48	–	Closed c.1976
	Clacton-on-Sea Pool, Pierhead	1934	165 x 60	–	Closed by 1989
	Colne Bank Avenue Pool, Chelmsford	1906	150 x 100	C Brown	–
	Southend Seawater Swimming Bath, Western Esplanade	1915	330 x 70	EJ Elford	–
Gloucs	Bathurst Pool, Lydney	1920	120	–	–
Gtr London	Alexandra Park Open Air Baths, Alexandra Park	1875	–	–	Closed c.1920s/30s
	Barking Open Air Pool, Barking Park	1931	165 x 90	RA Lay	Closed 1988, filled in
	Bellingham Open-Air Pool, Bromley Road	1922	150 x 60	W Owsley & H Higgins	Closed 1980
	Bexley Open Air Pool, Danson Park	1936	165 x 90	GA Joy	Closed 1980 Dem 1982
	Bickley Lido (see Bromley Open Air Pool)	–	–	–	
	Blue Pool, Uxbridge Road, Hillingdon	1933	–	–	Closed 1938 Savoy cinema
	Bromley Open Air Pool, Baths Rd, Bromley	1925	150 x 50	S Hawkins	Now Gatsby Spa
	Compton Leisure Centre, Bengarth Road, Northolt	–	–	–	Closed 2004
	Charles Crescent Lido, Bessborough Road, Harrow	1923	165 x 75	P Bennetts	Closed 1981, housing
	Craven Park Lido, Craven Park, Willesden	1935	165 x 60	F Wilkinson	Bombed WW2
	Durnsford Road Lido, Bounds Green	1934	165 x 92	EP Mawson	Closed 1989, garden centre.
	Ealing Northern Sports Centre, Greenford Road	–	100 x 50	–	–
	East Ham Open Air Baths, Central Park	1902	90 x 30	–	Closed 1923
	Edensor Baths, Edensor Road, Chiswick	1930	100 x 35	–	Closed 1980, indoor pool
	Eltham Park Lido, Glenesk Road	1924	150 x 60	Borough engineer	Closed 1990, derelict
	Enfield Lido, Southbury Road	1932	200 x 80	HR Crabb	Closed 1991, leisure complex
	Erith Outdoor Pool, Stonewood Road	1907	60 x 25	H Hind	Closed 1967
	Finchley Lido, High Road*	1932	165 x 80	P Harrison	Closed 1993, leisure complex
	Geraldine Mary Harmsworth Lido, St George's Rd, SE1	1938	90 x 90	–	Closed early 1980s
	Gladstone Park Open Air Pool, Dollis Hill Lane, Willesden	1903	240 x 78	–	Closed c1980s, bowling green
	Highbury Fields Lido, Highbury Crescent	1923	180 x 60	CA Smith	Closed 1980s, indoor pool
	Houndsfield Lido, Houndsfield Road, Edmonton	1927	150 x 100	–	Closed 1980, housing
	Kennington Park Lido, The Oval	1931	165 x 66	–	Closed 1988, now tennis courts
	King Edward's Pool, Donnington Road, Willesden	1911	165 x 75	–	Closed 1991
	Kingfisher Pool, Highams Park, Woodford Green	1934	–	–	–
	Kingsbury Lido, Roe Green Park, Kingsbury Road	1939	165 x 75	CS Trapp	Closed 1988
	Lagoon Bathing Pool, Lagoon Road, St Mary Cray	1933	–	E O'Sullivan	Closed 1939
	Larkswood Open Air Pool, New Rd, Chingford*	1936	220 x 90	SJ Hellier	Closed 1988, leisure centre
	Leys Open Air Pool, Old Dagenham Park	1939	165 x 50	FC Lloyd	Closed 1980
	London Fields Lido, Richmond Rd, Hackney	1932	165 x 66	–	Closed 1988, plans to re-open
	Martens Grove Heated Outdoor Pool, Bexleyheath	1939	100 x 35	FA Turner	Closed 1984
	Mill Hill Swimming Pool, Daws Lane, Mill Hill	1935	165 x 75	AO Knight	Closed c.1980, garden centre
	Millwall Open Air Pool, Recreation Gd, Cubitt Town	1925	150 x 60	H Weckford	Closed 1939, demolished 1960s
	Peckham Rye Bathing Pool, Peckham Rye Park	1923	180 x 60	–	Closed c.1987, parkland
	Poplar Open Air Baths, Violet Rd, Bromley-by-Bow	1924	100 x 40	H Weckford	Closed 1936, council depot
	Purley Way Lido, Purley Way, Croydon*	1935	100/60 & 200/70	CE Boast	Closed 1980, garden centre
	Roehampton Open Air Baths, Priory Lane, Roehampton	1934	120 x 60	GW Smith	Demolished 1970s, flats

Location	Name and Address	Opened	Size	Architect	Outcome
	Ruislip Lido, Reservoir Road, Ruislip	1936	–	GW Smith	Closed c.1990
	Silvertown Open Air Bath, Royal Victoria Gardens	1922	100 x 40	–	Closed 1948
	Southall Open Air Bath, Florence Road, Southall	1913	120 x 30	R Brown	Closed 1982
	Southlands Lido (see Bromley Open Air Pool)				
	Southwark Park Lido	1923	–	–	Closed 1989, arts centre
	Surbiton Lagoon, Raeburn Avenue, Surbiton	1934	165 x 90	HT Mather	Closed 1979, housing
	Teddington Lido, Vicarage Road	1931	120 x 48	HC Hunt	–
	Tottenham Lido, Lordship Lane	1937	165 x 75	H Wilkinson	Lido Square housing estate
	Twickenham Lido, The Embankment	1936	165 x 55	–	Closed c.1981
	Uxbridge Lido, Park Road*	1935	220 x 72.5	G Percy Trentham	Closed 1998, may re-open
	Valence Park Lido, Becontree, Dagenham	1931	150 x 50	TP Francis	Demolished
	Valentine's Park Lido, Perth Road, Ilford	1924	150 x 50	H Shaw	Closed 1995
	Victoria Park Lido, Grove Road, Hackney*	1936	200 x 90	H Rowbotham / T Smithson	Closed 1989, car park
	Wandle Park, Croydon	1913	150 x 50	–	Closed c.1970s
	Wandsworth Open Air Pool, King George's Park	1938	165 x 60	E Elford	Closed mid 1990s
	Wealdstone Open Air Baths, Christchurch Avenue	1934	165 x 75	P May	Closed 1997
	Wembley Open Air Baths, Vale Farm, Watford Road	1932	165 x 75	C Chapman	–
	West Ham Lido, Beckton Park, Canning Town	1937	165 x 90	WL Jenkins	Closed 1987, A13 on site
	West Hendon Lido, Goldsmith Ave, Colindale	1922	132 x 66	AO Knight	Closed 1980, housing
	Whipps Cross Lido, Walthamstow	1932	–	–	Closed 1983
	White City Lido, Bloemfontein Rd, Hammersmith	1923	150 x 75	R Hampton Clucas	Demolished 1984, indoor pool
	Wimbledon Open Air Bath, Wandle Park	1914	150 x 50	–	Closed 1936
	Yiewsley Pool, Otterfield Rd, Yiewsley	1934	120 x 30	–	Covered 1976
Hampshire	Andover Open Air Pool, London Street	1936	–	–	Indoor pool 1976
	Basingstoke Pool, West Ham Park	1906	100 x 25	–	Demolished 1966
	Central Baths, Gosport	1924	220 x 57	–	Closed 1982
	Ringwood Open Air Pool, Carver's Park	–	–	–	
	Bull Drove Bathing Place, Garnier Road, Winchester	1886	–	–	Closed c.1966
	The Lido, Worthy Rd, Winchester	1934	80 x 40	Mr Warwick	Closed 1973
	Recreation Ground, North Walls, Winchester	1911	135 x 70	City surveyor	Closed 1946
Herts	Berkhamstead Open Air Pool	1923	–	–	Closed 1990
	The Cloisters Swimming Pool, Letchworth	1907	–	–	Closed
	Harpenden Open Air Pool, Rothampstead Park	c.1965	–	–	Closed 1996
	Hemel Hempstead Pool, Park Road, Churchill	1937	165 x 60	A Murray	–
	Letchworth Garden City Baths, Pixmore Way	1908	75 x 40	–	Closed 1935, garden
	Rickmansworth Open Air Pool, Ebury Road	1909	100 x 36	–	Closed 1968
	St Albans Open Air Pool, Cotton Mill Lane	1905	105 x 30	G Ford	Closed 1970s
	Welwyn Garden City Pool, Stanborough Park	1935	50m	–	Closed 1998, Splashland
Humberside	Albert Avenue Pools, Anlaby Road, Hull	1908	80 x 60	–	–
Isle of Man	Ramsey Open Air Pool, The Seafront	1902	–	–	–
Isle of Wight	Seaclose Lido, Fairlee Road, Newport	1936	100 x 35	GA Gentry	Closed c.1979
Kent	Dartford Open Air Pool, Burnham Road	1910	90 x 36	–	Demolished 1976
	Folkestone Open Air Pool, Marine Parade	1936	165 x 90	EP Mawson	Demolished 1980s
	Gravesend Lido, The Promenade	1911	150 x 75	J Garrett Bennett	–
	Margate Lido, Seafront, Cliftonville*	1927	250 x 150	Mr Palmer	Closed 1977, sand
	Marine Terrace Sands, Margate	1937	320 x 250	EA Borg	Closed c.1990
	Walpole Bay, Margate	1937	450 x 400	EA Borg	Closed 1957
	Ramsgate Lido, The Seafront	1935	250 x 90	LG Mouchel	Demolished 1988
	Sheerness Lido, The Esplanade	1939	150 x 72	–	Demolished
Lancashire	Bubbles Swimming Centre, Marine Road, Morecambe	c.1981	Circular	–	Demolished 2001
	Edenfield Open Air Pool, Dearden Clough	1900	75 x 36	–	Demolished
	Fleetwood Open Air Pool, The Esplanade	1925	264 x 108	B Drummond	Demolished 1972
	Haslam Park & Ribbleton Park, Preston	–	–	–	Closed c.1970
	Marsden Park Open Air Pool, Walton Lane, Nelson	1930s	100 x 35	FV Alexander	Closed 1999
	Bathing Pool, Moor Park, Preston	1905	100 x 50	J Smethurst	Closed 1971
	St Anne's Bathing Pool, St Anne's	1916	240 x 120	F Harrison	Closed 1989
	Super Swimming Stadium, Morecambe*	1936	330 x 110	KMB Cross / CAL Sutton	Closed 1975
Leeds	Otley Open Air Pool, Wharfe Meadows Park	1935	–	–	–
	Roundhay Bathing Pool, Roundhay Park	1907	150 x 60	–	Closed 1980

Location	Name and Address	Opened	Size	Architect	Outcome
	Wortley Baths, Wortley Park	1906	–	–	–
Leicestershire	Hinkley Lido, Netherley Road	1935	–	–	Factory on site
Lincolnshire	Horncastle Pool, Coronation Walk, East Lindsey	1930s	–	–	–
	Boulthams Baths, Lincoln	1914	220 x 55	R Macbair	Closed 1970.
	Wickhams Gardens, Lincoln	1914	116 x 97	–	Closed 1939, roofed over
	Skegness Bathing Pool, Grand Parade	1928	330 x 75	WF Wills	–
	Cleethorpes Open Air Pool, The Seafront	1920	400 x 200	–	Demolished 1983
Liverpool	Burlington Street Open Air Baths, Vauxhall	1895	75 x 60	–	Destroyed WW2
	Gore Street Open Air Baths, Toxteth	1898	75 x 50	–	Destroyed WW2
	Green Lane Open Air Baths. Old Swan	1898	73 x 45	–	Closed post war
	Mansfield Street Open Air Baths, Everton	1899	75 x 30	–	Gymnasium also, destroyed WW2
	Queen's Drive Open Air Bath, Walton	1909	–	–	–
	Stanley Park Open Air Baths	1923	75 x 35	–	Closed post war
Manchester	Alexandra Park	1934	150 x 75	–	Closed c.1950s, playground
	Philips Park Open Air Pool	1892	200 x 70	–	Closed 1949, grass
Norfolk	Diss Open Air Pool	–	–	–	–
	Gorleston-on-Sea Lido, The Seafront	1939	150 x 48	–	–
	Great Yarmouth Open Air Pool, The Seafront	1922	300 x 75	SP Thompson	Demolished 1979
	Hunstanton Open Air Pool, The Seafront	1929	200 x 100	–	Dem 1967, sealife centre
	Norwich Lido, Aylsham Road	1934	75 x 36	–	Closed WW2, bingo hall
Northants	Daventry Open Air Pool, Ashby Road	1962	–	–	Closed 1990s
	Midsummer Meadow, Northampton	1908	247 x 80	A Fidler	–
	Overstone Solarium, Northampton	1934	–	–	–
	Upper Mount, Northampton	1936	100	J Prestwich	–
Notts	Bulwell Lido, Hucknall Lane	1937	170 x 70	RM Finch	Closed 2003
	Carrington Lido, Nottingham	1937	170 x 70	RM Finch	Playground
	Cranch Lido, Prior Well Road, Worksop	1910	100 x 35	G Rawson	Closed by 1992
	Highfields Lido, Highfields Park, Nottingham	1924	330 x 75	P Morley Horder	Closed 1981, arts centre
	Mansfield Open Air Pool, Pleasey Hill	1908	–	–	Closed 1948
	Newark Open Air Pool, Barnaby Gate House	1934	165 x 55	JH Clarke	Closed early 1970s
Oxfordshire	Abbey Meadow Open Air Pool, Abingdon	–	–	–	Closed 2004
	Banbury Lido, Woodgreen Avenue	1939	165 x 60	S Hilton	Closed 2002
	Carterton Open Air Pool	1970s	–	–	Closed 2003
Portsmouth	Stamshaw Open Air Pool, Gruneisen Road	1900	300 dia oval	–	Housing
Reading	Coley Open Air Baths, Reading	1912	200 x 60	–	–
	King's Meadow Men's Pool, Meadow Road	1860	260 x 80	–	Closed c.1960, now flats
	King's Meadow Ladies' Pool, Meadow Road	1902	120 x 45	A Collins	Closed 1974, listed Grade II
	Theale Green Open Air Pool, Church Road, Theale	1980s	25m	–	Closed 2003
Shropshire	Market Drayton Pool, Phoenix Bank	1933	165 x 50	JG Bailey	–
Sefton	Marsh Lane Open Air Baths, Bootle	1902	88 x 29	Anderson & Crawford	Destroyed WW2
	Canning Road Pool, Southport	1903	70 x 30	Mr Hirst	–
	Southport Sea Bathing Lake, Princes Park*	1928	330 x 212	AE Jackson	Demolished 1993
Sheffield	Longley Park Lido	1938	125 x 40	–	–
	Millhouses Lido, Abbeydale Road	1938	–	–	–
	Rivelin Valley Swimming Bath	1910	–	–	–
Somerset	Clevedon Marine Lake, The Seafront	1929	–	G Pimm	–
	Minehead Open Air Pool	1936	165 x 60	E Gunn	Demolished 1991, Aquasplash
	Princes Road, Wells	1938	100 x 25	R Tomlinson	Demolished by 1990
	Weston-super-Mare Lido, The Seafront*	1937	220 x 140	HA Brown	Closed 2000
Southampton	Southampton Lido, Western Esplanade	1854/1931	75 x 30	WB Bennett / SG Stanton	Closed 1977, demolished c.1982
Staffs	Tamworth Pool, Castle Pleasure Grounds	1937	100 x 50	AO Mitchell	Derelict by 1990
	Trentham Park Lido	1936	132 x 60	Wood & Goldstraw	Closed 1985
	Arboretum Open Air Pool, Walsall	1912	–	–	Closed 1956, café
	Readswood Park, Walsall	1931	–	–	Derelict by 1993
Suffolk	Broomhill Pool, Sherrington Road, Ipswich*	1938	165 x 60	E McLauchlan	Closed 2002
	Piper's Vale Pool, Ipswich	1937	150	E McLauchlan	Closed 1970s
	Lowestoft Bathing Pool	1920	–	–	–
	Oulton Broad Pool, Nicholas Everitt Park	1933	100 x 36	–	–
	The Pightle Pool, Swan Lane, Haverhill	1931	75 x 30	–	–

Location	Name and Address	Opened	Size	Architect	Outcome
	Stowmarket Open Air Pool, Ipswich Road	1937	100 x 40	–	Closed 1985
Surrey	Box Hill Open Air Pool, Box Hill Road, Tadworth	1932	100 x 30	–	–
	Sunbury Open Air Pool, Thames Street	–	120 x 40	–	Closed 1993
	Upper Deck, Hurst Rd, East Molesey	–	–	–	–
	Constitution Hill Recreation Ground, Woking	1935	165 x 90	GF Hawkins & RF Alner	Demolished 1986
Sussex E	Bexhill Open Air Pool, Egerton Park	1906	–	–	Flower beds
	Hastings Open Air Pool, Seafront, St Leonards*	1933	330 x 90	S Little	Holiday camp 1959, dem 1993
Sussex W	Burgess Hill Lido, St John's Park	1936	–	–	Closed 1998
	East Grinstead Open Air Pool, Brooklands Park	1911	80 x 35	–	Closed 1985, grass
	Horsham Open Air Pool, Horsham Park	1934	150 x 40	–	Demolished 1981
	Worthing Lido, The Seafront	1925	110 x 42	Adshead & Ramsey	Closed c.1988, fun fair
Trafford	Altrincham Open Air Pool, Castle Mill	1932	150	–	Demolished 1960
Tyneside N	North Shields, Hawkeys Lane	1909	100 x 40	JF Smillie	Closed 1971
	Tynemouth Swimming Pool, Beach Road	1925	–	Mr Forrest	Closed c.1990
Tyneside S	South Shields Open Air Pool, North Foreshore	1923	–	–	Closed 1939
Warks	Abbey Fields, Kenilworth	c.1985	–	–	–
	St Nicholas Park Pool, Banbury Road, Warwick	–	–	–	Closed mid-1970s
	Malvern Park Lido, Solihull	1983	–	–	–
Wiltshire	Chippenham Pool, Monkton Park	1930	–	–	Closed c.1990
	Devizes Open Air Pool, Colston Road, Rotherstone	1936	100 x 35	AW Jackway	Derelict by 1992
	Malmesbury Outdoor Pool, Old Alexander Road	1961	–	–	Closed 2003
	Marlborough Open Air Pool, Kennet Place	1919	–	–	Demolished by 1990
	Salisbury Open Air Pool, Castle Street	1932	110 x 40	–	Demolished c.1970s
	Trowbridge Bathing Pool, The Park, Brown Street	1939	100 x 45	G Clarke	Closed 1992, supermarket
Wirral	Bebington Open Air Pool, Birkenhead	1932	300 x 90	L Birch	–
	Rock Ferry Swimming Baths, Birkenhead	1933	–	R Furniss	–
	Hoylake Open Air Pool, The Promenade	1913	100 x 129	–	–
	Derby Pool, Harrison Drive, Wallasey	1932	330 x 75	L St G Wilkinson	Demolished 1980s, pub
	New Brighton Pool, Marine Promenade*	1934	330 x 75	L St G Wilkinson	Demolished 1991
Worcs	Droitwich Spa Lido	1935	132 x 66	TH Mawson Ltd	Closed 2000 / savedroitwichlido.org
	Evesham Open Air Pool	1926	100 x 35	–	–
	Kidderminster Open Air Pool, Stourport Road	1900	100 x 100	Mr James	–
	Malvern Bathing Pool, Priory Park	1925	100 x 30	–	Demolished by 1992
Yorkshire	Redcar Bathing Pool, Coatham Enclosure	1930	Oval-shaped	J Locking	Closed 1950, wasteland
	South Bay Pool, Scarborough*	1915	350 x 90	HW Smith	Closed 1989
	Whitby Open Air Pool, West Cliff	–	–	–	–
	Withernsea Open Air Pool, Lee Avenue	1911	100 x 40	–	–
	Yearsley New Baths	1909	150 x 50	F Rowntree	Covered 1965

Scotland

Location	Name and Address	Opened	Size	Architect	Outcome
Aberdeenshire	Tarlair Open Air Pool, Macduff	c.1935	–	–	Closed 1996
Angus	Arbroath Open Air Pool	1934	–	–	Closed 1980
Argyll & Bute	Dunoon Open Air Pool	1937	–	–	–
	Helensburgh Outdoor Swimming Pool	1929	–	–	Closed 1977, playpark
	Rothesay Bathing Pool	1937	–	–	–
Ayrshire E	Cumnock Open Air Pool, Woodroad Park	1936	–	–	Demolished 2003
Ayrshire N	Saltpans Bathing Pool, Saltcoats	–	–	–	–
Ayrshire S	Prestwick Open Air Pool	1931	–	–	Closed 1972
	Troon Open Air Pool	1931	–	–	Closed 1986
Dumfries	Warriston Open Air Pool, Moffat	–	70 x 30	–	–
Edinburgh	Portobello Bathing Pool, Rosebank Lane *	1936	330 x 150	I Warner / WA Macartney	Closed 1979, indoor bowls
Fife	Burntisland	1936	–	–	Closed 1977
	St Andrews Ladies' Pond	1904	160 x 60	–	–
	St Andrews Step Rock Bathing Pool, Men's Pond	1902	340 x 102	–	–
	Spinkie Den Swimming Pond, Leven	1920	–	–	Filled in 1950s
Highland	Invergordon Open Air Bathing Pool	–	–	–	–
Lothian E	Dunbar Open Air Pool	1929	–	–	–

Location	Name and Address	Opened	Size	Architect	Outcome
	North Berwick Pool, Harbour Esplanade	1900	–	Henry & MacLennan	Closed 1990s
	Port Seton Open Air Pool	1931	–	–	–
Moray	Strathlene Open Air Pool, Buckie, Findochty	1933	–	–	Derelict by 1989
Wales					
B Gwent	Abertillery Open Air Pool				
	Ebbw Vale Lido	1930	–	–	Closed 1961, indoor pool
	Tredegar Swimming Pool	1940	–	–	–
Caerphilly	Blackwood Pool, Treowan Park	1938	130 x 40	–	Closed c.1992, playground
Cardiff	Bathing Pavilion, Splott Park	1922	–	–	Closed early 1970s
	Open Air Pool, Western Avenue, Cardiff	–	–	–	–
	Llandaff Fields Pool, Cardiff	1930s	150	–	Closed c.1990
Carmarthen	Hendy Open Air Pool	1932	150 x 60	–	Closed 2002
Conwy	Rhos-on-Sea Open Air Pool, Colwyn Bay	–	–	–	–
	West Shore Bathing Pool, Llandudno	1934	–	–	–
Denbighshire	Prestatyn Lido, The Seafront	1923	–	H Robertson/JM Easton	–
	Rhyl Swimming Pool, The Promenade	1930	330 x 90	AA Goodall	
Glamorgan	The Knap Swimming Pool, Knap Way, Barry*	1926	360 x 90	J Pardoe / ER Hinchsliff	Closed 1997
Gwynned	Bryn-mawr Open Air Pool	–	–	–	–
Merthyr Tydfil	Edwardsville Swimming Baths, Treharris	–	–	–	–
	Merthyr Tydfil Open Air Pool	–	–	–	–
Monmouth	Bailey Park Pool, Abergavenny	1939	–	–	Closed c.1995
Newport	Caerleon Pool, Underwood Leisure Centre, Llanmartin	–	81	–	–
Powys	Ystalyfera Open Air Pool	c.1930s	100	–	Closed 1993
Rhondda	Aberdare Open Air Pool	1902	–	–	–
	Cymmer Open Air Pool	–	100	–	Closed c.1995
	Ferndale Pool, Rhondda Valley	1909	130 x 40	–	Closed c.1994
	Porth Open Air Pool, Bronwydd Park	1937	130 x 40	–	Closed c.1992
	Treherbert Swimming Pool, Rhonda Valley	1936	130 x 42	–	
	Ynysangharad Park, Pontypridd	1923	irregular	–	Closed 1990
Swansea	Blackpill Lido, Swansea	–	–	–	Paddling pool on site
	Clydach Open Air Pool, Nr Swansea	1935	–	–	Closed 1990s

Operating lidos and open air pools

The following lidos and open air pools were known to be open as of June 2005. The list does not include naturally formed tidal or rock pools.

Name: SP = Swimming Pool OP = Outdoor Pool OAP = Open Air Pool LC = Leisure Centre SC= Sports or Swimming Centre
Size: all measurements in metres
Water: B = Brine F = Freshwater P = Pond R = Riverwater S = Seawater H = Heated U = Unheated
Owner: BC = Borough Council CC = County Council C = Council DC = District Council PC = Parish Council TC = Town Council
MC = Management Committee

• denotes open all year round   * indicates location is subject of case study in this book   † indicates pool facing possible closure

England

Location	Name and Address	Opened	Size / Water	Owner	Tel	www / notes
Beds	Eversholt SP, Church End, MK17 9DU	1910	23 x 7.3 / FH	Pool MC	01525 280515	–
	Woburn OAP, Crawley Road, Woburn MK17 9QB	1911	22 x 10 / FH	Woburn SP Trust	01525 290168	–
Berks	Northcroft LC, Newbury RG14 1RS	c.1970s	75 x 10 / FH	West Berkshire C	01635 31199	leisure-centre.com
Bucks	Aqua Vale, Park Street, Aylesbury HP20 1DS	1935	20 x 12 / FH	Aylesbury Vale DC	01296 488555	aylesburyvaledc.gov.uk
	Chesham Town SP, Moor Road HP5 1SH	c.1964	24 x 11 / FH	Chesham TC	01494 783068	chesham.gov.uk
	Holywell Mead OP, High Wycombe HP11 1QX	1954	33 x 15 FH	Wycombe DC	01494 514265	wll.co.uk
	Wolverton Pool, Milton Keynes MK12 5HT	1960s	33 x 12 / FH	MKeynes C	01908 322200	mkweb.co.uk
Cambs	Cottenham OP, High Street, Cambridge CB4 8UA	1967	23 x 9 /FH	Cottenham Vllge Cllge	01954 288751	cottenhampool.org.uk
	Jesus Green OP, Cambridge	1923	92 x 14 / FU	Cambridge City C	01223 302579	jesusgreenoutdoorpool.co.uk
	Peterborough Lido, Bishop's Road PE1 1YY*	1936	50 x 18 / FH	Peterborough City C	01733 343618	dcleisurecentres.co.uk
Cheshire	Nantwich OP, Wall Lane CW5 5LS	1934	30.5 x 15 / BH	Crewe & Nantwich BC	01270 610606	crewe-nantwich.gov.uk
Co Durham	Weardale OAP, Castle Pk, Bishop Auckland DL13 2LY	1974	25 x 13 / FH	WOASP Association	01388 528466	woaspa.co.uk
Cornwall	Hayle SP, Memorial Walk TR27 5AA	1978	25 x 12.5 / FU	Hayle TC	01736 752568	beehive.thisiscornwall.co.uk
	Jubilee Pool, Penzance TR18 4HH*	1935	100 x 74 / SU	Penwith DC	01736 362341	jubileepool.co.uk
Cumbria	Askham SP, Penrith CA10 2PN	1972	20 x 8 / FH	ASP MC	01931 712474	–
	Greystoke SP, Church Road, Penrith CA11 OTW	1973	18 x 7.5 / FH	G&Dist Sports Assoc	01768 483637	–
	Lazonby SP, Townfoot CA10 1BL	1964	20 x 8 / FH	L&Dist SP Assoc	01768 898224	–
	Shap SP, Penrith, CA10 3NR	1988	17 x 8.5 / FH	Shap SP MC	01931 716572	(highest lido in England)
Derbyshire	Open Air SP, Hathersage S32 1BU	1936	30 x 12 / FH	Hathersage PC	01433 650843	hathersage.org.uk
Devon	Ashburton OAP, Love Lane TQ13 7DW	–	FH	Teignbridge DC	01364 652828	–
	Bovey Tracey, Newton Road, TQ13 9BD	1968	25 x 12 / FH	BTSP Association	01626 832828	boveyswimmingpool.co.uk
	Chagford SP, Dartmoor TQ13 8BB	1934	35 x 10 / RH	Chagford Rec Trust	01647 432929	chagford-parish.co.uk
	Chudleigh Community SP, Chudleigh TQ13 OLS	1997	20 x 8 / FH	Chudleigh Comm Project	01626 854780	coombe.moor.clara.net
	Kingsteignton SP, Meadowcroft Drive TQ12 3PB	1979	21 x 12.5 / FH	KSP & Rec Association	01626 366480	–
	Moretonhampstead OAP, Court Street TQ13 8LG	1980	25 x 12.5 / FH	SP Trust	01647 441165	(solar-heated)
	Mountwise SP, Plymouth PL1 4HG	1934	25 x 13 / SU	Plymouth City C	01752 306265	plymouth.gov.uk (free entry)
	Tinside Lido, Hoe Road, Plymouth PL1 3DE*	1935	55 dia / SU	Plymouth City C	0870 3000042	plymouth.gov.uk
	South Dartmoor LC, Ivybridge PL21 OSL	c.1986	25 x irreg / FH	South Hams DC	01752 896999	–
	Teignmouth Lido, Eastcliff Walk TQ14 8TA	1976	25 x 12 / FH	Teignbridge DC	01626 779063	teignbridge.gov.uk
	Topsham SP, Fore Street, Topsham EX3 OHF	1979	25 x 10 / FH	TSP Association	01392 874477	–
Essex	Brightlingsea OAP, Colchester CO7 OHH	1933	50 x 20 / FU	Tendring DC	01206 303067	tendringleisure.org
	Chelmsford LC, Chelmsford CM1 1FG	1962	20 diameter/ FH	Chelmsford BC	01245 615050	riversideiceandleisure.com
Gloucs	Bathurst SP, Lydney GL15 5DY	1920	37 x 18 / FU	Lydney TC	01594 842625	–
	Sandford Parks Lido, Cheltenham GL53 7PU*	1935	50 x 27 / FH	Cheltenham BC	01242 524430	sandfordparkslido.org.uk
	Cirencester OAP, Thomas Street GL7 2BA	1870	27 x 14 / FH	COAP Association	01285 653947	cirenopenair.co.uk
	Stroud OAP, Stratford Pk LC, Stroud GL5 4AF	1937	50 x 18 / FU	Stroud DC	01453 766771	stroud.gov.uk
	Wotton Pool, Symm Lane, Wotton GL12 7BC	1961	20 x 8 / FH	Stroud DC	01453 842086	wottonpool.co.uk
Gtr London	Brockwell Park Lido, Brockwell Park SE24 OPA*	1937	50 x 27 / FU	Lambeth BC	020 7274 3088	thelido.co.uk
	Charlton Lido, Hornfair Park, SE18 4LX	1939	50 x 20 / FU	Greenwich BC	020 8856 7180	gll.org.uk
	Hampstead Heath Bathing Ponds	–	PU	Corp of London	020 7485 4491	cityoflondon.gov.uk
	Hampton Heated OAP, High Street TW12 2ST•	1922	36.5 x 14.5 / FH	Hampton Pool Ltd	020 8255 1116	hamptonpool.co.uk
	Oasis SP, 32 Endell Street WC2H 9AG•	1946	27 x 10 / FH	Camden BC	020 7831 1804	camden.gov.uk
	Park Road Pools, Hornsey N8 8JN	1929	50 x 23 / FH	Haringey BC	020 8341 3567	haringey.gov.uk
	Parliament Hill Lido, Gordon House Road NW5 1LP*	1938	70 x 30 / FU	Corp of London	020 7485 3873	cityoflondon.gov.uk

Location	Name and Address	Opened	Size / Water	Owner	Telephone	www / notes
	Pools on the Park, Twickenham Road TW9 2SF	1965	33 x 13 / FH	Richmond BC	020 8940 0561	richmond.gov.uk
	Serpentine Lido, Hyde Park W2 2UH	1931	100 x 50 / RU	The Royal Parks	020 7706 3422	serpentinelido.com
	Tooting Bec Lido, Tooting Bec Road, SW16 1RU*•	1906	92 x 31 / FU	Wandsworth BC	020 8871 7198	slsc.org.uk
Hants	Aldershot Lido, Guildford Road, Hants GU12 4BP	1930	irreg shape / FU	Rushmoor BC	01252 323482	rushmoor.gov.uk
	Hilsea Lido, Portsea, Portsmouth PO2 9RP*	1935	67 x 18 / FU	Portsmouth City C	023 92664608	portsmouth.gov.uk
	Lymington Seawater Baths, Bath Road SO41 3RU	1833	90 x 30 / SU	New Forest DC	01590 674865	hants.gov.uk
	Petersfield OAP, Heath Road GU31 4DZ	1962	25 x 10 / FH	Petersfield OAP Trust	01730 265143	petersfieldpool.org
Herts	Hemel Hempstead SC, Park Road, HP1 1JS	–	25 x 12 / FH	East Herts DC	01442 228188	eastherts.gov.uk
	Hitchin SC, Fishponds Road, Hitchin SG5 1HA	1938	50 x 18 / FH	North Herts DC	01462 441646	northherts.gov.uk
	Hoddesdon OAP, High Street, Hoddesdon EN11 8BE	1933	23 x 9 / FH	Broxbourne TC	01992 461592	broxbourne.gov.uk
	Letchworth OAP, Icknield Way, Letchworth SG6 4UF	1935	50 x 20 / FH	North Herts DC	01462 684673	northherts.gov.uk
	Royston OP, Newmarket Road, Royston SG8 7DX†	1934	23 x 9 / FH	Letchworth Palace Ltd	01763 245577	northhertsgov.uk
	The Lido, Priory Street, Ware, SG12 9AL	1934	30 x 9 / FH	Ware TC	01920 460703	hertsdirect.org
Kent	Faversham SP, Faversham ME13 8PW	1964	33.3 x 12 / FH	MC	01795 532426	(1,3 & 5 m diving bds)
	Gillingham SP, Pier Road, Gillingham ME7 1TT	1896	25 x 25 / FU	Medway C	01634 573176	medway.gov.uk
	Tonbridge SP, The Slade, Tonbridge TN9 1HR	1910	20 x 13.5 / FH	Tonbridge & Malling BC	01732 367449	tonbridgepool.co.uk
Leics	Hood Park, Ashby de la Zouch LE65 1HU	–	30 x 13.5 / FH	NW Leics DC	01530 412181	nwleics.gov.uk
Lincs	Billinghay Community SP, Fen Road LN4 4HU	1972	25 x 10 / FH	North Kesteven DC	01526 861470	sarcastix.mcmail.com
	Bourne Outdoor SP, Abbey Lawns, Bourne PE10 9EP	1932	48 x 12 / FH	Bourne Utd Charities	01778 422063	bourneoutdoorswimmingpool.org
	Embassy SP, Grand Parader, Skegness PE25 2UG	c.1980s	25 x 13 / FH	East Lindsey DC	01754 610675	e-lindsey.gov.uk
	Jubilee Park SP, Woodhall Spa LN10 6QH	1937	33 x 13 / FH	East Lindsey DC	01526 353478	e-lindsey.gov.uk
	Metheringham SP, Prince's Street, LN4 3BX	1975	15.5 x 8.5 / FH	M & Dist SP Assoc	01526 320840	mspa.org.uk
Northants	Daventry Open Air Pool, Ashby Road NN11 5DB	1962	33 x 10 / FH	Daventry DC	01327 312317	daventrydc.gov.uk
North'land	Haltwhistle OAP, Greencroft Avenue NE49 9BP	1975	25 x 10 / FH	Social Welfare Centre	01434 320727	hslc.freeserve.co.uk
Oxon	Chipping Norton Lido, Fox Close OX7 5BZ	1972	25 x 14 / FH	CN Lido Ltd	01608 643188	chippylido.co.uk
	Hinksey Pools, Lake Street, Oxford OX1 4RP	1934	Freeform / FH	Oxford CC	01865 467079	oxford.gov.uk
	Riverside Park & Pools, Wallingford OX10 8EF	1955	20 x 10 / FH	South Oxon DC	01491 835232	soll-leisure.co.uk
	Woodstock SP, Shipton Road OX20 1LW	–	25 x 8.5 / FH	West Oxfordshire DC	01993 811785	wll.co.uk (has springboard)
Shropshire	Highley Pool, Bridgnorth Road, Highley WV16 6JG	1970	25 x 10 / FH	Bridgnorth DC	01746 860000	severncentre.co.uk
	Market Drayton SC, Newtown Road TF9 1JU	c1995	16.5 x 14.5/FH	North Shropshire DC	01630 655177	northshropshiredc.gov.uk
Somerset	Greenbank SP, Wilfrid Road, Street BA16 OEU	1937	30 x 12 / FH	Greenbank SP Trust	01458 442468	greenbankpool.co.uk
	Huish Episcopi SC, Langport TA10 9SS	1970s	25 x 8.5 / FH	Somerset CC	01458 251055	somerset.gov.uk
	Portishead OAP, Portishead BS20 7HD	1962	33 x 12.5 / FH	North Somerset DC	01275 843454	n-somerset.gov.uk
	Shepton Mallet OP, Shaftgate Avenue BA4 5YA	c.1950s	33 x 10 / FH	Mendip DC	01749 342126	avalonleisure.co.uk
	Wiveliscombe Community SP. Recreation Ground	1927	27 x 10 / FH	WCSP MC	01984 624720	wiveliscombe.com
Suffolk	Beccles SP, Puddingmoor, Beccles NR34 9PL†	–	33 x 16 / FH	Waveney DC	01502 713297	waveney.gov.uk
	Halesworth Open Air Pool, Dairy Hill IP19 8JS†	–	25 x 8.5 / FH	Waveney DC	01986 872720	waveney.gov.uk
Surrey	Abbey Fit SC, School Lane, Addlestone KT15 1TD	1977	22 x 9 / FH	Runnymede DC	01932 858966	abbeyfit.co.uk
	Guildford Lido, Stoke Road, Guildford GU1 1HB*	1933	50 x 28 / FH	Guildford BC	01483 444888	guildford.gov.uk
Sussex E	The Pells Pool, Brook Street, Lewes BN7 2PQ	1860	40 x 20 / FU	PP Comm Association	01273 472334	pellspool.org.uk
	Saltdean Lido, Brighton BN2 8SP*	1938	25 x 15 / FH	Brighton & Hove City C	01273 888308	saltdean.info
Sussex W	Arundel OAP, Queen St, Arundel BN18 9JG	1960	25 x 10 / FH	Arundel TC	01903 882404	arundellido.com
	Aztec Pool, Triangle LC, Burgess Hill RH15 8GA	–	Freeform / FH	Mid Sussex DC	01444 876000	midsussex.gov.uk (splashpool)
Warks	Abbey Fields SP, Bridge Street, Kenilworth CV8 1BP	1986	25 x 10 / FH	Warwick DC	01926 855478	warwickdc.gov.uk
Wilts	Highworth Rec Centre, Swindon SN6 7DD	1970	25 x 10 / FH	Swindon BC	01793 762602	swindon.gov.uk (temp. closed)
Yorkshire	Atlantis Water Park, Scarborough YO12 7TU†	1938	70 X 18 / FH	Scarborough BC	01723 372744	yorkshire-coast.co.uk
	Open Air Pool, Baxtons Lane, Helmsley YO62 5HT	c.1965	20 x 8 / FH	Feversham Mem Trust	01439 770617	–
	Ingleton Swimming Pool, Ingleton LA6 3EL	1933	20 x 8 / FH	Ingleton RCA	015242 41147	ingleton.co.uk
	Ilkley Lido, Denton Road, Ilkley LS29 OBD	1936	46 diameter / FU	Bradford DC	01943 600453	visitbradford.com

Scotland

Location	Name and Address	Opened	Size / Water	Owner	Telephone	www / notes
Aberdeen	Stonehaven OAP, Queen Elizabeth Park*	1934	50 x 18 / SH	Aberdeenshire C	01569 762134	stonehavenopenairpool.co.uk
Ayrshire	New Cumnock SP, New Cumnock KA18 4AH	1968	23 x 12 / FH	NC Env Regen Vol Grp	07985 381051	–
	Magnum Leisure Centre, Irvine KA12 8PP	1993	Circular/ FH	N Ayrshire C	01294 278381	naleisure.co.uk
Inverclyde	Gourock OAP, Albert Road PA19 1ND	1909/35	34 x 15 / SH	Inverclyde C	01475 631561	inverclydeleisure.com

Wales

Location	Name and Address	Opened	Size / Water	Owner	Telephone	www / notes
Carmarthen	Brynamman SP, Station Road SA18 1SF	1920s	27 / FU	Carmathernshire C	01269 824907	–

Links

Where no publisher listed assume self-published by author or lido users' group.

Website details for individual pools are listed in the Directory (*see pages 182-183*).

History general

Public General Acts & Measures 1936-7 HMSO (1937)
Colquhoun A *Modern Architecture* OUP (2002)
Hillman & Cole *South for Sunshine* Capital Transport (1999)
Manning-Sanders R *Seaside England* Batsford (1951)
Marsden C *The English at the Seaside* Adprint (1947)
Pimlott JAR *The Englishman's Holiday* Faber & Faber (1947)
Weinreb & Hibbert *London Encyclopaedia* Macmillan (1983)
Worpole K *Here Comes the Sun* Reaktion (2000)

Reports general

Case notes (various) The Twentieth Century Society
Managing Health & Safety in Swimming Pools HSC & Sport England (1999 & 2003)
Testing the Waters: The Sport of Swimming Select Cttee on Culture, Media and Sport, Second Report HC418 (2001)
Binney M et al *Taking the Plunge: The Architecture of Bathing* Save Britain's Heritage (1982)
Powers A (ed) *Farewell My Lido* Thirties Society (1991)

Swimming general

Deakin R *Waterlog* Chatto & Windus (1999)
Keil I & Wix D *In the Swim: The Amateur Swimming Association 1869-1994* ASA (1994)
Sprawson C *Haunts of the Black Masseur* Vintage (1992)

Articles general

Harrington R *Beyond the bathing belle: Images of women in inter-war railway publicity* Journal of Transport History 25/1
Sladen C *Holidays at Home in the Second World War* Journal of Contemporary History 37/1
Travis J *Continuity & Change in English Sea-Bathing, 1730-1900* Recreation & The Sea, Exeter (1997)
Worpole K & Greenhalgh L *The outdoor life: Volkspark and the lido movement* Landscape Design (March 1997)

Georgian and Victorian

Church R *The Royal Parks of London* Min of Works (1956)
Davenport P *Cleveland Baths, A Standing Building Assessment* Bath Archaeological Trust (2005)
Orme N *Early British Swimming 55BC-AD1719* Univ Exeter Press (1983)
Stow J *Survey of London, 1603* Oxford (reprinted 1908)
Stubbings Dr F *A Cold Bath* Emmanuel College (1994-5)

20th Century

Braggs S & Harris D *Sun, Fun and Crowds: Seaside Holidays Between the Wars* Tempus (2000)
Rollier Dr A *Heliotherapy* OUP (1927)
Sked A & Cook C *Post-War Britain: A Political History* Penguin (1993)
Surén H *Man and Sunlight* Sollux Publishing Co (1927)
Taylor M *Rustington: A Pictorial History* Phillimore (1998)
Wolfenden J *Sport in the Community* (1960)

London

Annual Report 1884 Royal Humane Society
Reports and Minutes of the London County Council Parks & Open Spaces Committee, 1923-39 London Metropolitan Archives
Clunn H *The Face of London* Spring Books (revised ed 1952)
Mernick P & Kendall D *A Pictorial History of Victoria Park* East London History Society (1996)
Wise D ed *Diary of William Tayler, Footman, 1837* Westminster (1998)

Design

Architectural Design & Construction *Swimming Pools and Sports Buildings Reference Section* (September 1939)
Health, Sport and Fitness Royal Institute of British Architects, exhibition catalogue (1938)
The Design and Construction of Open Air Swimming Pools Cement and Concrete Association (1938)
Cross KMB *Modern Public Baths* Amateur Swimming Association (1930, revised edition 1938)

Lido Life

Cane M & Griswold A (eds) *The Hungry Winter Swimmer* Kenwood Ladies' Bathing Association (2002)
Titmuss A (ed) *Breaking the Ice* Serpentine SC (1964)

Tooting Bec Lido, London

Smith Janet *Tooting Bec Lido* SLSC (1996)

The Knap Bathing Pool, Barry

Clemett T *History of Barry* (various newspaper articles)

Margate Lido, Cliftonville

Evans N *Dreamland Remembered* Whitstable (2003)

Finchley Lido, London
XIV Olympiad Souvenir, 1948 Finchley Borough Council

Guildford Lido
Mackey M *The Guildford Mayor's Work Fund and the Opening of the Guildford Lido, Stoke Park* Surrey History, Vol 4. No 3

Open Air Pool, Stonehaven
Mitchell M & MacDonald D *70 Years at Stonehaven Open Air Pool* (2004)

Sandford Parks Lido, Cheltenham
Denison A *Sandford Lido* 1935-1985

Hilsea Lido, Portsmouth
Smith Jane *The Book of Hilsea* (2002)
Smith Jane *The Story of the People's Pool* Hilsea Lido exhibition catalogue (1995)

Tinside Lido, Plymouth
Shaddick V *Pool of Dreams* (2003 unpublished ms)

Victoria Park Lido, London
Mernick P & Kendall D *A Pictorial History of Victoria Park* East London History Society (1996)
Sexby JJ *The Municipal Parks, Gardens & Open Spaces of London* Elliot Stock (1898)

Portobello Bathing Pool, Edinburgh
McKean C *The Scottish Thirties* Scottish Academic Press (1987)
Mekie M *Old Portobello* Stenlake Publishing (1999)

Super Swimming Stadium, Morecambe
Wade P *Echoes of Art Deco: Art Deco in Morecambe* (1999)

Larkswood Pool, Chingford
Davis L *Chingford Notes* Vol 6 No 18 Chingford Historical Society

Bathing Pool, Weston-Super-Mare
History of Knightstone Island North Somerset Museum
Official Souvenir Opening Programme Weston-Super-Mare Urban District Council (1937)

Saltdean Lido, Brighton
Atkinson C et al *A Guide to the Buildings of Brighton* McMillan Martin (1985)
D'Enno D *The Saltdean Story* Phillimore (1985)
Musgrave C *Life in Brighton* Rochester Press (1981)

Community
Hayter-Hames J *A History of Chagford* Rushford (2004)
Waites W *Cirencester Open Air Pool* (1981)

Journals
Architect & Building News; Architects' Journal; Athletic News; Baths & Bath Engineering; The Builder; Concrete; Country Life; The Municipal Journal & Public Works Engineer; Swimming (ASA); Swimming Pool Review

Newspapers
Blackpool Gazette & Herald; Blackpool Evening Gazette; Brighton & Hove Gazette; Brighton & Hove Herald; Bristol Evening Post; Bristol Mirror; Camden New Journal; The Cornishman & Cornish Telegraph; Daily Herald; The Daily Telegraph; East London Advertiser; Edinburgh Evening News; Evening Standard; The Finchley Press; The Guardian; Hampstead & Highgate Express; Hastings & St Leonards Observer; Hendon & Finchley Times; Holborn & Finsbury Guardian; Ilkley Gazette; The Independent; Isle of Thanet Gazette; Lancashire Evening Post; Morecambe Visitor; Peterborough Advertiser; Peterborough Standard; Scarborough Mercury; Scarborough Evening News; Scotland on Sunday; The Scotsman Magazine; Southport Visiter; Surrey Advertiser; The Times; Wallasey News; Walthamstow, Leyton & Chingford Guardian; Wandsworth Borough News; The Weston Mercury

Websites
www.english-heritage.org.uk
www.c20society.org.uk
www.s-parchitects.com
www.lidos.org.uk
www.londonpoolscampaign.com
www.so-dive-in.co.uk
www.prstubbs.btinternet.co.uk
www.river-swimming.co.uk
www.seasidehistory.co.uk
www.piscine-molitor.com

Played in Britain
for more information on English Heritage's *Played in Britain* series, see www.playedinbritain.co.uk

Published titles
Played in Manchester
Simon Inglis *(2004)*

Engineering Archie – Archibald Leitch, football ground designer
Simon Inglis *(2005)*

Liquid Assets – the lidos and open air swimming pools of Britain
Janet Smith *(2005)*

A Load of Old Balls
Simon Inglis *(2005)*

Played in Birmingham
Steve Beauchampé & Simon Inglis (2006)

The Best of Charles Buchan Football Monthly ed. Simon Inglis (2006)

Future titles
Played in Liverpool Ray Physick (2007)

Great Lengths – the indoor swimming pools of Britain Dr Ian Gordon (2007)

Uppies & Downies – Britain's traditional football games Hugh Hornby (2007)

Played at the Pub Arthur Taylor (2008)

Bowled Over – the bowling greens of Britain Hugh Hornby (2008)

Played in Glasgow Ged O'Brien (2008)

Played on Tyne & Wear Lynn Pearson (2009)

Played in London Simon Inglis (2011)

Credits

Photographs and images
Please note that in the credits listed here, where more than one photograph appears on a page, each photograph is identified by a letter, starting with 'a' in the top left corner of the page, or at the top, and continuing thereafter in a *clockwise* direction.

Special collections
The Cyril Farey painting of the Open Air Baths, Blackpool, on pages 64-65 is reproduced by kind permission of the Grundy Art Gallery, Blackpool and is © The Artist's Estate/Gallery Lingard. The map on page 31 was designed by Mark Fenton at English Heritage and is Ordnance Survey © Crown Copyright.

Agency, press and commissioned photographs
Aerofilms: 59a, 81, 91a, 100, 117, 133b, 148, 171; © Associated Newspapers / courtesy Edinburgh City Libraries: 121; Brighton Evening Argus: 149; Bob Croxford, Atmosphere Picture Agency: 97, 113; Sue Cutler: cover flap, 7, 10, 30ab, 37ab, 39bc, 57, 70a, 71b, 92a, 95abc, 101a, 102a, 105ab, 110, 146a, 150, 151, 158, 162, 163a, 164b, 165b, 187; Brian Donnan: 1; English Heritage, James Davies: 13; The Gazette, Blackpool: 63, 67b; Getty Images: 2, 20, 40b, 47; Ian Gordon: 28b; www.grantpritchard.co.uk: 83b; ©John Hinde Ltd: 24; Simon Inglis: 18a, 25, 26, 49bc, 52a, 56, 82a, 83ad, 140ab, 156ab, 157b, 169b, 173ab, inside back cover; Ipswich Star: 168; © Clive Landen / courtesy Weston Information Library: 137b; The News, Portsmouth: 45a; NRM/Science & Society Picture Library: 21, 60, 73, 93, 109, 134a; Mirrorpix: 125a; Martin Parr, Magnum Photos: 6; Qudos / Fusion Lifestyle: 141abc; S&P Architects: 9, 169a; Ian Segar: 11; Janet Smith: 50ab, 55, 61ab, 68a, 69b, 84a, 85abc, 108a, 111abc, 116a, 138a, 140d, 152, 155a, 170bc, 188; David Titchener: 161ab; Philip Trevennen: 8, 96; Wicksteed Leisure Ltd: 38b; Worcester News: 167a

Libraries, archives and local authorities
ASA: 44a; Atkinson Library, Southport: 72ab, 75; Barnet Local Studies Library: 76, 77, 78b, 79; Bradford Museums, Galleries & Heritage / courtesy Lancashire County Library & Information Service: 127; JC Clark Ltd: 161c; Corporation of London: 153b, 154, 155b, 157a; Croydon Local Studies Library: 22, 98, 99ab, 101b; Edinburgh City Libraries: 120a, 122; English Heritage: 142, 144b, 145b, 166ab; Guildford Borough Council: 83c; Hastings Reference Library: 80b; Hillingdon Borough Council: 106b; Hillingdon Local Studies, Archives & Museum Service: 106a, 107c; Ipswich Borough Council Museums & Galleries: 35a, 143, 144a; Islington Local History Centre: 12; Lambeth Borough Council Archives Department: 139; Lancashire County Library & Information Service, N Lancs Division: 41; Lancaster City Museums: 32, 48, 51, 129; Lifschutz Davidson: 174; Liverpool Record Office, Liverpool Libraries: 19 (H352COU/1900-01), 87a; londonstills.com: 140c; London Metropolitan Archives: inside front cover, 4, 27, 28a, 29a, 36, 44a, 49a,114ab, 115ab, 138b; Merseyside Maritime Museum / courtesy Wallasey Local Studies Library: 87b, 88ab, 89; National Monuments Record © Crown Copyright NMR: 14ab, 44b, 66, 107ab, 116b, 134b; North Somerset Museum: 135ab, 137a; Peterborough City Council: 118, 119; Plymouth City Council: 112; Portobello History Society: front cover, 40a, 45b, 120b, 124, 125b; Portsmouth City Council: 104a; Portsmouth Museum & Records Services: 102b, 103; RIBA Library Photographs Collection: 15, 29b, 34b, 39a, 146b, 147, 153a; The Ronald Grant Archive 43b; TP Roskrow / Penlee House Photographic Archive, Penzance: 94; St Andrews University Library: 130-1, 136; Scarborough Museums & Gallery: 58a; Southampton City Libraries Special Collections: 16ab; Stroud District Council: 172ab; Surrey History Service: 82bc; Vestry House Museum, London Borough of Waltham Forest: 37c, 132a, 133a; Wallasey Central Library: 23; 133a, 132a; Wandsworth Borough Council: 53ab; Weston Information Library: 43a

Donated photographs
Arundel & Downland Community Leisure Trust: 164a; Iain Barton, Sandford Parks Lido: 90, 175; Russell Beck, Pells Pool: 159; Darryl Chalkley, Broomhill Pool: 145a; Friends of Stonehaven: 84b; Matt Houghton, Sandford Parks Lido: 91b; Pete Jones, Hathersage Open Air Pool: 163b; Matt Lambourne, Cirencester Open Air Pool: 160; Save A Lido Today (SALT): 167b

Private collections
Tom Clemett: 68b, 69a; Ron Elam's Local Yesterdays: 54; Ian Gordon: back cover abcd, 16c, 17, 28c, 33abcd, 34a, 35b, 38a, 44a, 52b, 58b, 59b, 71a, 78a, 80a, 106a, 108b, 123a, 128ab, 132b, 170a; Sir Peter Heatly: 86, 126; Ted Lightbown: 42, 62, 67a; Ros Luxford: 92b; Jane Smith: 104b; Janet Smith: 46b, 70b; Marion Symes: 165a

Books
The Scottish Thirties by Charles McKean: 123b; Swimming: Badminton Library of Sports and Pastimes (1916): 46a

Acknowledgements

This book could not have been written without the help of a great many people. I am indebted both to longstanding friends and new acquaintances who have so generously assisted and supported me.

In particular, I should like to thank Dr Ian Gordon and Andrew Hoines for giving me free rein to their extensive personal swimming pool archives; Oliver Merrington for permitting me to use information from his invaluable website www.lidos.org.uk; and Ros and Doug Luxford for sharing their postcard collection with a complete stranger.

I have spent many happy hours researching in the London Metropolitan Archives, where the staff have been unfailingly helpful and efficient.

At English Heritage, Elain Harwood has been a wonderful source of knowledge, as has The Twentieth Century Society, whose members have done so much over the years to help save historic lidos.

I have also been given enthusiastic help at local history libraries and museums up and down the country. I should like to thank in particular: Helen Armstrong and Lesley Flood (Weston Central Library), Sue Ashworth (Lancaster City Museum), David Blake (Lancashire Record Office), Catriona Blaker (Thanet Council), Roger Bristow (Hastings Library), David Bromwich (Somerset Studies Library), David Buchanan (Scarborough Museums and Gallery), David Conway (English Heritage), Jennifer Done and Adrian Whalley (Wallasey Central Library), Gareth Edmonds (Rustington Library), Robert Ellwood and Jonathan Makepeace (RIBA Photographic Collection), Andrew Farthing and Matthew Tinker (Atkinson Library, Southport), Nick Goff (North Somerset Museum), Julie Gregson (Wandsworth Local History Library), Jonathan Holmes (Penlee House Gallery and Museum, Penzance), Martin Humphries (Ronald Grant Archive, London), Gwyn Jones (Hillingdon Local Studies), Lorna Lee, Gary Heales and David Pracy (Vestry House Museum, Walthamstow), Susan Orlowski and colleagues (Edinburgh Room, Edinburgh Central Library), Janet Morris (Emmanuel College, Cambridge), Susan Pugh and Andrew Sergeant (National Monuments Record, Swindon), Steve Roud (Croydon Local Studies Library), Jan Ruhrmund (Morrab Library, Penzance), Paul Stevenette (Peterborough City Council), Yasmin Webb (Barnet Local Studies Centre), and Lyn Wilman (Morecambe Reference Library).

A number of local historians, lido enthusiasts and architects have also generously given me the benefit of their expertise and allowed me to make use of their personal collections of photographs and memorabilia. I should particularly like to thank Harry Clark (Rustington Heritage Association), John Clarke (Penzance), Tom Clemett (Barry), Eddie Dangoor (Corporation of London), Jo Edwards (PTEa), Archie Foley (Portobello History Society), Sir Peter Heatly (Edinburgh), Roger Houghton (www.thebath.net), Dr Alan Jackson (Scarborough), Jeremy Lake (Cheltenham), Ted Lightbown (Blackpool), Graham Kelly (Glasgow), Fiona Marsden (Lewes), Mary Mitchell (Stonehaven), Vina Shaddick (Plymouth), Jane Smith (Portsmouth), Marion Symes (Chagford), Diana Tasker (Scarborough), Mary Taylor (Rustington) and Peter Wade (Morecambe).

My thanks also to *Played in Britain* series editor Simon Inglis for his considerable efforts in preparing the book for publication, to Jackie Spreckley of Malavan Media for her extra research and production management, to designer Doug Cheeseman for working his digital magic on the finished product, and of course to S&P Architects, without whose generous sponsorship this book might never have happened.

Finally, a very big thank you to Sue Cutler, who took many of the photographs, swam with me in most of the pools (the heated ones, anyway), and allowed me to share her tent.

Time for a swim, at Charlton Lido.

▲ Beached in Wales – the last inhabitant of the **Knap Bathing Pool** in **Barry** awaits the bulldozers in 2004 as yet another of Britain's precious liquid assets dries up and disappears.

During the two years I spent researching and writing this book for *Played in Britain*, eight lidos and open air pools closed. Another is destined to close at the end of 2005, while campaign groups are rallying to save at least seven more that are either currently closed or under threat of closure.

All outdoor pools, large and small, offer swimmers a potent mixture of physical exhilaration and inner peace that borders on the spiritual.

Back in London, shortly after I took this photograph, I went for a long and soothing swim in my home pool, Tooting Bec Lido, which next year celebrates its centenary.

As I stepped out of the crisp blue water, a fellow swimmer caught my sense of harmony.

'You look as if you've just found paradise!' he laughed.

He was right.

Janet Smith June 2005